"CHOPSTICKS ONLY WORK IN PAIRS"

SHANSHAN DU

"CHOPSTICKS ONLY WORK IN PAIRS"

Gender Unity and Gender Equality
Among the Lahu of Southwest China

COLUMBIA UNIVERSITY PRESS / NEW YORK

COLUMBIA UNIVERSITY PRESS

Publishers Since 1893

New York   Chichester, West Sussex

Library of Congress Cataloging-in-Publication Data

Du, Shanshan.

　　Chopsticks only work in pairs : gender unity and gender equality
among the Lahu of southwest China / by Shanshan Du.

　　　　p.　cm.

　　Includes bibliographical references and index.

　　ISBN 978-0-231-11957-3 (paper : alk. paper)

　　1. Lahu (Asian people) — Social conditions. 2. Lahu (Asian
people) — Marriage customs and rites. 3. Lahu (Asian people) —
Kinship. 4. Equality — China — Yunnan Sheng. 7. Marriage —
China — Yunnan Sheng. 8. Yunnan Sheng (China) — Social life
and customs. I. Title.

DS523.4.L33 D8 2002

305.8951 — dc21

2002071515

Columbia University Press books are printed
on permanent and durable acid-free paper.

Printed in the United States of America

Designed by Lisa Hamm

For my father, Du Yuting; for my Lahu "relatives" and friends; and for James R. Wilkerson and Alma Gottlieb, who sequentially introduced me to Chinese ethnology, Lahu culture, Western anthropology, and the anthropology of gender

In memory of my maternal grandmother, Li Jiayuan, a woman of love, strength, and wisdom, and Hu Calkheu, a great Lahu singer and passionate preservationist of Lahu oral literature

CONTENTS

TECHNICAL NOTES

LAHU ORTHOGRAPHY

The Lahu do not have their own traditional written language. The major systems of orthography that are now used to write Lahu terms are the Catholic, Protestant, Chinese, and a system designed by linguist James Matisoff. For the equivalence between these systems, see Matisoff (1988:21-25).

The orthography utilized to record Lahu terms in this book follows the Chinese system of romanization. In the table below, I list the Chinese system on the left, followed by the International Phonetic Symbols in brackets (Chang 1986:88).

CONSONANTS

p [p]	ph [ph]	b [b]	m [m]	f [f]	v [v]
t [t]	th [th]	d [d]	n [n]		l [l]
z [ts]	zh [tsh]	dz [dz]		s [s]	r [z]
c [tɕ/tʃ]	ch [tɕh/tʃh]		j [dʑ/ dʒ]	sh [ɕ/ʃ]	y [ʑ]
k [k]	kh [kh]	g [g]	ng [ŋ]	h [x]	x [ɣ]
q [q]	qh [qh]				

VOWELS

i [i]	e [e]	ie [ɛ]	a [ʌ]	aw [ɔ]	u [ʊ]
o [u]	eu [ɯ/ɤ]				

TONES

There are seven tones in the spoken Lahu language: middle, low falling, high falling, high rising, low checked, high checked, and very low. In spoken Lahu, no word ends with a consonant. All consonants appearing at the end of Lahu words are tone markers as used in standard Chinese orthography; these are never pronounced. The following table is based on the table provided by Chang (1986:88).

SYMBOLS	TONES	EXAMPLES
unmarked	middle	ma, "female"
l	low falling	mal, "thorny bamboo"
d	high falling	mad, "not," "many"
q	high rising	maq, "son-in-law"
r	low checked	mar, "war," or "military"
t	high checked	mat, "dream"
f	very low	maf, "teach"

MANDARIN ORTHOGRAPHY

All translations of Han Chinese terms in this book utilize the *pinyin* system of romanization of Mandarin (*putonghua*).

ILLUSTRATIONS

ACKNOWLEDGMENTS

I **OFFER** my first and deepest gratitude to God for making this book possible, especially for my miraculous survival from two traffic accidents on precipitous mountain roads during my fieldwork and for so many wonderful people I have met throughout the long timespan of the project. While my gratitude extends to all who have directly or indirectly helped me with this project, I can express my special appreciation here to only a few.

As an ethnographer, I am most indebted to my adopted Lahu family members for teaching me about their culture while offering me loving homes in my major fieldsites. I am grateful to my Lahu friends for sharing with me both their lives and their understanding of the issues related to my research. I also wish to thank many other individuals and families for kindly allowing me to peer into their lives, answering my numerous questions, and offering their time for lengthy interviews. While the rest of my informants must remain pseudonymous, I want to make an exception and specially thank one of my Lahu "relatives" named Hu Calkheu, the late Lahu folksong singer and preservationist of Lahu oral literature.

I would like to acknowledge several individuals, who are called ex-teachers in the United States but are considered lifelong mentors in Chinese tradition, for their enthusiastic support of both the project and my academic development. Particularly, I am deeply indebted to Alma Gottlieb for introducing me to the anthropology of gender and challenging me, with great care and sensitivity, to reach my intellectual and writing potential; to F. K. Lehman for his broad knowledge and many inspiring discussions; to Jacquetta Hill, Stevan Harrell, and Ann Anagnost for offering their respective specialties, the Lahu of Thailand, Chinese minorities, and gender in China; to my father, Du Yuting, for introducing me to Chinese ethnology and for constantly sending me relevant books and articles from

China; to James R. Wilkerson for introducing me to Western anthropology and offering comments on several drafts of the book.

Many of my colleagues, friends, teachers, and students have kindly helped me with the book at different stages. I am grateful to Hillary Crane, who generously volunteered to read through an entire draft of the manuscript and offered valuable comments when I was under enormous time pressures; to Anthony Walker, Clark Cunningham, Victoria Bricker, Alejandro Lugo, Monica Cable, April Middeljans, Amber Landis, Hu Yulan, Betty LeJeune, Richard Freeman, Mwenda Ntarangwi, Katherine Wiegele, Wuanhong Liao, Susan Sered, and Elise Bartosik for reading and commenting on varying portions of different drafts of the book; to Monica Cable for creating the maps and kinship chart in the text; and to Christopher Jones for checking the references in a draft of the manuscript.

I also wish to thank those who indirectly assisted me in accomplishing this project. In my first book written in English, I would like to acknowledge those who have helped me in attaining a Western education. I am deeply indebted to James R. Wilkerson for recommending me for anthropological training in the United States; to my husband, Zhong Shuming, and to Ms. Zhou for helping me get a passport when difficulties seemed insurmountable; to Peter Rendell, Ray Campbell, and Jack Barnes for insisting on lending $1,000 to me, a complete stranger, when I first left China and was stuck at the Hong Kong airport because the price of last-minute tickets had quadrupled. I would also like to thank the members of the Lancang subbranch of Hong Kong Oxfam (an international NGO) for allowing me to follow them to many remote villages, some of which I would not otherwise have had the opportunity to visit, during my fieldwork between 1995 and 1996. I am grateful to those who have offered me emotional and moral support: to my parents and my late maternal grandmother, who consistently and sacrificially encouraged me to focus on the project, especially during my fieldwork; to my father, brother, and sister-in-law, who helped me contact my Lahu adoptive relatives and friends after I left China; to my American adoptive family members (especially my adoptive parents, William and Clarice Behrence, and my adoptive sisters, Laurie Rubin, Cui Hong, Christine Jiau, and Li Ming), whose love transcends both biological bonds and the sociocultural gaps between East and West and between mainland China and Taiwan; to the members of the Department of Anthropology at the University of Illinois at Urbana-Champaign (UIUC) and of the Department of Anthropology at Tulane University for providing me with great intellectual and social environments.

I am grateful to several academic organizations and their members for offering me financial support for the research. Listed chronologically, the grants and awards I have received are as follows: two grants from the Yunnan Academy of Social Sciences (China); a summer grant from the Department of Anthropology at UIUC; two research grants from the Graduate College of UIUC; a Charlotte W. Newcombe doctoral fellowship and a doctoral grant in Women's Studies, both from the Woodrow Wilson National Fellowship Foundation; a fellowship from the Program for the Study of Cultural Values and Ethics at UIUC; and a summer fellowship from the Senate Committee on Research at Tulane University.

I would also like to express my gratitude to my editors, John Michel, Wendy Lochner, and Anne McCoy (managing editor) at Columbia University Press for their great support for the project and their extraordinary efficiency in producing the book; to Georgia Maas, my copyeditor, for her valuable comments and impressive professional dedication; to the anonymous readers for their helpful suggestions; and to Lisa Hamm, the designer of the book, and other staff at Columbia University Press for their effort and contributions to the book.

An earlier version of chapter 3 was first published in *American Anthropologist* 102, no. 3 (2000). Progressive concepts of the book were presented at the annual meeting of the American Anthropological Association (1997) and the annual meeting of the American Ethnological Society (1999). Earlier versions of parts of the book were presented on different occasions: chapter 2 at the annual meeting of the American Anthropological Association (1999), chapter 3 at the Midwest Graduate Student Conference on Southeast Asia (1996), and chapter 5 at the Conference for the Study of Kinship and Economy on the Yun-Gui Plateau (Academia Sinica, Taipei, 1999).

"CHOPSTICKS ONLY WORK IN PAIRS"

INTRODUCTION

WHILE THE CONCEPT of "gender equality" (or "sexual equality") has become increasingly popular in the global village at the beginning of the new millennium, it still represents primarily a beautiful dream to strive for. If we shift our attention away from utopian ideals, however, we may notice that gender-egalitarian societies, despite their scarcity and imperfection, do exist outside our dreamlands. Through an ethnographic study of the Lahu people of southwest China, I will explore in this book how gender equality has become a by-product of the worldview of gender unity, which is vividly expressed by the proverb "Chopsticks only work in pairs." According to this worldview, it is only right and natural that men and women, who are expected to unify in husband-wife teams, take joint roles as much as possible in all areas, including pregnancy, childbirth, childcare, domestic chores, subsistence work, and leadership. The principle of male-female dyads that is expressed by the chopsticks metaphor not only prevails in Lahu mythology and ideology but is also predominant in indigenous institutions and social practice. The Lahu example demonstrates both the existence of gender-egalitarian societies and the possibility of achieving such social conditions peacefully. Calling attention to the cross-cultural diversity of gender equality, this study encourages us to reflect on the obstacles, goals, and strategies of our own respective societies in the promotion of equality between men and women.

IS THERE ANY GENDER-EGALITARIAN SOCIETY ON EARTH?

Is there any gender-egalitarian society on earth? This question is almost unavoidable when we begin to explore gender equality. Different answers to the question constitute an integral part of the debates over the central concerns of both academic inquiries and feminist endeavors, especially how to define, measure, and achieve gender equality. As the remainder of this section suggests, various utopian ideals in feminist thought have turned the nonexistence of gender-egalitarian societies into a self-fulfilling prophecy. These idealistically oriented approaches have shaped the directions of comparative studies, hindering our understanding of societies whose mainstream ideologies and institutions are predominantly governed by gender-egalitarian principles.

GENDER EQUALITY AS UTOPIAN IDEAL

Mainstream feminism tends to perceive gender-egalitarian societies as utopian ideals. This tendency seems to be a reaction to the traditional Western ideology that polarizes male and female in both characteristics and values.[1] Specifically, men are defined as the positive One whose masculinity (especially when regarded as rationality) represents the ideals of humanity. Women, as measured against men, are defined as the Other, negative and lacking, and their femininity represents the failures of humanity (Beauvoir 1972 [1949]; Frye 1996; Jay 1981). Such dichotomous perceptions of male and female not only produce the ideology of gender hierarchy but also justify the inequality as a matter of course.

During the earlier waves of the women's movement that began in seventeenth-century England (Jaggar 1983:4), feminists' perceptions of gender equality were greatly confined by the strong ideological and social structures of patriarchy in their own societies (e.g., Gullett 2000; Lerner 1993). In particualr, the overarching power of the patriarchal systems created an unbridgeable gap between short-terms goals to improve women's status and the ultimate visions for a gender-egalitarian society and, consequently, turned the latter into fantasies. Despite the enormous progress in enhancing women's status in dominant Euro-American societies (e.g., Bryson 1999:2–3), the pessimistic legacy that perceives gender-egalitarian societies as desirable but nearly unattainable utopias has been retained in the most recent wave of the women's movement since the 1960s. As an extreme example, by identifying the cause of women's oppression with biological inequality between the sexes, Firestone (1970:12) places the hope for gender equality on future technology that would eradicate human reproductive roles. Along a similar line, some radical feminists trace gender inequality to "male hostility towards women" (Greer 1992:21), which is expressed especially in human sexuality

(Brownmiller 1976; MacKinnon 1987:66). At the turn of the new millennium, ambiguous attitudes toward, if not the denial of, gender-egalitarian societies still prevail in feminist thought, as expressed in the following statement by Littleton (1994:31):

> The various models of equality arise out of common feminist goals and enterprises: trying to imagine what a sexually equal society would look like, given that none of us has ever seen one, and trying to figure out ways of getting there, given that the obstacles to sexual equality are so many and so strong.

The chasm between utopian ideals and social realities is further deepened by the great diversity within feminism, especially by the fact that some major schools have promoted opposite ideals of, and opposite measurements for, gender equality. Deriving from different strands of Western philosophical and political thought, some feminists promote degrees of *sameness* between the sexes in a society (e.g., Beauvoir 1972 [1949]; Firestone 1970), while others insist on the essential *difference* between male and female by celebrating "womanhood" (e.g., O'Brien 1981; Ruddick 1989).[2]

Liberals and Marxist-socialists typically advocate increasing the sameness between male and female. From the liberal point of view, the achievement of gender equality relies on the full realization of liberals' ideals of individualism, which promise equal rights to individual members of society regardless of sex differences (e.g., Mill 1970 [1851]; Heilbrun 1973; Ferguson 1993). In contrast, collectively oriented Marxist-socialists envision another kind of ideal society in which citizens are primarily identified as members of a commune and are therefore free from any forms of social inequality, including gender inequality (Benston 1969; Engels 1972 [1885]; Fraser 1997). Despite the opposition between individualism and collectivism, liberals and Marxist-socialists agree that the social insignificance of, and the resulting indifference to, sex distinctions is a mark of the equality between men and women. In other words, both groups see the degree of *sameness* between the sexes as the ultimate measure of gender equality in a society.

Contrary to those who promote sameness between the sexes, many radical feminists insist on the natural and essential *difference* between men and women, especially highlighting "women" as a central social category. Some identify men as the oppressors or even the enemy of women (e.g., Daly 1979; Greer 1971; Solanas 2000). Perceiving masculine characteristics such as aggression and cruel rationality as the sources of women's subordination and of other major problems of humanity, some consider such feminine characteristics as nurturing and caring to be the salve to restore peace both socially and ecologically (Griffin 1984 [1978]). From such a perspective, efforts to increase sameness between male and female inadvertently perpetuate patriarchal values by assimilating women into masculine norms in the name of promoting gender neutrality and equality.

The utopian models for gender equality reflect different approaches and strategies for terminating the special kind of female subordination that is derived from the dominant ideology of gender dichotomy that favors males. Even the two opposing feminist schools are, in fact, attacking the same culture-specific gender hierarchy but from different positions. While agreeing with the dominant ideology concerning the innate differences between male and female attributes, radical feminists attempt to enhance women's status by reversing the traditional values that favor only masculinity. In contrast, identifying the ideology of gender dichotomy itself as the root of institutionalized sexism, liberal and socialist feminists attempt to promote gender equality by denying the social significance of sex difference. Nonetheless, the commonly shared idealistic approaches, coupled with various incoherent or even opposite ideals and standards for gender equality, perpetuate the common association of gender-egalitarian societies with utopian ideals.

IDEALISTIC BIAS AGAINST RECOGNIZING
GENDER-EGALITARIAN SOCIETIES

In the process of struggling for gender equality in their own societies, some Euro-American feminists have turned to other cultures for hope and inspiration. Accompanying the heated debate over the universality of female subordination in the mid-1970s, the search for gender-egalitarian societies also reached its peak.[3] Ironically, by projecting diverse utopian ideals into cross-cultural studies, the declaration of the nonexistence of gender-egalitarian societies became a self-fulfilling prophecy. After all, there is always an unbridgeable gap between a utopian fantasy and a real society because the latter never operates on seamlessly coherent principles. While not a single existing society on the planet can possibly match just one utopian model, it is even more impossible for a society to live up to the expectations of *many* utopian ideals, some of which hold conflicting standards for measuring gender equality. Not surprisingly, no agreement has been reached on vesting a single society with the title "gender-egalitarian," rendering infertile the debate over the universality of female subordination. Accordingly, since the late 1980s, many feminists have again assumed as a given that gender-egalitarian societies do not exist or that they are yet to be discovered. On the basis of this premise, they seek or try to imagine models of gender equality to strive for (Littleton 1994:31).

The different impacts of idealistic approaches on cross-cultural studies of women's status correspond to the different assertions denying the existence of gender-egalitarian societies. A society is sometimes classified as "male-dominant" despite the fact that its ideology and institutions are predominantly gender-egalitarian. For example, although women were observed playing similar and sometimes more conspicuous roles than men in many significant rituals, the society of the Crow Indians was categorized as "male-dominant" primarily because of the existence of menstruation taboos (Ortner 1996 [1972]:24).[4] According to this classificatory logic, a society is doomed to bear the label "male-dominant" if its egalitarian principles are not perfectly elaborated in every single symbol and ritual of the culture. In addition, Eurocentric bias can be embedded in the very criteria used to judge the "flaws" of an egalitarian gender system, such as, in this case, the existence of a menstruation taboo. According to some comparative studies, rather than necessarily being associated with pollution or other negative symbolism (Douglas 1984 [1966]), menstruation taboos can serve in some societies as positive symbols that empower women (Buckley and Gottlieb 1988). Along a similar line, while the Scandinavian welfare states have successfully promoted gender equality by empowering women as mothers, workers, and citizens, some feminists worry that such societal changes introduced by government social policies merely reflect a new kind of male dominance in public spheres (Siim 1987:255).

More moderate responses to the imperfection of a gender system disqualify the society in question from being "gender-egalitarian" rather than classifying it as "male-dominant." For example, some hunter-gatherer societies such as the Montagnais-Naskapi of Labrador (Leacock 1983) and the !Kung of the Kalahari Desert of southern Africa (Shostak 1981) are regarded either as an imperfect "past Eden" where the sexual division of labor still prevails (Yanagisako and Collier 1987:38) or as a society that is "somewhat short of having a perfectly balanced set of separate but equal gender roles" (Harris 1993:59). Interestingly, similar remarks are made about kibbutzim, Israeli utopian communes that practice collective ownership, production, consumption, and childcare (Agassi 1989; Spiro 1996). From a radical feminist perspective, although enthusiastically committed to eradicating gender difference in order to achieve gender equality, kibbutz pioneers rooted their institutions and practices in a male-defined ideology that was far from being a true emancipation of women (Fulop 1986:93). From the point of view of liberal and Marxist feminism, the kibbutz pioneers achieved temporary gender equality that was destroyed when their granddaughters chose to assume traditional feminine roles, especially in childcare.

Some scholars pay attention to the dominant egalitarian principles of a society rather than focusing on the imperfections in the implementation of these principles. Nevertheless, instead of directly using the term "gender-egalitarian" to describe the overall status of the society, they often place adverbs such as "possibly" (Ortner 1996 [1990]:157), "nearly" (Harris 1993:59), or "relatively" (Atkinson1990:59) in front of the term "egalitarian." By emphasizing the partiality or relativity of gender equality, these phrases suggest that the societies in question are not "genuinely" egalitarian in gender relations. While such expressions by themselves demonstrate academic rigorousness, they also reveal the subtle double standard in measuring gender equality and hierarchy. After all, although not a single society on earth can successfully implement its patriarchal ideology with complete coherence, nobody expects a researcher to modify the term "gender inequality" with adjectives such as "possible" or "relative" when referring to an extremely male-dominant society such as that of late imperial China.[5] In other words, according to the academic double standard, inequality and hierarchy can be of any degree, but equality must be perfect.

In brief, various utopian ideals have dominated both academic and popular perceptions of gender equality, generating either firm denials of or ambiguous attitudes toward the existence of gender-egalitarian societies. Furthermore, the double standard used to measure gender hierarchy and equality has reinforced the notion of the universality of female subordination. As I will show in the following section, much empirical evidence regarding the diverse ideologies and institutions of gender-egalitarian societies has long been overlooked because it is not able to meet multiple utopian expectations.

BEYOND THE SHADOW OF UTOPIAN IDEALS

Despite the strong utopian bias embedded in mainstream feminism, many studies have presented empirical evidence and theoretical interpretations of gender-egalitarian societies. Empirically, ethnographic and sociological studies have described gender-egalitarian principles that dominate societies spread across the continents, from the Pacific islands to East Asia and Southeast Asia, from Africa to North America, and from the Middle East to Scandinavia. Examples include the mountain-dwelling Arapesh (Mead 1963 [1935]) and the Vanatinai (Lepowsky 1993) of New Guinea, the Okinawans of Japan (Sered 1999), the Rungus of Borneo (Appell 1991), the Western Bontoc of the Philippines (Bacdayan 1977), the Aka of Congo (Hewlett 1991), the American Indians in the Ecuadorean Andes (Hamilton 1998) and Canada (Krosenbrink-Gelissen 1993, 1996), the kibbutz communes in Israel (Agassi 1989; Spiro 1996), and the welfare society in Sweden (Haas 1990; Nyman 1999). Whether they directly use "gender equality" or cautiously avoid the term for its conceptual complications, these studies have provided empirical evidence of gender-egalitarian societies.

Interestingly, the few scholars who use the term "gender-egalitarian" to describe the societies they study include some indigenous people who declare that their own cultural traditions are gender-egalitarian and thereby challenge the idealistic biases embedded in mainstream feminism. During the revivals of American Indian cultures in the 1980s, many male and female Indians in Canada declared that gender equality pervaded their widely shared cultural heritage and successfully linked sexual equality with folk law, aboriginal rights, and self-government (Krosenbrink-Gelissen 1993:14; 1996:155). With less political influence, some individual scholars criticize Western bias against the recognition of the gender-egalitarian nature of some non-Western cultural traditions. For instance, by demonstrating the precolonial concept of equality manifested in the dual-sex system of the Onitsha of Nigeria, Nzegwu (1994:84) calls for academic attention to the "varieties of [gender] equality" that may be obscured by Western feminist bias. Contrasting the cultural insignificance of gender difference in the precolonial Yoruba of Nigeria and the focus of Western scholars on the status of Yoruba women, Oyewumi (1997:43) even argues that the very concept "women" has itself been a Western invention.

On the basis of empirical data, some researchers have attempted to theorize the attributes of gender-egalitarian societies. Focusing on the economic aspects of social relations, Marxist feminist Eleanor Leacock (1978, 1983) argues that gender egalitarianism exists in nonstratified societies in which both sexes have equal control over the means of production as well as over their own labors. Pushing Leacock's argument a step further, Karen

Sacks (1979) suggests that, when relating to each other as siblings rather than as spouses, men and women can be institutionally equal even in patrilineal, patrilocal societies. Rather than focusing on the materialist dimension, some scholars theorize the ideological attributes of gender-egalitarian societies with concepts such as "sex-role plans" (Sanday 1981:3) and "egalitarian hegemonies" (Ortner 1996 [1990]:146). Integrating several sociological approaches, Chafetz (1990) uses "stability and change" to explore the transformation from gender hierarchy to gender equality.

Quantitatively, some comparative studies have demonstrated the extreme diversity and complexity of women's status across cultures, contributing to our understanding of gender-egalitarian societies by directly or indirectly revealing the fallacy of the notion of the uniformity of male dominance. Some scholars have developed comprehensive coding systems, including the sociocultural measurements for women's status in preindustrial societies (e.g., Sanday 1981; Schlegel 1972; Whyte 1978) and the index of gender equality in industrial or postindustrial societies (Harvey et al. 1990). Others have focused on more specific indicators of gender equality in cross-cultural settings, including housework (Baxter 1997; Doucet 1995), romantic love (de Munck and Korotayev 1999), and ecological determinants among hunter-gatherers (Hayden et al. 1986). While collectively demonstrating the diversity and complexity of gender status across cultures, some of these researchers also sharply point out the impossibility of quantitatively pinning down a coherent scale for measuring the general "status of women" from culture to culture (Whyte 1978:116).

In contrast to the predominant denials of the existence of gender-egalitarian societies, these studies have presented evidence and interpretations that collectively contribute to our understanding of gender equality. Nevertheless, since only a small proportion of these researchers directly argue for the existence of gender-egalitarian societies, their voices are often ignored in both academia and popular opinion.

Building on previous studies on the subject, I intend in this book to firmly reject the influences of the various utopian biases and to explore gender equality as a sociocultural phenomenon. Before proceeding to further discussion, I would like to clarify my use of the terms "sex" and "gender." By "sex" I mean the anatomical, hormonal, and/or genetic differences between the vast majority of men and women, particularly differences that determine women's exclusive roles in gestation, parturition, and lactation. In contrast, I use "gender" to refer to sociocultural constructions of male and female as well as their fundamental relationships.[6] Although I separate "sex" from "gender" from analytic necessity, I perceive their relationship as interactive rather than dichotomous, a conceptual fallacy that has been criticized from widely divergent perspectives.[7]

Approaching gender equality as a sociocultural phenomenon, I define a gender-egalitarian society as one whose dominant ideology, institutions, and social practices value its male and female members equally, regardless of the roles they play. By this definition, I acknowledge the inevitable inconsistency between ideal and practice as well as the existence of multiple gender ideals in a society. I prefer "gender equality" to "[gender] egalitarian hegemonies" (Ortner 1996 [1990]:146) to describe such a society in order to completely break the conceptual shackles of both the various utopian biases and the academic double standard imposed on gender equality and gender hierarchy.

Theoretically, I am concerned with the diversity of gender perceptions and institutions across cultures that may shape the forms and degrees of gender equality, paying attention to both ideological and material dimensions. I aim to explore the relationships between gender equality and gender motif—the main feature of the symbolic and institutional constructions of men, women, and their relationships in a given society. Applying this theoretical concern to my ethnographic study of the Lahu people, I demonstrate how the motif of gender unity prevails in their worldview, gender roles, and social structures. I also discuss how such a gender motif produces the ideology and institution of gender equality as a by-product.

The emphasis of this book on Lahu ideals, norms, and social structures requires me to warn against possible misinterpretations that may occur in regard to the idealistic pitfalls I have mentioned. I cannot emphasize enough that, despite the preeminence of the motif of gender unity, we cannot essentialize it as a monolithic and static principle that coherently governs the Lahu people. In particular, while the Lahu people are greatly diversified across regions and subgroups, the indigenous traditions of a particular community always have their own internal tensions and transformations because Lahu individuals are active social agents who continuously negotiate their social ideals in their daily lives. Additionally, the Lahu gender system has been transformed in various ways and to various degrees during a long history of interacting with both neighboring groups and the central Chinese government. While paying special attention to these issues, I am unable to address them as fully as I wish in this book because of length constraints and my concerns about readability.

THE LAHU PEOPLE

The Lahu are a Tibeto–Burman-speaking people (Chang 1986:1; Matisoff 1988:11) who are divided into several subgroups with mutually intelligible dialects and slightly different subcultures, including the Lahu Na, the Lahu Shi, the Lahu Nyi, and the Lahu Shehleh (Walker 1974). For example, the dialects of the Lahu Na and the Lahu Shi share over 80 percent of their vocabulary (Chang 1986). The archaic or poetic language used in Lahu song performances enjoys an even higher level of commonality among the Lahu across subgroups and regions. In 1923, the missionary M. Vincent Young and some Lahu Christians created a Lahu written system based on the Latin alphabet; this was later reformed by Chinese linguists (Xing 1992:76–77; Zhang et al. 1996:114).

The Lahu people from all subgroups refer to themselves as "Lahu," the meanings of which have remained controversial. Lahu studies in China predominantly associate the term "Lahu" with 'tiger hunting', 'tiger roasting' (Wang 1983; Wang and He 1999:10), or 'tiger worshipping' (Chen and Li 1986:7; Wang and He 1999:10). Nevertheless, some scholars believe the term means 'a people who live by the source of rivers or on the top of mountains' (Hu 1991; Wang 1996: 87; Wang and He 1999:11).

The Lahu people live in the mountainous region that constitutes a southerly extension of the Tibetan highlands along the border areas of the People's Republic of China (PRC), Myanmar (Burma), Laos, Thailand, and Vietnam. According to the 1990 census, the Lahu population in the PRC was 411,476 (Mackerras 1994:239), which is about two-thirds of the total Lahu population (Walker 1995:7). Almost all of the Chinese Lahu reside in Yunnan Province, the most ethnically diverse province of China, located in the most southwestern region of the current Chinese territory. In contrast to that of many other ethnic minorities in China, the national and international visibility of the Lahu people is extremely limited.[8]

Most Lahu people reside in rugged mountains, often at a height of more than 1,000 meters above sea level and influenced by a subtropical monsoon climate (Wang and He 1999:50; Zhang et al. 1996:61–62). The subsistence pattern of the Lahu is typically a mixture of farming, raising domestic animals, hunting and gathering, and fishing. At the beginning of the twenty-first century, while the Lahu are increasingly engaging in intensive agriculture (irrigated wet-rice), the slash-and-burn cultivation of hill rice, wheat, and buckwheat still persists to varying degrees, especially for those people in

Myanmar and Thailand. The growth of cash crops such as tea and sugarcane has also been increasing since the 1980s.

A Lahu village is usually located at the top or the middle of a terraced mountain (Zhang et al. 1996:117). A typical Lahu village contains twenty to sixty households. A traditional Lahu house (*yiel*) is rectangular with a roof of thatched cogon grass and walls of bamboo strips or mud-packed wooden boards. While Lahu houses in some areas are built above the ground with cattle living under the house, in most areas the houses are constructed directly on the ground. Since the 1980s, an increasing number of Lahu families have been able to afford houses built with brick walls and roofs made of corrugated cement tiles or aluminum.

Before the 1950s, most Lahu villages generally lacked social stratification; there were no strict markers for hierarchical status except for that of generation and age (Du 1996; Walker 1995). Varying degrees of economic and political hierarchies that were attributable to external influences could also be observed in different Lahu areas. For instance, increasing direct control by the central Chinese government among the Lahu in Lancang County during the first half of the twentieth century unevenly fostered political and economic inequality among Lahu villagers (Gen 1997:63–74; Zhang et al. 1996:115–116); this was later eliminated by the collectivization practices of the Mao era.

The high degree of gender equality among the Lahu is recorded in both the English (e.g., Hill 1985; Walker 1995:9–11) and the Chinese literature (e.g., Dong et al. 1995:809; Xu 1993:50; Wang 2001:167; Zhang et al. 1996:119). In particular, the Lahu people across subgroups and regions typically adhere to their indigenous values that greatly appreciate children and show preference to neither boys nor girls (Lei and Liu 1999:116; Wang 2001:31; Wang and He 1999:154, 292).

Households constitute the center of Lahu village life (Hill 1985) and serve as basic units for production and consumption. The Lahu people practice monogamy, and married couples tend to jointly own and manage their households. The Lahu kinship system is fundamentally bilateral although there are varying degrees of matrilineal or patrilineal skewing in different regions or subgroups. Varying degrees of bilocal tendency mark the patterns of postmarital residence among the Lahu in most areas. For example, the ideal pattern among the Lancang Lahu Na is that a couple stays several years with the wife's parents after the wedding, then several years with the husband's parents, and then establishes their own household.

Across countries, regions, and subgroups, the Lahu share similar beliefs in Xeul Sha, the creator of the universe and a supreme parental god. Rituals that pay special respect to both living and deceased parents, the extreme form of which is parental worship, often complement this belief. In addition, animist beliefs and practices prevail among many Lahu, especially among those who have experienced only limited external religious influences. Beyond indigenous beliefs, many Lahu have been influenced to different degrees by a wide variety of externally introduced beliefs, including those of Mahayana and Theravada Buddhism, Protestant and Roman Catholic Christianity, and communist atheism.[9]

The Lahu people have historically constituted part of an "ethnic mosaic" with their neighboring groups. In addition, the Yunnanese and other Chinese merchants have long incorporated the multiethnic regions in which the Lahu reside into their institutionalized trading networks between Yunnan and Southeast Asia (Hill 1998:47). The Lahu in China have been increasingly involved in local, regional, national, and global socioeconomic systems since the 1980s, resulting in drastically intensified interactions with other ethnic groups. Despite their increasing encounters with other groups, however, the Lahu living west of the Lancang River have still maintained a high degree of ethnic homogeneity at the level of the village, and interethnic marriage is uncommon in the first decade of the twenty-first century (Chen and Li 1986; Lei and Liu 1999:80; Zhang et al. 1996:118).

FIELDWORK SITES

The main site of my fieldwork was Lancang Lahu Autonomous County, which is named after the Lancang (Mekong) River on its eastern side. Lancang County (22° to 23° N. and 99° to 100° degrees E.) is located at the most southwestern corner of China's territory at the China-Myanmar frontier. The southernmost end of Lancang County shares a border with Myanmar for 80.6 kilometers. Rugged mountains, especially the five ranges that run roughly northwest to southeast, are the county's most significant geographic features. Among the numerous mountains spread all over the county's territory, more than 150 are over 2,000 meters high with the highest at 2,516 meters (Zhang et al. 1996: 62). Many rivers, deep valleys, and ravines run through these mountains. The important rivers are the Lancang (Mekong) River and the Black River. A year in Lancang County is clearly divided into the dry season (late October to mid-May) and the wet

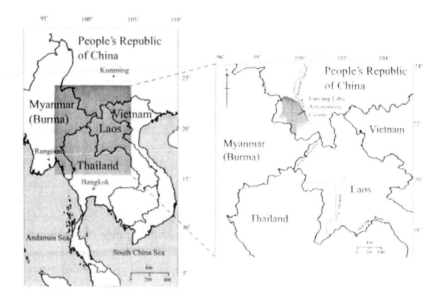

MAP 1 Approximate habitation area of the Lahu People (shaded square) Map by Monica Cable

MAP 2 Lancang Lahu Autonomous County (shaded area) Map by Monica Cable

season (mid May to late October). The average yearly rainfall is 1,626 millimeters. The climate varies greatly according to altitude, which divides the county into four major climate types: northern tropical, southern subtropical, middle subtropical, and cool.

Lancang Lahu Autonomous County is the only autonomous county in China that is solely dedicated to the Lahu people. Administratively, Lancang County belongs to the Simao prefecture of Yunnan Province. The seat of Lancang County is Menglangba ('the Menglang basin'). According to the 2000 census (Lancang Statistics Bureau), the population of Lancang County was 464,016, of which the Lahu population, at 195,796, accounted for 42.2 percent. The residents of Lancang County also represented thirty-one other ethnic groups officially recognized by the Chinese Communist Party (CCP), including the Han (23.3 percent), the Wa (11.7 percent), the Hani (9.9 percent), the Yi (6.7 percent), the Dai (3.9 percent), the Bulang (1.4 percent), and the Hui (0.6 percent).

The distribution of the major ethnic groups in Lancang County forms a vertical pattern that largely corresponds to the groups' different subsistence patterns (Zhang et al. 1996). The Han, the Dai, the Yi, and the Hui are the dominant inhabitants of the lowland regions. These areas are located in valleys, flat basins, and low hills whose altitudes are less than 1,400 meters above sea level. Most land in these regions is arable and fertile, making it suitable for the cultivation of irrigated paddy rice and other tropical and semitropical crops. In contrast, the Lahu, the Hani, the Wa, and the Bulang are the major occupants of the highland areas, i.e., the middle or upper level of the mountains whose altitudes are greater than 1,400 meters above sea level. These highland farmers used to practice slash-and-burn cultivation before the 1950s. Owing to a devastating combination of deforestation and rapid population growth, the rotation cycle of swidden land has greatly declined since the 1950s while the use of fertilizers and pesticides has increased. Among the highlanders, some residents of the middle range of the mountains build terraced fields to grow wet rice. Nevertheless, most of these terraced paddy fields are nonirrigated, which means that crop yield depends heavily on the weather. Although they practice horticulture, highlanders of Lancang County also frequently engage in hunting and gathering and fishing. The major crops are dry rice, wheat, corn, buckwheat, and potatoes.

The combination of agricultural constraints and lack of infrastructure in Lancang highland areas tends to cause constant threats of food shortages. As a result, this population constitutes a vast majority of the impoverished population of Lancang County, which is one of the most impoverished counties in China. According to official statistics in 1990, more than 180,000 Lancang farmers (41 percent of the county's farming population) lived below the poverty standards of China, a condition commonly called "unable to have one's back covered and belly full" (*wenbaoxian* in Mandarin) (Zhang et al. 1996: 178–181). The standards set by the government in 1985 were an average of 200 kilograms of grain and 120 *yuan* (about $15) per person per year. Food shortages among the highlanders are, in fact, even more severe given the lack of protein in their diet. Therefore, despite their demographic dominance, the Lahu are by no means the economically advanced ethnic group in Lancang County. Because the vast majority of the people are highland farmers, struggling to survive is the society's major challenge. The crop yield of highland farmers also tends to be more vulnerable to natural disasters, which compounds the shortage of arable and fertile land.

Located in the mountainous regions on national borders and isolated by poor transportation infrastructures, most Lahu villages in Lancang have retained a high degree of ethnic and cultural homogeneity at the beginning of the twenty-first century. Nevertheless, since they constitute part of the ethnic mosaic of the Lancang area, Lahu villagers have historically developed interethnic relationships with other groups, a tendency that has drastically intensified since the development of the market economy in the 1980s. An increasing number of Chinese from other provinces have arrived and traded in the county seat of Lancang, in local townships, and in some village markets. More and more young Lahu men have begun to work outside the village doing contract work in lowland areas of Lancang County. Many Lahu women have migrated, and some have been abducted, to other provinces of China, typically marrying Han peasants who are unable to pay the high bride-price for local women. In the county seat, the entertainment industry (mainly in the form of karaoke bars), along with the increasing commodification of women's bodies elsewhere in China (e.g., Anagnost 1997:132), has boomed since the 1980s.

In addition to participation in regional and national market economies, Lancang County has become increasingly involved in the global economy. Since the 1980s, trade between China and Myanmar has begun to open. With the flourishing of cross-border trading, Lancang County has also suffered from being situated at the frontier, which means it serves as a doorway for the infiltration of drugs into China. The threat of drug addiction has become very severe, especially among youth in the county seat, as I observed during my last field trip in 1995–1996. Beyond the neighboring countries, Lancang County has also become involved in economic and social interactions with some Western countries. For example, joining a delegation consisting of local leaders in Simao prefecture, the head of Lancang County visited the United States in 1996. The Motorola Corporation sponsored the trip in exchange for an agreement that those officials would purchase its products for their respective administrative areas. In 2000, seventy-two out of the 157 administrative villages of the county (46 percent) were already connected to a program-controlled telephone system.

Most of my fieldwork was conducted in the village cluster of Qhawqhat, one of the eight village clusters of Nuoba Township (*xiang*). In 2000, over 80 percent of the more than 20,000 residents of Nuoba were Lahu Na. The population of Qhawqhat was about 2,300, and 99 percent of the people were Lahu Na. Qhawqhat consists of eight villages, of which all but one are only a few minutes' walk from an adjacent village.

The Lahu in Lancang County generally consider the Qhawqhat village cluster one of the few village clusters in which Lahu traditions have been

FIGURE 1 View of the Lahu village cluster of Qhawqhat. Photograph by Shanshan Du

FIGURE 2 Close-up view of Qhawqhat. Photograph by Shanshan Du

systematically maintained. According to the local Lahu elders, prior to 1949 Qhawqhat was among the strongest village clusters in the region in terms of the defense of its autonomy, and its village heads maintained a strong determination to preserve Lahu principles. Although the lives of Qhawqhat villagers can by no means be regarded as representing a "relic" of the "authentic" Lahu traditions, their dominant ideologies and social institutions are indeed widely shared, in various forms and to various degrees, across most Lahu subgroups and regions.[10]

PROJECT DEVELOPMENT AND METHODS

Many coincidences led me to study the Lahu people, who are one of the least visible groups among the twenty-six ethnic minorities in Yunnan Province in southwest China. In a linguistics course I took in 1985, I met my first Lahu–a college instructor named Cal Nud from a remote Lahu village in Lancang County who was auditing the course for his own academic improvement. Pleased by the interest of several classmates in his culture, Cal Nud invited us to Yunnan Nationalities College to attend his Lahu language course, which I took in the spring of 1986. Consequently, when I conducted pioneering fieldwork in 1987, I chose Lahu as one of the ethnic groups (along with the Dai and the Jinuo) to visit despite the very limited information and literature that were available on the Lahu culture. After the exploratory fieldwork, I decided to focus my research on the Lahu people because I was both warmly accepted by the local people I met and deeply intrigued by the cultural phenomena I encountered.

The project of writing this book originated in my ethnographic training in China. The Lahu perceptions of male and female fascinated me when I studied Lahu oral literature and religion during my fieldwork in 1987. However, the biases of my own cultural background (especially yin/yang philosophy), which manifested itself in my initial conceptualization of the Lahu worldview (Du 1987), hindered me from comprehending the core meanings of the Lahu "pair" and, therefore, from pursuing the issue further. Drawing heavily upon the findings of my previous fieldtrips, my doctoral fieldwork between 1995 and 1996 focused on the extremely high rate of love-pact suicide among Lahu youth. Ironically, in the process of seeking answers to this tragic social problem, many of my conceptual blinders were removed, enabling me to more fully comprehend and appreciate the dyadic and egalitarian ideals that dominate Lahu gender institutions and practices. My field-work eventually suggested to me that the dramatic increase in the number of Lahu suicides beginning in the 1950s was itself the result of a devastating clash between Lahu gender constructions and the radical socialist transformations imposed upon the Lahu during the Maoist era. Meanwhile, I also found it unrealistic to thoroughly examine this subject in my first extended piece of writing because of the extraordinary challenge of conceptualizing the Lahu gender system in the face of the scarcity of appropriate theoretical frameworks and ethnographies on the Lahu. This realization, combined with the thrill of putting together the pieces of a puzzle whose solution had once eluded me, made me decide to shift the focus of my dissertation to the Lahu gender system and to leave the suicide problem for my next large writing project. This book is the result of that decision.

The data for this project were gathered through a combination of archival research, a total of eighteen months of ethnographic fieldwork, and ongoing correspondence with my Lahu host families. From 1987 to 1990, I conducted six months of fieldwork in Yunnan, China, including three trips to Lancang County, two trips to Menglian County, and two trips to Jing-hong County and Menghai County. In the summer of 1992, I conducted two months of fieldwork among the Lahu and some other highland ethnic groups in northern Thailand. From October 1995 to August 1996, I conducted ten months of fieldwork in Lancang Lahu Autonomous County. My continuous correspondence with my designated Lahu relatives in Lancang has provided the most recent updates.

The ways in which individual Lahu perceived and received me greatly shaped both my fieldwork experiences and the ethnographic data of this book. Despite its salience in public and other contexts, my identification as a Han (the ethnic majority of China) by no means determined my interactions with the Lahu. Notwithstanding some negative perceptions of the Han that are widely shared by the Lahu, I did not detect a collective Lahu resentment of the Han, nor did I experience particular Lahu projecting their traumatic experiences in the political upheavals during the Maoist era upon individual Han. Living in a region that had its own complex ethnic mosaic, most Lahu villagers were aware of the fact that their neighboring ethnic groups, including the Han, experienced similar traumas. I personally never experienced any problem with my Han ethnic identity during my numerous encounters with Lahu individuals, nor did I observe any systematic animosity or tension between the Lahu and the few Han villagers living in the village cluster in which

I resided. In addition, for reasons of personal and intellectual history, my own identity as Han has been so decentered and mediated that it lacks the gravity necessary for a typical "problemization" in terms of "ethnic identity" (James Wilkerson 2002, personal communication).

If my ethnic identity by itself offered little more than an abstract, experience-distant identity, my various localized identities, which grew out of multiple webs of connectivity with Lahu individuals, offered the experience-near identity that framed the contexts within which I pursued the ethnography in this book. My official identity in the Lahu areas of China I visited was primarily as a Han student who came from Kunming (and later from a university in the United States) to learn Lahu culture and traditions. As a Chinese woman with junior social status and a personal preference for keeping a distance from institutional authorities, I usually drew little official attention, receiving neither the suspicion and constraints (Ruf 1998:xiii) nor the honors and support (Harrell 2001:7) experienced by some foreign ethnographers. Nevertheless, most individual officials I interacted with, especially those in the villages where I stayed relatively long, were all friendly and cooperative.

Many Lahu villagers with whom I had limited contact in different places and contexts offered me various nonofficial identities, including *hiet ma* ('Han woman'), *dawd peuq shief ma* ('wise or knowledgeable woman'), *awlha thawf shief ma* ('picture taker' or 'photographer'), or *jizhe* ('journalist'). My flattering informal identities, such as a "good friend of Lahu people" and "promoter of Lahu culture," were mostly introduced to villagers by Hu Calkheu, the very distinguished late Lahu singer and collector of folk songs who, beginning with my first fieldtrip, taught me Lahu oral literature and took me to villages. Influenced by his grandfather, a famous singer and ritual healer, Calkheu became one of the best folksingers in the surrounding village clusters before he left at the age of eighteen to work for the government at the county seat. As a preventive-healthcare worker, he had the opportunity to frequently visit villages all over the county. He often initiated antiphonal singing after work with the best local singers, both for entertainment and as a result of his passion for preserving the Lahu cultural heritage, especially the various creation myths. Accordingly, although lacking official recognition, he was extremely popular and revered among Lahu villagers and was also honored by the scholars who learned from him as "the living encyclopedia of Lahu oral literature." Benefiting from Calkheu's connections and reputation, I was well received by many Lahu elders and folksingers who were the specialists of Lahu "high culture."

My Lahu host families and friends constituted the most important personal and ethnographic resources for me in Lancang. In the township of Menglangba, the county seat of Lancang, I had two host families who sincerely and warmly took me in as their family member. As a humorous expression of intimacy, the elder relatives of one of my adoptive families sometimes called their own daughter "Xiao Na Gaf" ('younger silly girl') and me "Da Na Gaf" ('older silly girl'), especially when they saw us laughing over our own private little talks. Through these two families, I was connected to many of their extended families in rural Lancang areas, including my host families in Qhawqhat and in Banlo. In 1989, my Banlo family adopted me with a series of ceremonies including a touching ritual that named me as "Na Thawd." Elders from several related households chose the name because *thawd* means both 'rabbit' (my birth year) and 'stability,' which represented their perception that I had brought stability and hope back to the village after the devastating earthquake that had killed many villagers. Nevertheless, I decided not to conduct my long-term fieldwork in Banlo because I was overwhelmed by the contrast between the great hospitality of the villagers and the hostility of certain village officials who made up rumors about me, including some about my having antirevolutionary intentions in going to Lancang. Their resentment of me derived from the criticism and penalty they received after I presented to the county government the deep grievances of many villagers against the officials' ongoing corruption and abuse of power in the midst of earthquake relief.[11]

In stark contrast to my highly emotionally-charged relationships in Banlo, relaxation and calmness marked my social relations in the village cluster of Qhawqhat, where I conducted most of my fieldwork between 1995 and 1996. I was very comfortable with my junior status among Qhawqhat adults, being called "Yad Mid" (an endearing name for a young woman or girl) by my older adoptive relatives and "Xiao Du" ('Little Du,' a Han way of addressing junior colleagues) by officials. My host family consisted of a couple (Cal Pheud and Na Nud) and their two young children. I had known Cal Pheud since 1989 when his two cousins, whose ancestors were founders of the present-day Qhawqhat village cluster, accepted me as their designated sister (or cousin). The couple's house was located in the village of Abo, the center and one of the oldest villages in the village cluster. This living place provided me easy access to news and events of village life because it was located close to the ritual center of Qhawqhat, the intersections of several other villages, the administrative office (*cungongsuo*), and several village shops.

The major part of my participant observation was interwoven with my daily interactions with several Lahu families in Qhawqhat. I joined the domestic work of my host family on a daily basis and occasionally participated in their work in the fields. As did most Lahu villagers, the couple engaged in intense reciprocity with their relatives and therefore led me to extensive interactions with several other households in the village. These relations and communications provided me with opportunities to observe the dynamics of Lahu gender relations—especially in labor allocation, decision-making, conflict resolution, and inter- and cross-generational relationships. This greatly enriched my understanding of the relationship between Lahu gender ideals and practice. While interacting daily with several Lahu households, I also participated as much as possible in the public activities of the village cluster, including festivals, life-cycle rituals, the public antiphonal singing of Lahu folk songs, mass-media entertainment, and political events such as meetings of local cadres. Observation of these public events has helped me to understand Lahu symbolism and ideals as well as social interactions and transformations.

To complement participant observations, I also used interviews to elicit descriptive, autobiographical, evaluative, and reflective information from different sectors of the Lahu population. Most frequently, I engaged in spontaneous conversations during my daily interactions with villagers, especially with my adoptive relatives and friends. I also conducted intensive interviews to systematically obtain topical and normative information from knowledgeable individuals such as elders who served as traditional village heads, spiritual specialists, and respected local singers. On such occasions, I relied heavily on the guidelines and questions that I had previously prepared, and I recorded many such conversations by taking notes on the spot. In addition, I conducted group interviews to obtain different opinions on controversial issues such as the identity of the Lahu god Xeul Sha. While most groups were spontaneously formed in houses where rituals were being held or where relatives were gathered for Lahu festivals or events, I also organized focus groups of individuals chosen for their knowledge and interest in specific topics, such as retrospective surveys on the incidence of suicide in the village. While I used the Lahu language in some of my surveys, most of my interviews on specialized topics were conducted in the Yunnan dialect of Chinese with Lancang accent, which many local Lahu spoke. Occasionally, I also received help from local translators when I was unable to communicate with some elders on special topics or when I briefly visited villages of other ethnic groups such as the Wa and the Hani.

Beyond observations and general interviews, I conducted household surveys, the methods of which were developed gradually through my fieldwork, corresponding to my increasing understanding of the relationships between Lahu marriage, the kinship system, and gender relations at large. Before conducting such surveys, I usually drew maps on which I marked and numbered each house according to its geographical location in the village. The questions on household surveys focused on the head couples in the households and were often developed to quantitatively assess the norms I had found in my interviews. Topics included the couple's kinship relations prior to marriage, choice of marriage partners, residence patterns, land and/or household inheritance, and the allocation of labor in domestic and field work. To enhance the reliability of the results of these surveys, I further cross-checked my results in different contexts. If the information on certain households appeared unclear or conflicting after my preliminary analysis, I conducted follow-up interviews with members of the household or their close relatives. As my fieldwork progressed, I began to use household surveys to explore the historical dimensions of Lahu social life in order to identify the complex impact of radical social transformations on Lahu life at the household level.

Throughout my fieldwork, I conducted preliminary analysis on a regular basis. In addition to highlighting and summarizing significant information, such analysis helped me to identify unclear or conflicting information, which then generated questions for follow-up interviews and plans for future observations. Along with the preliminary analysis that regulated my day-to-day research, I also reviewed my data periodically with an eye to my overall project. I compared data on certain issues in order to continuously reconceptualize them and remain in touch with the theoretical concerns of my project as much as possible. This process frequently inspired me to move in new directions for further investigations to test and/or enrich my new hypothesis, thus modifying my research plans.

Some of this book's data came from archival research, mainly in Kunming, Lancang County, and in Chiang Mai of northern Thailand. My archival research in Kunming relied chiefly on publications preserved at the Yunnan Institute for Regional History, the Yunnan Nationalities College, the Library of Yunnan Province, and the Yunnan Academy of Social Sciences. This research provided me with information on Lahu history that had been recorded by official historians prior to the Chinese Communist Party (CCP) regime as well as literature concerning Lahu history, culture, and society that has been published during the CCP regime. My research in the Lancang Archives in Menglangba (the seat of Lancang County), which contain a complete record of official county documents, provided me with information on the history of the CCP rule in Lancang County and its impact on Lahu life since the 1950s. The documents in this archive included information on the county's major political and economic policies as well as reports from different administrative levels of policy implementation. My research focused on local implementation of policies on communization, the Cultural Revolution, and the economic reforms since the 1980s. In northern Thailand, I conducted archival research mainly at the Tribal Institute of Chiang Mai University and in the Chiang Mai Public Library. In both places, I collected many documents, unpublished manuscripts, and government reports on the Lahu of northern Thailand as well as some of the neighboring groups. These archival data covered a wide range of topics, and the authors included scholars in different disciplines from both Thailand and the Western world and from national and international development organizations, as well as government officials in a variety of departments.

Because of the sensitivity of my original research on suicide (Du 1994), I paid special attention to protecting the privacy of my interviewees even though my project focus gradually shifted away from this topic. I developed a coding system to record their names in order to prevent any breach of confidence in case my notebooks were lost or read without my permission. I recorded this code in a small booklet that was kept separately from my field notebooks. Although most of my interviewees stated that they would not mind their real names being used in my publications, I consistently use fictitious names to prevent those who preferred the use of pseudonyms from being indirectly identified. I made the exception of using the real name of Hu Calkheu in order to honor his extraordinary contribution to the preservation of Lahu oral literature.

THE AIM AND ORGANIZATION OF THE BOOK

The goal of this book is to conceptualize the fundamental cultural logic and social institutions of Lahu gender, which reveal both the existence and the diversity of gender-egalitarian societies. While primarily addressing academic audiences—especially those in the fields of anthropology, women's studies, and Asian studies—I also wrote this book with the intention of introducing the Lahu principle of gender unity to a more general audience that is interested in cultural diversity in gender equality. Personally, I thus hope the book to be accessible to my undergraduate students, many of whom are not majoring in anthropology, as well as to my friends outside academia. I particularly hope that, if the book were translated into Chinese, my literate Lahu friends would find the book accessible and worthy of discussion with me. With these considerations in mind, I have, whenever possible, avoided jargon and dense theoretical discussion that could form an obstacle for interdisciplinary and general readers. Many of the theoretical implications of the Lahu gender system and its transformations have been discussed (Du 1995, 1996, 1999a, 2000, 2001), or will be pursued, elsewhere.

This book consists of six chapters, organized into three parts dealing, respectively, with mythology and ideology, gender roles, as well as social structures and antistructures. Part 1—which includes chapters 1 and 2—demonstrates the symbolic elaboration of gender unity in traditional Lahu perceptions of the world and human life. Chapter 1 explores the dominance and prevalence of a dyadic worldview in mythology, rituals, classifications, and language. Chapter 2 discusses the application of such a worldview to the classification and symbolism of the life cycle, which is marked by the great emphasis on the joint social status of husband and wife throughout the life course and beyond.

The second part of the book—chapters 3 and 4—examines the ideals and practices of joint gender roles, epitomized by the dyadic teams of husbands and wives in labor, ownership, and leadership. Chapter 3 examines the joint responsibilities of a couple in both reproductive and productive tasks. Chapter 4 examines gender unity in the arena of ownership and leadership, manifested in the institution of "head couples" who are in charge of both households and some village offices.

Chapters 5 and 6—which comprise the third part of the book—examine the social structures that generate and perpetuate husband-wife dyads as well as the tensions and conflicts within those structures. Chapter 5 discusses the ways in which husband-wife dyads constitute the basic building blocks of Lahu kinship structures, in which the married man and woman are, in effect, regarded as a single social entity, which I call a "dyadic ego" or a "paired ego." Chapter 6 explores the tension between individual needs to dissolve marriages and social pressures to maintain them, a tendency that is built into Lahu traditions but has been exacerbated by the radical social changes since the 1950s.

In the conclusion, I discuss the theoretical implications of this study. After examining how certain historical, socioeconomic, and environmental factors have fostered the institutionalized equality between Lahu men and women in rural Lancang, I explore several forms and underlying principles of gender equality across cultures.

This book's organization reflects my intention to offer a balanced description of both gender ideals and practices among the Lahu. Specifically, following the first two chapters, which focus on overarching gender ideals, chapters 3 and 4 deal with gender roles, with special attention to the varying degrees of conformity to these gender ideals. While chapter 5 examines the social institutions that ground the husband-wife dyads, chapter 6 emphasizes the extreme forms of conflicts and deviance, including divorce, elopement, and love-pact suicide.

Despite my focus on the mainstream Lahu gender ideologies and institutions, I pay special attention throughout the book to locating Lahu gender and its transformation in historical context. In addition to focusing in chapter 6 on how radical social changes have drastically intensified the internal tensions and conflicts of Lahu gender structures, I also interweave data in other chapters concerning the ways in which state-imposed social changes have undermined Lahu gender ideologies, institutions, and social practices. More comprehensive and in-depth engagement of relevant theories and comparative studies will appear in some of my future writings, especially in the project on Lahu love-pact suicide.

PART 1

MYTHOLOGY AND IDEOLOGY

CHAPTER 1

"EVERYTHING COMES IN PAIRS": A DYADIC WORLDVIEW

GENDER IDEOLOGY constitutes an integral, or even the central, part of the dominant worldview of a culture. The Lahu ideology of gender unity is deeply rooted in the dyadic worldview that is expressed by the common saying, "Everything comes in pairs; aloneness does not exist" (*laiq ceol-laiq yal awl cie feuf, awl tif mad cawl*). In this chapter, I first examine the Lahu indigenous concept of "pair" (*awl cie*)—a single entity that is made up of two similar yet distinguishable components. I then explore the ideal pairs in Lahu mythology, which suggest a cosmological order of male-female dyads. After discussing the extreme pervasiveness of dyads in other domains of Lahu culture, I conclude with the argument that, by declaring an identical human nature and morality that is shared by both sexes, and by denying any epistemological predestination of sex difference in reproduction, the dyadic worldview generates the ideology of gender equality as a by-product.

"BOTH ONE AND TWO": PAIRS AS DYADS

Pairing appears to be a universal way in which cultures impose order upon the world people live in, including mythological realms, physical objects, social organization, and languages.[1] However, the patterns of pairing differ across cultures, depending on the diverse perceptions of and different emphasis on the relationship between the two parts and the relationship between the parts and the whole. While researchers often use the same category—"dualism"—to analyze pairs, many have revealed, explicitly or implicitly, alternative cultural principles of pairing, including the dichotomous, the complementary (Fox 1989:44–47; Nzegwu 1994), the dialectic

(Almagor 1989:165–166; Maybury-Lewis 1989:2–3), and the dyadic (Atkinson 1990:65; Errington1987).[2]

According to the Lahu indigenous worldview, the concept of the pair is predominantly dyadic. The dyadic principle focuses on the wholeness of the pair and highlights the similarities and harmony between the two components, which identify with each other through their shared membership and joint function in the whole. A dyad is comparable to an organic compound consisting of two elements in which neither element has an essential nature of its own and, therefore, no internally bounded identity. Being *one* entity that consists of *two* parts, the dyadic "pair" can be considered both "one" and "two," depending on the linguistic context.

Before I go on to discuss intrinsic connections between Lahu mythology and the dyadic principle, I would like to discuss the crystallization of the principle in two important objects in Lahu village life: chopsticks and ritual beeswax candles. The proverb "Chopsticks only work in pairs; a single chopstick cannot pick up food," typically used by parents to persuade their children to marry, reveals the dyadic nature of the Lahu concept of "pair." Although the two pieces of a pair of chopsticks are not physically connected to each other, a single stick is useless unless it joins with the other piece to form a unified tool. Since neither stick has any autonomous identity as a food-picking-up utensil, the two pieces must coexist symbiotically and function harmoniously within their shared identity in the pair. Additionally, the two sticks are identical in nature, and any superficial differences are often ignored, in contrast with the differences between the two components of a complementary pair such as a pair of shoes.

The paired beeswax candles offered to the Lahu supreme god go a step further in demonstrating the great salience of "oneness" in an ideal Lahu "pair." Made by folding and pressing together a thin beeswax stick while it is warm and flexible, each pair of traditional ritual candles consists of two inseparable parts. A single wick goes through the beeswax stick and is lit at both ends during rituals. Accordingly, a dyadic candle often has two flames although they may converge into one larger flame if the two ends of the candle are very close to each other (see figure 3). Such a ritual candle tangibly demonstrates the ideal Lahu pair, in which the two parts are so unified that they are not only inseparable but also barely distinguishable, functioning as a single entity. In this sense, any effort to discern the exact number of candles that constitute such a dyadic piece would be fruitless. The images and symbolism of chopsticks and ritual beeswax candles can

FIGURE 3 A Lahu household altar displaying paired offerings, including beeswax candles, rice cakes, and bowls of water, to Xeul Sha and the paired guardian spirits of the household. Photograph by Shanshan Du

help us comprehend the more abstract dyads embedded in Lahu mythology and beyond.

TWIN-DYADS IN ORIGIN MYTHS

The mainstream Lahu worldview and gender ideals have been greatly shaped by the extremely rich origin myths, which have been most completely preserved, typically in the form of the antiphonal singing of poetic songs, in Lancang Lahu Autonomous County.[3] Lahu origin myths are preoccupied with dyadic relationships, which are neither the mother-infant symbiosis described by Shakespeare in his poem "The Phoenix and the Turtle" (Bock 1987:258), nor the perfect sexual union (the reunion of the two halved souls) elaborated by Aristophanes in Plato's *Symposium* (de Botton 1999:719). Instead, similar to that in Balinese mythology (Boon 1990, Errington 1987), the ideal pair in Lahu mythology is identified with cross-sex twins. Born as a pair and acting as one, the Lahu supreme god Xeul Sha, Xeul Sha's Senior Daughter and Senior Son, and the first human couple epitomize the ideal male-female dyad, which can be considered both one and two.

SUPREME GOD XEUL SHA: THE PRIMORDIAL TWIN-DYAD

Lahu people across subgroups, regions, and countries share the beliefs in a supreme god named Xeul Sha. The perception of Xeul Sha as the creator of the universe is commonly held by the Lahu Na and Lahu Shi in China (Du 1996; Lei and Liu 1999:57) as well as by the Lahu Nyi (Lewis 1984; Walker 1986) and Lahu Shehleh in Thailand (Plath and Hill 1992). The great prevalence of Xeul Sha in Lahu symbolism and in daily lives leads some scholars to characterize Lahu culture as "Xeul Sha culture" (Gen 1997:191) and Lahu religion as "Xeul Sha religion" (Lei and Liu 1999:58). Even the Lahu who have accepted world religions have preserved their indigenous supreme god to varying degrees. For instance, Xeul Sha is Buddha for the Lahu who practice Buddhism (Walker 1986; Wang and He 1999) and God for those who have adopted Protestant or Roman Catholic Christianity (Wang and He 1999; Ge 1997:226).

According to Lahu origin myths, Xeul Sha is a pair of cross-sex twins, representing the primordial dyad and the ultimate cosmological order.[4] While colloquial Lahu calls the paired god by the single name Xeul Sha, the poetic versions of origin myths usually separate the pair and refer to the twins as Xeul Yad and Sha Yad. Although the two names themselves are not gender-specific, most Lahu elders consider it common sense that Xeul Yad is male and Sha Yad is female. As suggested by the following verses, which are found in many versions of origin myths in Lancang, the twin gods came into being simultaneously from the void prior to the existence of the universe (Cal Yawl 1989:1):

A long time ago / There was no sky for Xeul Yad to live in,
In the very ancient times / There was no earth for Sha Yad to stay on.
Xeul Yad was as thin as a hair / Sha Yad was as small as a leg hair.
Xeul Yad raised Xeul / Sha Yad raised Sha [Xeul Sha raised themselves].
Xeul Yad turned around / Xeul Yad grew big,
Sha Yad stretched out / Sha Yad grew tall.

The twin gods are often depicted as if they were a single joint entity who created the universe and human beings. After making a few male-female pairs to serve as assistants, Xeul Sha created the earth (female) and the sky (male), the sun (female) and the moon (male), the water and the vegetation that cover the earth, and then the animals (Du and Hu 1996; Lei and Liu 1999:57–60). In order to solicit offerings, Xeul Sha also created and raised a pair of demigods called Xeul Sha's Senior Daughter and Senior Son, who were eventually punished with death for their rebellion (Du and Hu 1996; Hu 1996). To replace them, Xeul Sha then created the original humans, a pair of twins who came out of a gourd. Xeul Sha raised the first human twins, taught them how to hunt and farm, and instructed them to marry. Xeul Sha looked after the offspring of the first human couple—who became the ancestors of the human population—and taught them hunting, farming, and customs such as clothing styles and the Lahu New Year celebration as well as guiding them to live in different places. The following verses of Lahu origin myths exemplify how the twin gods acted as a single concordant entity during the entire process of creation (Cal Yawl 1989:15–16):

> There was no sun / Day was unable to divide,
> There was no moon / Night was unable to divide.
> This was not too difficult for Xeul Yad / This was not too hard for
>   Sha Yad.
> Xeul Yad had an idea / Sha Yad had a plan,
> Xeul Yad wanted to make / a flower in the sky,
> Sha Yad intended to create / a flower on the earth.
> The sky flower of Xeul Yad / was the sun in the sky,
> The earth flower of Sha Yad / was the moon in the sky . . . .
> Xeul Yad rubbed out hand-scurf [detritus resulting from sloughed skin
>   and dirt],
> Made gold from the scurf [later used to smelt the sun].
> Sha Yad rubbed out foot-scurf,
> Made silver from the scurf [later used to smelt the moon].

While undertaking joint roles in creation, the dyadic supreme gods also demonstrate identical capacity, rationality, emotions, and morality. The commensurate capacity of Xeul Yad and Sha Yad to reason is shown in many commonly used expressions such as "The wisdom of Xeul Yad is endless, the intelligence of Sha Yad is infinite" and "Xeul Yad thought back and forth, Sha Yad pondered deeply." The identical morality and reasoning of the twin gods are most profoundly reflected in their effort to educate their Senior Daughter and Senior Son regarding filial piety and their difficult decision to punish their rebellion with death. Additionally, the twin gods exhibit the same emotional reactions to circumstances. For example, after the death of their Senior Daughter and Senior Son, "Xeul Yad cried for three days, Sha Yad cried for three nights . . . their tears formed a large lake." In contrast, when a bee messenger reported the birth of Only Man–Only Woman's nine pairs of children, "Xeul Yad was joyful, Sha Yad was glad."

According to the available versions of Lahu creation myths, the twin gods always acted as if they were one entity with the exception of one situation in which their efforts were not perfectly coordinated (Hu Calkheu 1987, personal communication):

> When Xeul Yad built the sky / Xeul Yad was conceited about [his] strength;
> Frequently drank tea and rested / The sky was made small.
> When Sha Yad created the earth / Sha Yad was not conceited about [her] strength;
> Worked diligently day and night / The earth was made big.

To solve the problem caused by their lack of coordination, Xeul Sha shrank the earth with a net, causing the formation of mountains, valleys, and rivers. Similar explanations of the origin of the earth's topography exist in many versions of Lahu creation myths (e.g., Cal Yawl 1989:10–11; Sanit 1974:146; Walker 1995:3).[5]

Focusing on the dyadic identity of the supreme god, Lahu origin myths trivialize and sometimes even disguise the sexual identities of the twins. Specifically, they are described as having emerged simultaneously as identical twins, acting concordantly and sharing the same intellect and emotion. Therefore, without close examination through an academic magnifying glass, male and female parts of Xeul Sha are barely distinguishable in Lahu creation myths. According to the Lahu folksingers I interviewed in Lancang, the poetic versions of lengthy myths reveal the male and female identities of the twin gods only in a few verses found in the most comprehensive versions. Even the late folklorist and local singer Hu Calkheu, who was strongly critical of academic ignorance about the issue, could identify only the following verses that clearly specify that Xeul Yad is male and Sha Yad is female:[6]

At the very beginning / At the very start,
There was no sky in the world / There was no earth in the world.
Xeul Yad came into being / Sha Yad came into existence.
At the time when Xeul Yad was born / At the moment when Sha Yad was
  born,
Xeul Yad was as thin as a hair / Sha Yad was as small as a leg hair.
Xeul Yad turned around and grew big / Sha Yad stretched out and grew tall.
Xeul Yad took the name of Cal Pul [male name],
Sha Yad took the name of Na Pul [female name].

Beyond these verses that offer Xeul Yad and Sha Yad gender-specific names, no Lahu folksingers I interviewed could find any descriptions of morphological and reproductive differences between the cross-sex twin gods in Lahu origin myths. Therefore, the identities of Xeul and Sha join with each other so tightly that they not only share nearly identical features but are also almost indistinguishable. The blending of identities and attributes of Xeul and Sha contrasts sharply with Zeus and Hera in Greek mythology, who represent, respectively, the opposite features that are associated with masculinity and femininity. While Hera constantly creates trouble and chaos out of unpredictable emotions, Zeus always plays the key role in restoring order.

The dyadic nature of the Lahu supreme god manifests itself beyond mythology. On the one hand, the wholeness of twin gods is highly emphasized. Most important, the paired gods frequently appear in Lahu colloquial conversations referred to by only the single name Xeul Sha. Accordingly, during festivals and rituals, Xeul Sha is worshipped as an inseparable entity, as shown in the symbolism of the traditional beeswax candles. On the other hand, Lahu symbolism often recognizes the two components of the dyadic god, especially in the form of supernatural dual parents, as in the saying "*Apa Xeul o, A-e Sha o*" or "*Apa Xeul Sha-o! A-e Xeul Sha-o!*" ('Xeul is father, Sha is mother') (Hu 1996; Wang and He 1999:179). Worshipping the parental god Xeul Sha and honoring one's natural parents jointly mark the core symbolism of important Lahu festivals, especially the New Year Festival and the New Rice Tasting Festival. All offerings to Xeul Sha are conventionally expected to be in pairs, including beeswax candles, bowls of water, rice cakes, and stalks of sugarcane (see figure 3).

Some village clusters in Lancang have developed local traditions that highlight the dyadic nature of the Lahu supreme god. For example,

Qhawqhat villagers call the three nearby mountain peaks the cooking-stones (or the hearth) where Xeul Yad and Sha Yad are believed to have cooked together during their creation of the sky and the earth. During the Lahu New Year Festival, villagers ritually walk through these three mountain peaks to "dump weed seeds" (*mur yawd pud bal*) at Xeul Sha's hearth so that fewer weeds will sprout in their fields in the coming year. More dramatically, Fulqhat villagers built two adjacent Buddhist temples in the center of their village cluster to worship Buddha, who has been transformed into the indigenous god Xeul Sha (Du 2001). According to villagers and the chief monks, because Xeul Sha (Buddha) is a pair, they need a pair of temples in which to rest.

Most Lahu villagers I interviewed in Lancang recognized Xeul Sha as a male-female pair although generational difference is obviously reflected in such recognition.[7] Similar perceptions of the Lahu supreme god have also been found in different Lahu subgroups in northern Thailand. For instance, Sanit (1974:146) recorded that the Lahu Nyi considered their supreme god to consist of the father Xeul Sha and his wife Ai Ma. Bearing more resemblance to many Lancang Lahu in China, Lahu Shehleh tended to reply that Xeul Sha was both male *and* female when asked whether Xeul Sha was a male or a female.[8]

While many Lahu villagers (especially the elders) in Lancang and elsewhere take for granted that Xeul Sha is a pair of male and female, the two-in-one nature of the Lahu supreme god generates conflicting interpretations in academia. The vast bulk of Chinese literature on the Lahu implies that Xeul Sha is a single god whose sexual identity is often either unspecified by the author (Wang 1983:258; Wang and He 1999:179) or described as "ambiguous"(Chen and Li 1986:78). In contrast, some scholars occasionally identify Xeul Sha as a male by using third-person masculine pronouns (Gen 1997:191; Lei and Liu 1999:58), and others describe Xeul Sha as a female who has a husband (Wang 2001:246). Meanwhile, a few scholars also recognize that Xeul Sha is a male-female pair (Du 1996; Du and Hu 1996; Wang and He 1999:179).

The nature of the Lahu supreme god is hidden in the indigenous cultural fabric, expressed only by the seemingly universal term "pair" rather than being highlighted and elaborated as a unique cultural concept. Therefore, it is extremely difficult for people from a different cultural background to comprehend the dyadic nature of Xeul Sha. Interestingly, even if an indigenous scholar were to notice the academic misunderstandings and inform a

fortunate researcher that Xeul Sha is a pair, the researcher would be in-
clined to understand the concept "pair" according to his or her own cultural background and therefore miss the "two-in-one" dyadic ideal. By il-
lustrating the turning point of such a fortunate researcher (myself) in
understanding the issue, the following story may help some readers better
comprehend the identity of Xeul Sha in particular and the dyadic nature of
the Lahu pair in general.

During my first visit to Lancang in 1987, the Lahu singer and folklorist Hu
Calkheu informed me that Xeul Sha was actually a pair; this was supported
both by his citations from Lahu creation myths and by my later interviews
with Lahu villagers (Du 1987, 1996; Du and Hu 1996). Until the time of my
conversations with one of the most knowledgeable elders in the Fulqhat village cluster in 1996, however, I understood Xeul Sha only as two gods, no
matter how unified they were in presentations in Lahu mythology and ritual
symbolism. Hoping to elicit more information on the distinctions between
the male and female halves, I once pointedly reoriented my question to the
elder regarding the identity of Xeul Sha by using the phrase "one or two,"
rather than "pair or alone" or "male or female." He paused for a moment,
then replied that Xeul Sha was one. While startled by his "inconsistency," I
also realized that he was the first Lahu elder I encountered who seemed to
deny that Xeul Sha was two gods. I sharply pointed to his previous statements
that Xeul Sha was a pair of male and female (thus unquestionably two from
my perspective) and expected him to solve the "contradiction" by making a
definite choice. Smiling, he replied, "Xeul Sha is a pair. One is right. Two is
[also] right." Challenged by the illogical yet plausible statement of Xeul Sha
as "both one and two," I finally realized that my analytical bias derived from
the yin/yang philosophy of my own culture, which focuses on the dialectic
interactions between the *two* components (Du 1987).

THE DYADIC DEMIGOD: THE REBELLIOUS TWINS

As an integral part of Lahu origin myths and local beliefs, the story of a
dyadic demigod explains the origins of the life and death of human beings.
As a supernatural male-female pair, the demigod signifies the ideal of dyadic
unity, possessing power and intelligence close to that of the supreme god. As
a dyadic moral being, however, the demigod sets up an extremely negative
example that serves as a lesson for humans.

Created simultaneously by Xeul Sha out of the same substance and for the same purpose, the paired demigod can also be considered cross-sex identical twins. According to the origin myths that are widespread in Lancang villages (Hu 1996), after creating the universe and the animals, Xeul Sha set up four altars, one for each of the four directions of the sky and the earth. The animals proved disappointing because they failed to understand how to make offerings. After much deliberation, Xeul Sha created Senior Daughter–Senior Son (Nie Xeul–Yad Xeul) out of the skin scurf of Xeul's foot and Sha's hand, respectively. While the name of the demigod directly reveals Senior Daughter–Senior Son's different sex identities, their bodily builds are described as similar in verses such as "Senior Daughter's body was as huge as half the sky, Senior Son's body was as large as half the earth."

Unlike the creator Xeul Sha, who emerged from the void with ultimate intelligence and wisdom, Senior Daughter–Senior Son came into being as children who lacked the knowledge to survive despite their enormous body forms. Lahu myths offer detailed descriptions of how Xeul Sha taught the twins to survive and manage the natural environment, particularly slash-and-burn cultivation and hunting skills (Hu 1996). In the process of their socialization, the twins demonstrated identical intellectual capacity as well as supernatural strength in applying their knowledge as a single concordant unity, as shown in the following verses (Hu 1996:66).

Nie Xeul–Yad Xeul burnt the land / Not knowing what to do next
Sought guidance from white-headed Xeul / Requested advice from yellow-headed Sha . . . .
Xeul Yad rubbed out foot-scurf / Sha Yad rubbed out some hand-scurf.
Xeul Yad created plow and rake / Handed over to Nie Xeul [Senior Daughter],
Sha Yad made water-buffalo / handed over to Yad Xeul [Senior Son].
Nie Xeul–Yad Xeul went to plow with joy,
Completed nine mountains and nine valleys in seven days and seven nights.[9]
Not knowing what to do the next / Nie Xeul–Yad Xeul sought guidance again . . . .[10]
[During harvest] Senior Daughter could carry rice, nine kangs and nine bags on each trip,
Senior Son could carry rice, nine bags and nine kangs on each round . . . .
Senior Daughter–Senior Son hunted animals and cooked meals,
Ate new rice seven days and seven nights.

In contrast to the animals, Senior Daughter–Senior Son were created with the capacity to learn how to produce rice, which could be used to make offerings to their creator. More significantly, the twins were created as moral beings who not only possessed the capacity to recognize their creator but also had the free will to decide whether they wanted to honor their parents and fulfill their filial responsibility to make offerings to Xeul Sha.

Parallel to their identical experiences of learning and laboring, the moral stands of the paired demigod also developed simultaneously as a seamless entity. After their first successful harvest, Senior Daughter–Senior Son jointly decided to neglect, and thus rebel against, Xeul Sha. Senior Daughter–Senior Son ate alone, neglecting Xeul Sha and failing to offer new rice to their white-haired parents. Senior Daughter–Senior Son claimed that she-he had produced the rice through their own strength, ability, and hard work. Thus, Senior Daughter–Senior Son made offerings of new rice to their own knees and wrists, and ignored their parents Xeul and Sha.

Attempting to encourage Senior Daughter–Senior Son to fulfill their filial responsibility, Xeul Sha made the following remarks (Hu 1996:66):

> Senior Daughter, your body is as huge as half the sky, yet you were brought up by us; Senior Son, your body is as large as half the earth, yet you were raised by us. We provided you seeds . . . taught you production, why don't you offer us the newly produced rice?

Nevertheless, "Nie Xeul did not listen to the words of Xeul, Yad Xeul did not obey the words of Sha" (Hu 1996). Thus, the paired demigod jointly resisted recognizing, let alone honoring, their relationship with and obligation to Xeul Sha. To declare their rebellious and newly independent identity, Senior Daughter–Senior Son renamed themselves Na Hie [female name]–Cal Hie [male name]. Although also bearing the positive connotation 'strong', the term *hie* is extremely derogative when used to describe personality in Lahu culture, meaning 'harsh', 'boasting', 'arrogant', and 'aggressive.'

Xeul Sha eventually gave up hope for the demigod twins and determined to eliminate them. In the process of thwarting Xeul Sha's several attempts to kill them, the paired demigod acted as one entity and demonstrated a supernatural creativity, finding ingenious methods for surviving floods as well as the heat brought by nine suns and the cold caused by nine moons. Finally, Xeul Sha came up with the idea of taking advantage of the arrogance and ill temper of the demigod. Xeul Sha created a pair of insects that had strong, sharp stingers and made loud noises that sounded as if they were bragging of their strength and placed them on the path of the demigod. Irritated and offended by the noises, Senior Daughter stepped on one insect and Senior Son swatted the other. Unable to remove the stingers from her foot and his palm, they had to ask Xeul Sha for treatment. Following Xeul Sha's advice, they used an ax to remove the stingers and bound up the wounds with cattle dung and flies. When they opened their bandages after seven days and seven nights as suggested, maggots had eaten up to her knee and to his elbow. They eventually died, after putting some poisonous medicine offered by Xeul Sha on their rotten limbs. At this point, the narration of the myth renames the demigod Cal Nud–Cal Pie—nud refers to 'cattle' and pie refers to 'bind up'—symbolizing their dishonorable and repulsive death. The ground powder of the twins' corpses was transformed into mosquitoes and a kind of thorny plant, both of which are harmful to humans.

The story of the demigod associates arrogance and rebellion with the ultimate immorality that destroyed the potential immortality of the supernatural twins. Additionally, the shared sin of the demigod twins seems to have destroyed the potential for a perfect cosmic order represented by a presumably everlasting relationship between the dual parents and the twin children. While the story serves as a transitional section leading to human origin in the framework of Lahu mythology, it is most frequently sung during wakes to explain the origin of death. Many local customs in Lancang are consistent with the negative image of the demigod twins. For instance, it is taboo to sing the story at weddings, where Lahu creation myths are a popular theme, in order to protect the newlyweds from the misfortune of bearing unfilial and irresponsible children who, in real life, are accused of being Cal Nud–Cal Pie.

It is worthwhile noting that there exist in China both villain and hero versions of the stories of the Lahu demigod that represent different moralities and gender ideologies. As an integral part of Lahu origin myths and well-known among Lahu villagers, the villain stories depict the demigod as rebellious cross-sex twins who set up a negative moral example for humans. In contrast, the hero versions always appear as independent Lahu epics or folk stories that mention neither Xeul Sha's creation nor the names Senior Daughter and Senior Son (Du and Hu 1996; Liu 1988:114–118). This official version of the story portrays Cal Nud–Cal Pie as a single male hero who righteously rose up against the oppressive authority of the supreme god.[11] When the hero epic first reached Lahu villages through the broadcast station of Lancang County in the 1970s (during the Cultural Revolution), villagers' complaints pressured the officials to stop the program. However, the heroic version remains so dominant in both the official and academic representations of Lahu mythology that many educated Lahu have adopted it with ethnic pride. While several Lahu scholars I know strongly disagree with the hero version of the story without voicing their objections in public, some argue that "We Lahu people also need an ethnic hero."

THE ORIGINAL TWIN-COUPLE AND HUMAN MORALITY

Consistent with other parts of Lahu mythology, the original humans were also presented as an ideal dyad, i.e., a pair of cross-sex twins. Unlike the immortal supreme god and the potentially immortal demigod, the first human twins were created to be mortal beings whose reproductive necessity generated the division of sex roles (especially in pregnancy and childbirth). Nevertheless, Lahu origin myths tend to trivialize, rather than essentialize, such a division by denying the existence of any epistemological predestination.

Like the demigod dyad, the first human twins were created simultaneously by Xeul Sha out of the same substance and for the same purpose: making offerings to the parental god. According to Lahu origin myths, among which there are only minor variations, the first humans came out of a gourd rather than being created directly from the scurf of Xeul Sha (Cal Yawl 1989:40; Lei and Liu 1999:60; Liu 1988:24–41). After overcoming their grief at the deaths of Senior Daughter–Senior Son, Xeul Sha created a gourd seed out of their scurf and planted it. From the gourd came the first human male-female pair, called Cal Tif–Na Tif ('Only Man–Only Woman'). Xeul Sha raised Only Man–Only Woman identically, and their sex difference is manifested only in gendered names. The following verses portray the identical vulnerability of both twins and of their extreme dependence on Xeul Sha (Cal Yawl 1989:60; Liu 1988:41):

> Xeul Yad raised Cal Tif [male twin]/ Sha Yad raised Na Tif [female twin] . . . .
> All the beasts wanted to eat Cal Tif / All the birds desired to eat Na Tif.
> Cal Tif's face turned green from fear / Hurried to tell Xeul Yad;
> Na Tif's face turned pale from terror / Rushed to report to Sha Yad . . . .[12]

When Only Man–Only Woman reached physical maturity, the ideal twin-dyad began to be challenged by the necessity of sexual reproduction, which was a nonissue for both Xeul Sha and the paired demigods. Xeul Sha, although believed to be both male and female, produced "children" by using their body parts (scurf), thus involving neither sex differentiation nor sexual encounters. With potential immortality and supernatural strength sufficient to farm all the land under the sun, the demigod twins had never needed to reproduce themselves. In contrast, the first pair of human beings were created as mortal beings, and sexual reproduction became a necessity.

According to Lahu origin myths (e.g., Cal Yawl 1989:62–66; Liu 1988:44–47), Xeul Sha suggested that Only Man–Only Woman marry each other so that they could produce children. Acting as a single moral being, the twins declined Xeul Sha's proposal, invoking their siblinghood. Attempting to inspire the only pair of human beings, Xeul Sha requested each twin to take one half of a grinder, consisting of two large round stone pieces that grind against each other to produce a powdered or liquefied substance, and roll it down a mountain. Although the male and female pieces of the grinder ended up in a conjoined position, the twins claimed that siblings should not follow the example of the stone grinder. Failing in several other similar attempts to inspire and convince the human twins, Xeul Sha offered them an aphrodisiac without telling them its function. After drinking it, Only Man–Only Woman "stayed together" (a euphemism for 'having sex'). The couple jointly experienced such intense feelings of guilt and shame that they begged those who witnessed their sinful actions (an eagle and a leopard) not to tell Xeul Sha, promising them rights to the livestock of their offspring in the future. On the other hand, strong cultural adoration of the mystical ideal dyad is also manifested in some local customs that allow a pair of cross-sex twins to marry if they wish because they are believed to be matched by Xeul Sha before birth (Wang and He 1999:154).

Violation of the incest taboo transformed the ideal twin-dyad into a sexual union, resulting in the division of reproductive roles between the sexes. Since Xeul Sha created the twins without clear role assignments, Lahu mythological explanations of the origin of sex difference in human reproduction are filled with coincidences, experiments, and negotiations. While some versions described the twin sister's pregnancy and childbirth without explanation (Cal Yawl 1989:67), I have not found a single version of Lahu origin myths suggesting that Xeul Sha assigned the role of pregnancy and childbirth exclusively to Only Woman. Interestingly, many versions of origin stories claim the same initial reproductive capacity for both twins and explain how some roles were later assigned exclusively to women. According to some versions of origin myths (e.g., Walker 1995; Lei and Liu 1999:115; Liu 1988:47–48), the twin brother first became pregnant and carried the fetuses inside his calves until they accidentally fell out while he was walking. Fortunately, the twin sister caught the fetuses and wrapped them up inside the front of her garment where they penetrated her belly and remained until she delivered them. Along a similar line, another version more clearly states that the twin sister altruistically took over the reproductive burden from her brother out of compassion and wisdom. The close association between the decision of Only Woman and the origin of women's reproductive role is shown by the following story (Wang 1990:40–41):

> Carrying the fetuses within his calves rather than within his belly, the brother [Only Man] was unable to walk or work, thus the sister [Only Woman] had to cut trees and dig the ground alone. After each childbirth, the sister had to kill cattle to feed the brother [for his recovery], thus, they had fewer and fewer cattle left. . . . During a particular pregnancy, the brother carelessly kicked the threshold and the fetuses miscarried from his broken toes, suffering from the pains that almost killed him. Out of sympathy, the sister said, "Brother, while carrying fetuses in calves, you cannot work and you have difficulty in labor. After childbirth, cattle have to be killed to feed you. When all cattle are killed [one day], how can we plow the vast mountainous fields? [Therefore], let me become pregnant and give birth to children from now on. I will carry fetuses within my belly, thus I can normally walk and work, and will have little difficulty in giving birth. After childbirth, it will no longer be necessary to kill cattle; several chickens will do." From then on, pregnancy and childbirth became women's tasks, and chickens are killed after childbirth.

Like pregnancy and childbirth, nursing and raising children are not depicted as tasks naturally and exclusively assigned to Only Woman in Lahu mythology. Rather than demonstrating the "natural instinct" of motherhood, Only Woman left behind the many newborn twins because she did not know how to handle them. After rescuing the infants and using various animals to nurse them (Cal Yawl 1989:71–73; Liu 1988:54–55), Xeul Sha was actively involved in raising and teaching them. These newborns then became the ancestors of different ethnic groups.

By representing the supreme god, the demigod, and the first human couple as three pairs of cross-sex twins, Lahu mythology expresses a cosmological order that is based on male-female dyads. The two halves of the ideal dyads are so tightly connected to each other that their gender difference is not marked and does not demonstrate any essentially different attributes that are comparable to the dichotomy between femininity and masculinity. In addition, Lahu mythological stories of Only Man–Only Woman tend to trivialize the epistemological and symbolic significance of sex difference in reproductive roles, thus contributing to the social expectations of husbands' maximum participation in the pregnancy and childbirth of their wives (see chapter 3).

THE PREEMINENCE OF DYADS

The dyadic worldview imposes its order on Lahu lives beyond mythological figures and human beings. The pervasiveness of pairs is expressed by the common saying "Everything comes in pairs; aloneness does not exist," a phrase appearing frequently in oral literature, wedding ceremonies, and daily conversations. The effort of the Lahu people to conform to the paired cosmological order can be observed in almost all areas of their lives, especially in rituals, folk beliefs, language, and folk classification systems.

RITUALS AND LOCAL BELIEFS

The dyadic cosmological order prevails in Lahu symbolism (Wang 2001:235), especially in rituals and festivals. According to the conventions of many rural Lahu across subgroups and across many regions, a complete wedding ceremony is a dyadic process, one part held at the house of the bride's parents and the other at that of the groom's parents (Lei and Liu 1999:84; Wang and He 1999:104–105). In general, the rituals performed at both locations are similar. Nevertheless, the rituals held on the bride's side precede those held on the groom's side and tend to be more elaborate. While such distinctions by gender seem to suggest the symbolic advantage of women over men, all of the villagers I interviewed denied any association between gendered values and the differences between the two parts of a wedding. Therefore, when arranging a wedding into a pair of male-female parts, Lahu villagers focus on completing a dyadic entity in accordance with their cosmological order rather than on essentializing the contrast between the two parts.

The Lahu New Year Festival is also a male-female dyad consisting of a female period and a male period. This custom is widely shared by the Lahu across subgroups and regions. Typically, "Women's New Year Festival" (also called the "Big New Year Festival") precedes "Men's New Year Festival" (or the "Small New Year Festival"), and the former tends to contain more days than the latter. Some folk stories trace the origin of Men's New Year Festival to a historical event when women decided to create it for the men who had missed the festival because they returned late from hunting (Wang and He 1999:245; Lei and Liu 1999:97). Again, Lahu villagers denied any gendered values associated with the differences between the male and female parts of the Lahu New Year Festival. The customs that require local villagers to ensure that the New Year Festival comes with paired or even days are also found among the Lisu people (Gillogly 2000), who are closely related to the Lahu both linguistically and culturally.

The effort to make a paired festival is shown in some local responses to the officially established ethnic festival of the Lahu people—the Gourd Festival celebrated mainly in Lancang. For the sake of increasing ethnic awareness among the Lahu, the government of the Lancang Lahu Autonomous County designated the fifteenth to the seventeenth day of the tenth month in the lunar calendar as the Gourd Festival (*Aq Phor-Aq Lor Ni*) in 1992 (Wang and He 1999:244). Although the county government promotes the ethnic festival by organizing large-scale annual celebrations at the county seat, only a few village clusters (such as Fulqhat) had incorporated the new festival into their local traditions in 1996. In Fulqhat, the three-day official festival was turned into a paired festival composed of a six-day female period, a four-day male period, and a two-day rest period in between. One of the most articulate elders clearly explained their rationale: "Everything comes in pairs; aloneness does not exist. This is the principle of our Lahu (*Ladhof ve awl lid*). The new Lahu festival needs to be practiced according to the principle."

Parallel to the traditions that expect some rituals and festivals to be celebrated as pairs, social etiquette requires most of the offerings and gifts for rituals and festivals to be presented in dyadic items. As discussed earlier, the beeswax candles are made as an inseparable paired entity, the two components of which are hardly distinguishable. Other major offering items such as pieces of sticky-rice cakes, sticks or bundles of incense, bowls of water, and stalks of sugarcane are made into pairs by arranging them in even numbers. Interestingly, although many villagers claim that the gifts and offerings represent male-female pairs, most of these pairs are indistinguishable in shape and size.

The ideals of gender unity are also manifested in the paired guardian deities at various levels including the guardian deities of the household (*yiel sheor*), the village (*sha sheor* or *qhaw shief phad lawf shief phad*), and the village cluster (*fuf shief phad*) (see details in chapter 4). Although these deities seem to be absent in Lahu oral literature, local religious beliefs in Lancang consider them to be Xeul Sha's servants (*zi yad*), who are responsible for protecting villagers' daily well-being. Villagers recognize the paired nature of these deities in their offerings, which are ritually presented in pairs, as are the offerings to Xeul Sha. Likewise, the female and male halves of these deities are hardly distinguishable in rituals and oral representations. Lahu villagers do not make statues of their household and village guardian deities, so there are no visual images of them. All of the elders I interviewed were very certain that these deities are cross-sex pairs, and some supported their statements with the common saying "Things are manageable only when a pair of male-female masters rule together" (*shief phad shief ma qha peif thar kuad xad*).

Another significant dyad in Lahu local beliefs is "the world of the living" (*chaw chit khie*) and "the world of the dead" (*si mud mil*). According to Lahu cosmology, the combination of the two subworlds constitutes the whole world, which is in the care of the supreme god Xeul Sha (Du 1987). The dyadic existence of the two worlds reaches to the level of the village and the household. It is widely believed that the villages and households in the world of the living are made whole by the existence of their counterparts in the world of the dead. The death of a person in the world of the living corresponds to the birth of a person in the world of the dead. Any increase of property in the world of the living suggests a loss in its counterpart household in the world of the dead. Although some star-crossed lovers idealize the world of the dead when planning double suicides, and many elders tend to depreciate it in order to combat the suicide epidemics (see chapter 6), the dominant belief considers it similar to the world of the living.

The significance of making a pair in rituals is manifested in certain funeral symbolism of the Lahu Shi village cluster of Fulqhat. The local custom demands that people attend a funeral in even numbers so that nobody is left without a partner, thus avoiding the risk that a lone soul may be persuaded to stay in the world of the dead after the ceremony. In other words, regardless of the size of the crowd, the soul of an individual is situated in the miserable state of being "alone" (*awl tif*) as long as he or she cannot make a pair with another soul. What matters here is simply "making pairs" in order to avoid anyone's being left alone, an emphasis that renders both sex and age irrelevant on such occasions.

CLASSIFICATION AND LANGUAGE

The Lancang Lahu simultaneously use two folk classification systems, which make pairs according to dyadic and dichotomous principles. In accordance with the mythological genesis of dyads, one system organizes the natural world and phenomena into pairs by focusing on the unity of two components in making a complete whole rather than on contrasts or oppositions between the two. On some occasions, as in the often-cited phrase "Tree and bamboo are a pair, mountain and river are a pair," the companionship and concomitance are so focused that the two halves of a dyad are rarely gendered.[13] On some other occasions, gender distinctions are made between two dyadic objects or phenomena such as the sun (female) and the moon (male). Lahu villagers also classify two nearby mountains as a paired entity in which the higher one is female and the lower one is male. A rainbow is classified into a female half (brighter) and a male half (dimmer). In such linguistic contexts, the slight differences between the gendered objects or phenomena tend to highlight, rather than undermine, the unity of the male-female dyad. In other words, what matters in such classification is making pairs, thus imposing the cosmological order on the world.

In contrast to the dyadic system, dichotomous classification is used to represent contrasts or opposite features. For instance, while high and perilous peaks are classified as female, small peaks that slope more gently are categorized as male. Likewise, streams that flow swiftly and turbulently are classified as female in contrast to the male streams, which flow slowly and calmly. Similarly, wide-ranging rains are classified as female, and isolated showers are classified as male.

The dichotomous principle is systematically applied to a popular flora classification method in rural Lancang. In this system, "female" (*awl ma*) and "male" (*awl paf*) are used to represent series of opposite features regarding a plant's capacity to blossom and to bear fruit and also describing the qualities of the fruit. Specifically, those plants that yield fruit (such as peach trees) are female, contrasting to the male plants that blossom but do not bear fruit (such as azaleas). Likewise, among the fruiting plants, those with edible fruits are female while those bearing inedible fruits are male. Among the plants that bear edible fruits, those bearing delicious fruits are female in contrast to the male plants whose fruits have an unpleasant taste. In addition to representing certain botanical features, female and male are also used to classify the status of a plant according to the manifestation or realization of such features in particular contexts. For instance, "female" and "male" can be used, respectively, to represent particular peach trees that bear fruit versus those that are barren, or to identify the trees whose fruits have good versus bad tastes. Similarly, the azalea plants that blossom in season are classified as female in contrast to the male azalea plants that do not bloom.

In general, in the dichotomous classification system, "female" tends to represent desirable or powerful features—such as bright, large, fast, influential, fruitful, and edible—while "male" symbolizes the opposites. From an anthropological perspective, I reasoned that such binary symbols suggest gender asymmetry that slightly favors women (Du 1987). Nevertheless, all the Lahu individuals I interviewed firmly denied the validity of my interpretations, and several further lectured me on the Lahu principle that "men and women are the same." In other words, from an indigenous point of view, the binary classifications bear no symbolic implications for—let alone value assignments to—the relationship between men and women.

The tendency to universalize the "pair" also manifests itself in the Lahu language, which tends to construct pairs of words, phrases, and verses. In contrast to Lahu classification systems, pairs in the Lahu language are predominantly dyads in which the two components are either identical or similar. The pairing features of the Lahu language resemble what James Fox (1974) refers to as "ritual parallelism," except that Lahu parallelism exists far beyond the limit of ritual contexts.[14] More specifically, appearing in both colloquial and poetic contexts, Lahu linguistic pairing tends to use a mixture of identical words or coupled synonyms (absolute ones or those that have shades of difference). Since one of the paired words in a phrase or sentence is sufficient for semantic purposes, such dyadic structures often appear to outsiders to be redundant, especially when a single mythological theme is depicted by hundreds or even thousands of poetic verses. However, by symbolically and aesthetically making phrases or sentences "complete," the pairing structures are extremely appealing to the Lahu, who can more fully appreciate their oral literature.

The dyadic wording structures in the colloquial Lahu language typically take the following four forms (Chang 1986:15; Du 1987):

Type 1: AA-BB.
Example: *hit hit-nad nad*—'rocky', 'swaying', or 'shaky.' Both *hit* and *nad* mean 'swaying' and 'rocky.'

Type 2: AB-AB.
Example: *kheu lat-kheu lat*—'lame', 'lamely.' *Kheu* means 'foot', *lat* means 'lame.'

Type 3: AB-AC.
Example: *ha liel-ha qa*—'glad', 'happy', and 'joy.' Both *ha liel* and *ha qa* mean 'happy', 'glad', and 'joy.'

Type 4: AB-CB.
Example: *mad jad-pie jad*—'enormous amount of', 'many.' Both *mad* and *pie* mean 'many', 'a large amount of'; *jad* means 'very.'

In contrast to colloquial Lahu, dyadic expressions in Lahu poetic oral literature are much more coherent and strict, taking the form of "canonical parallelism . . . in which all or most semantic elements are paired in dyadic sets, structured in formulaic phrases, and expressed as couplets or parallel verses" (Fox 1989: 40). In the context of antiphonal singing and ritual chanting, great appreciation is offered both for the singers' knowledge of conventional verses and for their creativity in composing coupled verses and paragraphs. As I observed during a wedding of Hu Calkheu's relatives, such singing sessions, where a few equally talented singers rotate to sing antiphonally to each other, may last as long as three days and nights in a household. While such songs appear to be extremely redundant to those unfamiliar with the aesthetic standards of pairing, they tend to draw large crowds of thrilled listeners. I have introduced some poetic verses from origin myths in the previous section; the breakdown of the following three paired verses may demonstrate canonical parallelism in Lahu oral literature in more detail.

EXAMPLE 1

Xeul Yad ('the male god') *mad feof* ('not establish') *chi* ('this') *mad cawl* ('not exist')
Sha Yad ('the female god') *mad feof* ('not establish') *chi* ('this') *mad paw* ('not exist')

The running translation of the verses is: 'If Xeul Yad had not established it, it would not have existed. If Sha Yad had not established it, it would not have existed.' This paired sentence is frequently used in antiphonal songs as well as in ritual chanting to express the idea that something under discussion (such as a substance, phenomenon, or custom) was established by the supreme god Xeul Sha. In this paired sentence, "Xeul Yad" and "Sha Yad" constitute a pair although they are addressed by one name, Xeul Sha, in ordinary language. As synonyms, *cawl* and *paw* constitute another pair. Although the rest of the words in each verse are identical to each other, they also function as pairs to make the two verses complete as a one-pair sentence. In such contexts, stating only one verse of the sentence will leave the listeners hanging even though they can predict the meaning.

EXAMPLE 2

Mud ('sky') *kheud* ('fertile') *lal* ('arm,' 'hand') *ziq* ('joint') *zhid* ('deep')
Mil ('earth') *kheud* ('fertile') *kheu* ('leg,' 'foot') *ziq* ('joint') *zhid* ('deep')

Translated as 'The fertile soil in this land is so deep that it reaches one's elbow, / The fertile soil in this land is so deep that it reaches one's knee', these verses are a common metaphor for the extreme fertility of a place. They are often used in the antiphonal singing of creation myths and love songs. This paired sentence is made of two distinguishable pairs ("sky-earth" and "leg-arm"), as well as three identical terms.

EXAMPLE 3:

Qhaw ma ('mountain range') *cie* ('seven') *qhaw* ('mountain') *je* ('converge') *keul lo* ('place')
Lawlma ('river bank') *cie* ('seven') *lawl* ('river') *je* ('converge') *keul lo* ('place')

Meaning 'at the place where many mountains converge, at the place where many rivers converge', these descriptive verses often appear in Lahu creation myths and migration legends.[15] In this paired sentence, while "mountain" and "river" and other identical words constitute corresponding pairs, "many mountains" and "many rivers" simultaneously comprise a paired word group within each verse.

In summary, Lahu language tends to construct dyadic pairs in which the two components are either identical or similar. While some Lahu classification systems are governed by dyadic orders, others are governed by dichotomous principles, which associate the two parts of a pair with opposite features yet imply no value differentiation between the sexes.

CONCLUSION

While the common saying "Everything comes in pairs" encapsulates the preeminence of dual principles in Lahu culture, the metaphor "Chopsticks only work in pairs" vividly reveals the dyadic nature of the conceptualization of the "pair." In accordance with the worldview that perceives male and female as symbiotic dyads, gender difference is minimized and trivialized in mythological representations of human nature and in ideological definitions of moral and aesthetic standards as well as in rituals and language.

The worldview of male-female unity generates as a by-product the ideology of gender equality, which is manifested as the joint identity and value of the two components of a symbiotic dyad. Accordingly, the Lahu translate the Mandarin term *nannü pingdeng* ('equality between men and women') into their own phrase *yad mid hawq qhad qhe yol*, meaning 'men and women are the same.' This saying by no means implies that the Lahu people cannot or do not distinguish men from women; instead, it indicates that they do not distinguish them as separately valued social categories.

CHAPTER 2

HUSBAND-WIFE DYADS IN THE LIFE CYCLE

DEFINITIONS OF personhood throughout the life cycle serve as overarching expressions of cultural ideals and norms for male and female, elaborating dominant gender ideologies that are often implicitly embedded in mythologies and general worldviews. In many patriarchal societies, the oppositions between the two sexes are encoded in childhood socialization, highlighted by puberty rites and masculine-versus-feminine ideals, institutionalized by assigning prestigious social roles and positions exclusively to men, and finalized in the spiritual realm by worshiping only male ancestors. In contrast, gender-egalitarian societies tend to highlight the motif of gender unity, or that of complementarity, in their own culture-specific mappings of the life cycle.

In this chapter, I discuss the manifestations of the Lahu dyadic worldview in the conventional classifications of the life cycle (see table 1), in which a married couple is defined as a single social entity throughout the life course and beyond. I first discuss how the formation of a husband-wife dyad in the wedding ceremony serves as the watershed dividing childhood and adulthood. I then examine the ideal life cycle, in which a married couple goes through the life journey together, sharing responsibility, prestige, and authority. After fulfilling their joint responsibilities in life, husband and wife are believed to reunite in the afterlife, jointly holding an honorable and authoritative position in the spiritual realm. In contrast, those who die before marriage or before fulfilling marital responsibilities are marginalized in the Lahu cosmological order and are typically treated as lone souls in mortuary rituals. Corresponding to the minimal gender difference in the classifications of the life cycle, in which husband and wife are defined as a dyadic social and spiritual entity, identical ideals are imposed on both men and women. I conclude that by simultaneously initiating a boy and a girl into adulthood in a wedding and then allocating joint prestige and authority to the couple, the dyadic perceptions of personhood cultivate gender equality throughout the life cycle.

TABLE 2.1 STAGES AND SUBSTAGES OF THE LIFE CYCLE

RED-AND-NAKED CHILDREN: THOSE WHO ARE UNABLE TO TALK AND WALK.

YOUNG CHILDREN: THOSE WHO ARE ABLE TO TALK AND WALK BUT ARE UNMARRIED.

A. Little children: Those who are unable to understand love songs and sexual remarks.
B. Unmarried youth: Those who are able to understand love songs and sexual remarks.

ADULTS: THOSE WHO ARE, OR ONCE WERE, MARRIED.

A. Married youth or junior adults: Those who have no grandchildren.
B. Elders: Those who have at least one grandchild.
C. Senior elders: Those whose children have all established (or inherited) households.
D. Parental spirits: The spirits of those who died as elders or senior elders.

THE WEDDING AS THE RITE OF PASSAGE TO ADULTHOOD

In many cultures, the rites of passage to adulthood initiate boys and girls separately into manhood and womanhood, thereby highlighting gender differences.[1] In contrast, the Lahu threshold for adulthood is the wedding, which unites two socially immature individuals into a single social entity and transforms them into full members of society. Serving as a rite of passage to simultaneously initiate a boy and a girl into adulthood, the symbolism and rituals of the Lahu wedding focus on elaborating the sacredness, endurance, and harmony of a husband-wife dyad.

The sacredness of the transformation into a paired social entity is encoded in the Lahu terms for 'wedding', which include *pied tuq, uq qof peu*, and *cied dar*, respectively meaning 'lighting [beeswax candles]', 'kneeling down and bowing', and 'becoming a pair.' In most Lahu areas, a wedding consists of two ceremonies, conforming to the dyadic ideology. The first and more elaborate ceremony is held at the house of the bride's parents, and the second is held at the house of the groom's parents. At each ceremony, a pair of beeswax candles is lit for Xeul Sha.

The connotations of the Lahu terms for 'wedding' derive from the major rituals of the ceremony, especially the joining of two lives in front of Xeul Sha. After lighting the paired candles on the altar, the bride and groom kneel down side by side facing the altar. In the Lancang area, the standard ritual texts include "Xeul and Sha make a pair, sky and earth make a pair, mountain and river make a pair, tree and bamboo make a pair, chopsticks make a pair. Today, this boy and girl become a pair as you Xeul and Sha." Singers also perform ritual wedding songs, *haw thaw-lawd jid* (Cal Yawl 1989), which trace the origin of human marriage to Xeul Sha's arrangement of the marriage of the sun (female) and the moon (male). These texts suggest that, by becoming a pair, the new couple has conformed to the cosmic principle set by the paired god.

During the ceremony, the bride and groom ritually close a traditional Lahu lunch box, which is made of bamboo strips.[2] The bride holds the container with her left hand, and the groom holds the cover with his right hand. Standing side by side, they cross their arms in an interlocked position to unify the box into one, representing their sexual and social unity. The bride and groom then ritually eat the sticky rice in the lunch box, symbolizing the cohesion of the couple in life, especially their joint role in work.

In addition to symbolically elaborating the sacred turning point when the boy and the girl join their lives in marriage, moral teachings are offered to the couple, emphasizing the social expectations of their newly acquired status as adults. According to convention, the oldest brother of the bride's mother offers the moral teachings when the ceremony is held at the house of the bride's family, and the oldest brother of the groom's mother gives the speech when the ceremony is held at the house of the groom's family. Although the length of such speeches varies according to individual speakers, some standard texts are widely shared, conveying the core ethics for a husband-wife dyad.

The first motif of a wedding speech is the exclusive legitimacy of heterosexual monogamy, which is clearly declared by the principle that "A husband can have only one wife, and a wife can have only one husband." Specifically, the speaker requests the couple to defend the principle by staying away from any extramarital sexual relations. Such a moral demand is expressed by the metaphor that "You should never admire or touch the knife or cloth-bag that belongs to any other man or woman," symbolizing the prohibition against exchanging any personal items as tokens of mutual affection with members of the opposite sex. Practically, the speaker orders the couple to return after the wedding any headcloths belonging to other "boys" or "girls," symbolically severing any previous emotional attachment to other members of the opposite sex.

Another major theme of a wedding speech stresses the expectation of lifelong commitment to marriage, claiming the impossibility of divorce under any circumstances. According to the conventional texts, "Rather than treating each other as baskets or bags that one can carry and put down at will, two of you should live together until [your] hair turns white and yellow. You can never abandon each other even if one suffers from sickness or pain." Emphasizing the ethic of unbreakable marriage, wedding speakers also metaphorically pronounce the social prohibition of divorce. For example, "You should not even think of asking for divorce unless you demonstrate to the wedding participants that you can swallow and excrete in its full shape the bamboo table on which a pair of ritual candles is lit." Obviously, it is impossible for anyone to swallow such a traditional Lahu table, which is made of bamboo strips and is about one meter in diameter. Such sayings also symbolically suggest that requesting a divorce not only brings shame to all the relatives witnessing the wedding but also blasphemes the supreme god Xeul Sha, to whom the pair of candles on the table is lit. Another phrase commonly used in wedding speeches to demonstrate the impossibility of divorce is "You may ask for divorce only if you can compensate your spouse with ninety-nine infertile cows and hens." There are many similar metaphors asserting the prohibition of divorce in many Lahu areas (Lei and Liu 1999:142; Wang 2001:172).

The third motif of a wedding speech is advice to the couple on how to maintain harmonious relationships with each other and with their relatives. Most important, the couple must share all the work of their household: "Whatever needs to be done in your family, two of you should do it together with warmth and joy (*ha liel-ha qa ted gie te*), rather than simply watching the other [performing the task]." Settling and forgetting disagreements as soon as possible is another important piece of advice: "You must drop a quarrel at either the head or the end of a field plot [wherever it occurs], rather than carrying it back home to upset your parents." Additionally, the couple is instructed to respect and take care of both sets of parents and to be generous to relatives from both sides.

A wedding speech typically concludes with a strong statement that abiding by these principles will result in abundance, and abandoning them will incur misery (Lei and Liu 1999:85). Usually, when the couple ritually drinks water from one bowl, the elder explains that if the couple "listens to the words of the elders," what they drink will become the "water of blessings" (*bo xeul shiq xeul*) on all dimensions of their lives. They will have many offspring, will prosper in the crops they grow, and will enjoy abundance in the livestock they raise. If the couple disobeys, however, what they drink will become the blood of cattle (*nud paf sif xeul*), symbolizing the curse of pollution and destruction.

The wedding reinforces the ideology that marrying a member of the opposite sex is the exclusively natural way of life. The cultural equation between marriage and adulthood is internalized in early childhood socialization. Adults or boys and girls frequently tease a little child by saying that he or she will "make a pair with" (marry) a member of the opposite sex with whom he or she likes to play, or whose parents are close kin or friends. Although unable to fully comprehend the meanings and thus having few emotionally charged reactions, little children often tease one another by pointing out that "so-and-so is your husband or wife." Sometimes they also tease one another by remarking that one will become an "old and unmarried" man or woman. Reflecting the strong socialization of the cultural emphasis on marriage, none of my Lahu interviewees considered remaining single a reasonable way of life, let alone a desirable alternative.

The close association between the wedding ceremony and social adulthood also puts pressure on those who remain single for many years after the onset of physical maturity. In the 1990s, increasing pressures to marry were usually put on those in their twenties. Lahu parents often nudged their children to look for a spouse by invoking the sayings "Chopsticks only work in pairs" and "A single chopstick cannot pick up food." Those who remain single in their late twenties or older often bring shame to themselves and their families. Behind their backs they are called "old and unmarried men" (*haq hu paf*) or "old and unmarried women" or "spinsters" (*haq hu ma*), degrading terms that seem to resolve the semantic conflicts between calendar age and the social category of "young children."

The number of individuals who are affected by the ideological discrimination against those who remain unmarried beyond a certain age seems to be very limited. After all, it is extremely rare in rural Lahu areas for individuals to remain single all their lives. In the Qhawqhat village cluster, I found no individuals who had never married before the age of thirty-five during the 1990s. Some elders recalled two cases in village history in which the individuals had remained unmarried throughout their lives because of severe chronic health problems. These two individuals were taken care of first by their parents and then by their married siblings. Despite the strong ideological discrimination against those who remain unmarried after physical maturity, close relatives are expected to care for disabled singles.

In brief, by transforming a male and a female "young child" into a paired social entity, the Lahu wedding serves as a rite of passage, initiating the two incomplete individuals into adulthood. After the ceremony, a couple is expected to be bound together to move jointly through the rest of the life cycle, sharing the responsibilities, authority, and prestige corresponding to the different substages of "adulthood."

THE JOINT JOURNEY OF MARRIED COUPLES IN LIFE

After the wedding ceremony, the couple simultaneously achieves the social rank of "adult" (*chaw mawd*).[3] Such a cultural definition of adulthood depends solely on one's marital status and is irrelevant to age and sex. Prior to the 1950s, some Lahu individuals in arranged marriages may have acquired the status of adulthood when they were as young as eleven years old. In contrast, the social category *chaw mawd* ('adult') excludes all those who have never married, even if they are over sixty years old.

Occupying the longest span in the cycle of life and afterlife, the stage of "adult" can be further divided into four substages—"married youth" or "junior adults," "elders," "senior elders," and "parental spirits." In this section, I examine how a married couple is jointly given different responsibilities, authority, and prestige in the first three substages of adulthood, covering the time span from their wedding to their deaths. As I will show, the accomplishment of raising children defines the substages and the corresponding social status of the couple.

MARRIED YOUTH OR JUNIOR ADULTS

From their wedding until the birth of their first grandchild, a couple is categorized as "married youth" or "junior adults" (*al niel*), contrasted with other married couples who already have grandchildren. Although the ages of junior adults vary according to the time of their own marriage and the marriage of their children, the typical age is roughly between twenty and forty-five.

At the substage of "junior adults," married couples are usually loaded with the heaviest responsibilities including feeding household members (*kheor cad*), raising children (*yad hu*), and caring for elderly parents (*chaw mawd ni*). Most junior Lahu couples indeed take on such responsibilities jointly in both domestic and outdoor work, basically conforming to the Lahu ideal of "husband and wife do it together" (see chapter 3).

Along with their heavy responsibilities and hard work, a junior Lahu couple also jointly goes through a series of transformations and attains expanded autonomy and authority. The authority of a couple relates mainly to their position in the household in which they reside. After their wedding, a couple is obligated to reside in the household of the bride's parents for three years; after that, they move to the household of the groom's parents for two to three years. The length of bride-and-groom service is flexible and is determined by negotiations between the two sets of households and the labor and land situations of the couple's respective parents. During this time, the newly married husband and wife mainly serve as laborers for the household in which they reside. Since each household is co-headed by the couple's parents, the young couple has no formal authority in rituals or decision-making. After the husband and wife complete their labor obligations in serving both sets of parents, they eventually establish and co-head their own household.

ELDERS

From the birth of their first grandchild until they retire from their joint position of household co-heads, a husband and wife are categorized as "elders" (*chaw mawd* in one of its narrow senses) within the general category "adults" (*chaw mawd* in its broad sense). From the perspective of parental status, a couple is promoted from "junior adults" to "elders" when they have a grandchild. The typical age of elders is between forty and sixty-five.

During this substage of life, a couple has fulfilled the responsibility of raising their children, and the struggle to feed their household members is generally lessened. They begin to receive labor input from their unmarried children and newly married children and children-in-law. At this stage, the core reciprocal network of the couple has gradually shifted from their parents and siblings to their children and the parents of their children's spouses.

The social authority of the couple reaches its peak when they become elders because many of their children have become the co-heads of their own households. During the Lahu New Year Festival and the Festival of Tasting New Rice, such elders are invited to feast at the households co-headed by their children and enjoy a revered ritual status that is second only to that of Xeul Sha and parental spirits. Likewise, on the day before the Lahu New Year, a couple classified as "married youth" is conventionally expected to carry loads of firewood to the houses of their two sets of elder parents to offer ritual respect and honor.

SENIOR ELDERS

When all of their children are married and have established their own households, a couple is promoted to the status of "senior elders" (*chaw mawd qo*), which is the last substage of physical life. In Lahu terms, a couple becomes "senior elders" when their "children have divided the household completely" (*yad tuf yiel piel – qa piel piel-ol*). At this stage, at least some of a couple's children have had grandchildren and have thus become elders themselves. Most senior elders are older than sixty years of age.

Having completely fulfilled their responsibilities in life, senior elders are entitled to be cared for by their children, or to "eat the strength" of their children, as the reward for their lifelong hard work. They usually live together with one of their children and his or her spouse who have jointly inherited their house and have succeeded them as household co-heads. They also receive various forms of support and care from their other children and children-in-law. The social expectation for the senior elders to live a relaxed life is so intense that they are sometimes pressured to quit their work in the fields. If they continue to work outside, the senior elders may be pointedly and sympathetically questioned as to whether or not they have children, and their children may be criticized for "not understanding the principle" (*awl lid mad shif*) and treating their parents or parents-in-law poorly.

A decline in social authority and an increase in ritual and spiritual authority mark the substage of senior elder in the life cycle. At the moment when a couple is transformed from "elders" to "senior elders"—when their last child and child-in-law have inherited their house and household—they are formally retired from the position of household co-heads. Although retired couples often offer advice to their children and children-in-law, formal responsibility and authority to make decisions for the household are shifted to their successors. At the same time, however, the ritual prestige of senior elders reaches its peak. This is because all of their children have become household co-heads who are responsible for performing rituals honoring Xeul Sha and other deities as well as living and deceased parents.

In brief, a married couple is counted as a single social entity and progresses jointly through each substage of adulthood, which is defined mainly by parental roles. The married couple jointly holds the status, prestige, and authority of each of the hierarchical stages and substages of the life cycle. Revered status and prestige are intrinsically intertwined with a couple's accomplishment of their social responsibilities, especially their responsibility as parents.

THE REUNION OF ACCOMPLISHED COUPLES IN THE AFTERLIFE

By fulfilling the responsibility of raising their children to adulthood, elders and senior elders are greatly revered for living a complete and accomplished life. Therefore, those who die at these two substages receive great respect and honor in mortuary rituals. As I will show in the remainder of this section, rituals are performed to appropriately and honorably send the souls of elders and senior elders to the world of the dead and to let them symbolically pass down blessings to their children and children-in-law before their burials. Most important, funeral symbolism guarantees that the deceased elders and senior elders will reunite with their spouses in the afterlife, ensuring the full force of their joint responsibility and authority in the spiritual realm.

The death of a senior elder or elder constitutes a significant social event, obligating an entire village cluster to pay respect to their accomplished lives. Typically, two sequential gunshots are fired immediately after the death, and more shots are fired when the corpse is placed into the coffin, loudly announcing the news to the village and to neighboring villages. Since the illnesses of all senior elders or elders are usually well known, many villagers can guess the identity of the deceased from the direction of the gunshot, and some immediately visit the household even if it is late at night. One night when I was in the village interviewing an elder named Cal Lie, gun shots occurred. Cal Lie looked very alert, stayed motionless for a while, and said softly, "Cal Xad from Beul Tawt [a village on the west of the Qhawqhat] just died." When I walked out of the house a few minutes later, the quiet village night had been disturbed by the barking of dogs, and shifting lights from flashlights from different sections of the village moved toward the west, where the household of the deceased was located.

A wake is required for a deceased elder or senior elder, lasting two days for the former and three days for the latter. The most important ceremony during a wake is the ritual singing that symbolically sends the soul of the deceased to the world of the dead. The songs typically begin with a vivid description of the life and work of the deceased prior to death. Drawing from part of the Lahu creation myth, the singers then review the origin of the death of human beings, i.e., the dishonorable death of the rebellious Senior Daughter and Senior Son of Xeul Sha that rendered the next generation of creatures mortal (Hu 1996). In this way, the funeral songs implicitly reinforce the Lahu ethic of parents' revered status and authority, which is equivalent to the highest order in the universe (Du and Hu 1996). Afterwards, guided by the songs, ritual specialists and all the attendants at the wake symbolically send the deceased step-by-step to the mirror village in the world of the dead, delivering the soul to the spirits of his or her parents and of the head couple of the village.

The wake for an elder or senior elder becomes an occasion to celebrate and honor the accomplishments of the deceased in the world of the living. Consequently, the basic emotional tone of the events is cheerful and even celebratory rather than mournful, although the deceased's loved ones are sometimes grieving.[4] In fact, one of the implicit responsibilities of the ritual participants is to keep the household lively and jolly, which is believed to be emotionally and spiritually beneficial. The house in which the wake is held is often bustling with noise and excitement that can be heard far away. While corn liquor is passed around, the crowd breaks into small groups chatting, joking, and singing. I finally found the location of the wake for Cal Xat when I was guided by the noise, especially some popular Chinese songs (in Mandarin) played on a boombox. Weeping or crying is not forbidden on such occasions, but it is very rare and happens on an individual basis rather than being part of the ritual. The only time when an atmosphere of sadness covers the majority of the crowd is typically at the beginning of the wake songs, which vividly review the life and work of the deceased. I observed that when the singers described specific geographic places where the deceased had worked along with some members of the audience, some related men and women were moved to tears.

The wake obligates many households to send their representatives to attend even if the death occurs in busy seasons for agriculture. If the deceased is a senior elder, the obligated households include all of the relatives who live in the village cluster as well as core relatives who live in neighboring village clusters. If the deceased is only an elder, relatives in neighboring village clusters, except for the children of the deceased, are not obliged to participate. Because of the extreme inclusiveness of the Lahu kinship system (see chapter 5), the attendance at the wake for an elder or senior elder usually exceeds one hundred people. For example, when I went to Cal Xat's wake at about midnight, there were over seventy people packed in the hosting house alone—sitting or squatting beside the hearth, on the beds, and occupying every other place available in the room. About fifty people were gathered in the front yard and in the neighboring house. The major responsibility of the crowd is to keep the surviving household members company, a practice called *yiel shaw* ('house-sitting' or 'keeping watch over the house'). Additionally, visitors voluntarily help the host family in various tasks such as preparing food and carrying the coffin, following the Lahu saying that "at the death of [elder] people, there is no need to look for labor" (*chaw si xad mad ca*).

Marking the end of the wake, a special ritual—called *qawd hawq lor* ('circling underneath a coffin') or *chaw mawd hawq awl shiq piel* ('dividing blessings from under the deceased parents')—is held for the deceased to pass down blessings (*bo*) to his or her married children and children-in-law.[5] The ritual is performed in the courtyard when the coffin, with the feet of the corpse facing the front, is removed from the house to be buried in the graveyard. While bearing the coffin, the pallbearers stop in the middle of the front yard of the house. A spiritual specialist (*mawq paf*) stands at the front of the coffin, facing away and holding a basket that is filled with popped rice. Meanwhile, the married children and children-in-law of the deceased line up in pairs at the end of the coffin where the head of the deceased is located. When the spiritual specialist starts to blindly throw popped rice backward, the married couples start to circle through underneath the coffin, which is held up very high by the pallbearers. They take off their headcloths, headscarves, or hats and hold them stretched out between their hands. Then they bow their heads and cross underneath the coffin in a counterclockwise direction. After the entire line has circled underneath the coffin three times, they wrap up their headcloths, scarves, or hats, unfolding them only when the coffin is taken away from the front yard.

Any items that may be found in these unfolded headcloths, scarves, or hats are considered signs of the spiritual inheritance that is being passed down from the deceased parent. Popped rice that has landed in the head-cloths and hats symbolizes rice production. The more a couple receives, the more productive their rice field will be in the future. Besides popped rice, many other symbolically significant items that were not contained in the ritual specialist's basket may also mysteriously appear in those headcloths, scarves, and hats. Such items include grains, chaff, chicken feathers, and pig and cattle hair, which symbolize, respectively, a promised prosperity in producing crops, and in raising chickens, pigs, and cattle. Since the spiritual specialists have not thrown them, these items when received are considered signs of special favor that the deceased parent has shown toward a couple. My interviewees could not explain how those items get into the headcloths or scarves, and most believed that they arrived in a mystical way related to the parental spirit. At the funeral of a woman who died during my fieldwork in June 1996, several of her children and children-in-law found in their headcloths and hats such auspicious items as pig and cattle hair; the news spread widely in Qhawqhat. All of the items collected in the ritual will be saved by the recipients in a special basket. According to villagers, in the case of an unfilial child or child-in-law, the couple will receive rice hulls, which symbolize poverty. Nevertheless, I did not hear any reports of such incidents in the village.

While rural Lahu of different regions tend to share similar ceremonies at their wakes, there is a division in the practices during the last stage of mortuary rituals. In contrast to most Lahu villagers, who place the dead in a coffin and bury him or her directly in the ground, some cremate the body and bury the container of ashes in the ground.[6] Although the farmers of an entire village cluster typically share the same type of burial method, there are a few village clusters in Lancang whose residents follow different traditions. Despite the division between ground burial and cremation, however, burial rituals express in different ways a common belief in the reunion of an accomplished couple in the world of the dead and in their joint rights and authority in receiving offerings from their offspring. In the remainder of this section, I focus only on the rituals practiced by those who bury the dead directly into the ground, as is the custom in Qhawqhat and many other Lahu village clusters.

According to Qhawqhat traditions, burial rituals begin in the late afternoon and must finish before sunset, which is considered a good time for the deceased to enter the world of the dead because the sun is about to rise there, and people have not yet gone to work. For a couple who has reached the substages of elders or senior elders, the funeral symbolism centers on their reunion in the world of the dead.

In the funeral for the first deceased member of a couple, the most important task is choosing an appropriate gravesite, which represents the location of the prospective "house" of the couple in the world of the dead. Grave locations mirror the patterns of house arrangement in the world of the living, emphasizing the belief that married couples who die at the stage of senior elder and elder are entitled to establish their independent households in the afterlife. Following the pattern of an independent house in a village, the gravesite is ideally one row below and to the west of the grave of the set of parents from whom they inherited their houseland (see chapter 4). Such spatial arrangements symbolize the belief that the couple inherits their "houseland" in the world of the dead from the same set of parents from whom they inherited their houseland in the world of the living. While the range of socially appropriate space is predetermined, the first deceased member of a couple is considered responsible for choosing the exact location of the "house" site in the afterlife. A ritual called "throwing an egg" is performed to allow the deceased to express his or her will. A spiritual specialist blindly throws an egg backward over his head and chants, "If you don't like this place, please catch the egg with the front of your garment [so that the egg will not break]." Eventually, wherever the egg breaks is believed to be the burial spot favored by the dead spouse.

Whereas the spatial symbolism of the gravesite represents a house with the potential for an independent household in the afterlife, the grave mound arrangement emphasizes the incompleteness of the "house" by the symbol of the "front door" of the "house." In the world of the living, the door of a Lahu house is composed of a pair of wooden flaps that swing open and closed vertically from the center. Any household that lacks such a double door does not qualify as an independent household either socially or spiritually. Mirroring the house in the living world, a symbolic half-door is built

FIGURE 4 A half-(stone) "door" grave of a married woman. A man digs the other half to bury her husband. Photograph by Shanshan Du

FIGURE 5 The couple's joint grave, which has a complete "door" with two flaps. Photograph by Shanshan Du

in front of the grave mound of the first deceased member of a couple, expressing the belief that an independent household cannot be established until the couple reunites. This "half-door" is made of the stones picked up in the creek on the way to the graveyard and mimics the one flap of the pair of wooden front doors of a house. The stone "half-door" is located in such a way that, when the "house" of the couple is eventually completed on the death of the surviving spouse, the two "half-doors" can make a completed "door" with two flaps (see figure 4).

Burial rituals for the second deceased member of a couple focus on completing the couple's "house" or reestablishing an independent household in the world of the dead. The digging begins at about five *cun* (about 0.2 meter) away from the deceased spouse's "half-door," and the diggers are required to be especially careful and dig straight down in order to protect the old coffin from being broken. Before placing the new coffin into the grave pit, one gravedigger digs a hole in the middle of the thin wall that was kept between the two grave pits during the digging process. This hole between the two grave pits symbolizes the door inside the house between rooms, which is called the "small door" (*yiel miq yied*) of a house.

After placing the coffin in the new grave pit, one single grave mound is built by piling the displaced dirt on top of the two coffins. Then, the other half of the "door" for the "house" is built with stones. The extra stones are used to pave the "front yard" of the completed "house." The emphasis on the completed (paired) "door" of the "house" is symbolically exaggerated by retaining a space of one *zha*—a Lahu (and Han) unit for measuring length, representing the span from the thumb to the middle finger when both fingers are outstretched. Such a space between the two stone half-doors symbolizes the gap between the two half-doors in a house (see figure 5). Finally, a pair of beeswax candles is lit and stuck to both sides of the completed "door." This ritual formally recognizes the couple as household co-heads in front of the paired household guardian gods and Xeul Sha, who is believed to control both the world of the living and that of the dead.[7] After the ritual, a new "household" is considered established for the reunited couple in the world of the dead.

Upon their symbolic reunion in the world of the dead, the spirits of the deceased couple are believed to reach another peak of prestige and authority. While co-heading their own "household" in the world of the dead, they are also believed to play a crucial role in the well-being of the households of their children, especially those who have inherited their house or land. The symbolic ties between the spirits of a deceased couple and their married children are so tight that the Lahu typically use a single term—*chaw mawd*—to refer to living parents, elders, and the spirits of deceased parents. They only occasionally modify the term *chaw mawd* with a suffix *ned* ('spirit') when specification is necessary. The frequent Lahu use of the same word for 'parental spirits' and 'parents' signifies a conceptual and structural continuity between the two categories that is not severed by physical death.

According to the beliefs of most Lancang Lahu, the influence of parental spirits on the lives of their children is so strong that it is considered second only to that of Xeul Sha. Parental spirits are appeased on most important ritual occasions. For example, they are ritually invited to attend feasts for the Lahu New Year and the Festival of New Rice Tasting. Additionally, they receive offerings and honors at the annual grave-repairing ritual held by their children. After the ceremony, their children divide the offerings, which are called "blessed rice or liquor." Through chicken-bone divination, the couples read the wills of their parental spirits toward their own households. Corresponding rituals and offerings have to be held to appease the parental spirits by those households whose chicken-bone divinations show inauspicious signs. Otherwise, lacking protection from the spirits of deceased parents, the members of the children's household risk losing their well-being and even their lives.

Having fulfilled the responsibility of raising their children to adulthood, those who die as "elders" or "senior elders" receive the highest honors in mortuary rituals, and their spirits are believed powerful in the spiritual realm. Beyond celebrating and paying respect to such a complete life, mortuary rituals also symbolically reunite elders or senior elders with their spouses in the afterlife.

MARGINALIZING LONE SOULS

Whereas many Lahu indeed live long enough to become "elders" or "senior elders," certain individuals fall short of the social expectation. Specifically, some die before marriage, others die as "married youth," breaking husband-wife dyads before fulfilling their share of the responsibility of raising children to adulthood. As I will show in the remainder of this section, those who die premature deaths at different stages of the life cycle constitute challenges to Lahu dyadic ideologies and social values and are therefore marginalized in the Lahu cosmological order.

Death before marriage directly contradicts the Lahu worldview that "Everything comes in pairs; aloneness does not exist," especially defying the social ideal of husband-wife dyads. Accordingly, those who die at the stages of "red-and-naked children" or "young children" are usually considered life's worst failures or even lesser humans in the cosmological order. According to a popular belief found in many Lahu village clusters of Lancang, those who die before marriage are an ambiguous form of human, doomed to be lone souls because of their odd nature. The story goes that "normal" people always die after marriage, ideally after their children are also married. After death in the world of the living, they are reborn in the world of the dead. After a complete life in the world of the dead, they die and are reborn into the world of the living. In contrast, those who die before marriage have an ambiguous status in the cosmos because, while migrating between the two worlds, they always turn into birds before they are transformed into human beings. Those lone souls are believed to enter the world of the living as birds waiting to be eaten by humans so that they can be born as human babies. Nevertheless, such babies will again die before marriage and will reenter the world of the dead to be transformed once more into birds waiting to be reborn as human forms. This cycle will perpetuate until a bird's lifetime is completed without being eaten by humans. Influenced by this popular belief, some Lahu villagers are cautious about shooting birds who may appear to be abnormally lethargic, suspecting them to be such lesser humans and fearing that eating them may result in producing children who are doomed to die prematurely.

Mortuary treatment of those who die before marriage directly expresses a strong sense of social depreciation toward them. In sharp contrast to the deaths of elders or senior elders, no gunshots are fired to publicly announce such deaths so that attention from the village is avoided. No wake is held for the deceased, and no rituals are performed to appropriately and honorably send the souls to the world of the dead. Additionally, nobody in the village is obligated to visit the household of the deceased although some core relatives may visit to demonstrate emotional support for the surviving household members on the first night after the death.

While mortuary treatments for red-and-naked children and for young children are both marked by neglect and disrespect, they differ drastically regarding the degrees of dishonor. Occupying the lowest stage of the life cycle, red-and-naked children are treated as lesser humans. Located on the way to the village graveyard, the special burial ground for infants and young babies (*yad ni quiq tuf keul*) represents a place of limbo between the world of the living and the world of the dead. Rather than being placed in a coffin, the corpse is usually wrapped in a mat made of bamboo strips. Although a small grave mound is formed out of the displaced dirt, no stone is placed in front of the mound to represent even half a door, symbolizing the homelessness of the spirit in the world of the dead.

Compared to deceased red-and-naked children, those who die as "young children" (including "little children" and "unmarried youth") receive much more respectful mortuary treatment. Most important, they are buried in the village graveyard, suggesting that they are symbolically accepted in a mirror village in the world of the dead. Rather than being wrapped with a mat, the deceased young children are often put in crude coffins. Depending on the feelings of the surviving members of the household, a deceased young child may even receive some special favors.[8] While mortuary rituals treat deceased young children as full humans, burial sites and grave arrangements also emphasize the belief that their spirits are not full members of society. Even the burial site of an "unmarried youth" of adult age is half a row down from the (anticipated) grave of the co-heads of their former household, symbolizing a continuous affiliation to the household in the spiritual realm. The grave of a young child consists of only one stone in the middle that represents a "half-door," suggesting that the corresponding spirit remains a lone soul in the world of the dead.

While those who die before marriage are culturally doomed to be lone souls both in life and in the afterlife, those who die as "married youth" risk becoming lone souls in the world of the dead because their surviving spouses often remarry. The degrees of such risk are complicated by the age span, which ranges from the newly married to those with children close to marriage. In general, the earlier a death occurs in the substage of married youth, the higher the probability that one will become a lone soul in the world of the dead. If the death of a married person occurs before the couple have established their own household, the deceased is buried symbolically as a dependent member affiliated with the household in which he/she resided before death. In this case, the grave is identical to that of an "unmarried youth," half a row down from the (anticipated) gravesite of the household co-heads, and the grave has only a "half-door" that will never be complete.

In other words, the deceased is downgraded from "adult" to "child" in the transition from the world of the living to the world of the dead. If the death occurs when the person's children are close to marriage, however, the deceased has great opportunity to reunite with his or her spouse in the world of the dead, being recognized as an adult and worshipped as a parental spirit by his or her offspring. In the case of the remarriage of the surviving spouse, children from both marriages decide on the burial before the death of the one who has married more than once. Although all of the children hope their own parents will be buried together, the decision is based mainly on the number of children each marriage has produced.

By departing from the world of the living before raising any children to adulthood, the spouses who die as "married youth" are severely blamed for abandoning the responsibilities they ought to have shared with their surviving spouses. According to my interviewees, such a junior adult "leaves his or her spouse alone when a couple should 'work hard together to eat,' raise children, and care for elders." Since the entire responsibility for feeding and caring for household members is shifted from two people to only one, the surviving spouse often "takes care of one thing and can hardly manage others." Even after remarriage, the life of a surviving spouse is still perceived to be harder than usual, because "it is hard to teach children who are not born from the same parents." Therefore, the surviving spouses of junior adults, called *mied chawd paf* ('widower') or *meid chawd ma* ('widow'), are considered the most miserable people in the world. Many villagers I interviewed remarked that only orphans have a comparable life of misfortune. Although not living up to the ideal husband-wife dyad that lasts throughout the life cycle, widows and widowers typically suffer no social discrimination because they tend to remarry soon and receive sympathy and support during the transitional period. While some widows and widowers with grown children may decide not to remarry, they are still respected because of their status as elders or senior elders.

Responding to the damage that the deaths of "married youth" bring to their surviving spouses and children, their mortuary rituals publicly announce their downward mobility in the spiritual realm, demonstrating the negative evaluation given to such an incomplete life. Specifically, rather than treating them as adults, mortuary rituals for "married" youth treat them as if they were young children. Socially, the responses to death are limited to the household and are neglected by the village as a whole. Spiritually, the transition from life to death is ambiguous because of the absence of a wake and of the appropriate rituals that send the soul to the corresponding village and household in the world of the dead. In practice, however, mortuary rituals for married youths are flexible, depending on the feelings of the surviving spouse, the economic condition of the household, and the popularity of the deceased in the village.[9]

In brief, those who die prematurely are depreciated to different degrees depending on the stage at which they died. According to how far a premature death causes a person's life to fall short of the social expectation for a complete life, mortuary symbolism, respectively, marginalizes the soul as a lesser human, a lone spirit, or a spirit with ambiguous status in the afterlife.

BLENDING FEMININITY AND MASCULINITY IN GENDER IDEALS

By defining and evaluating personhood according to one's standing in the husband-wife dyad, Lahu classification and symbolism of the life cycle fully elaborate the cosmological ideal of male-female unity. While placing social ideals for personhood on the joint entity of the married couple in both the life course and the afterlife, the ideals for men and women also converge in multiple ways. Specifically, Lahu ideals for men and women tend to blend femininity and masculinity in their religious definitions of human nature and ultimate morality, as well as in personality, social traits, and standards of beauty.[10]

The indistinguishable ideals for men and women in the life cycle of husband-wife dyads are rooted in Lahu mythology, which assigns the two sexes identical essence and morality in the scope of cosmology. According to Lahu oral literature, the offspring of the first twin couple began to develop husband-wife dyads, pairs that the two halves married into, which thus became less homogenous than the twin-dyads into which each half had been born. While describing humanity's departure from the primordial ideal of twin-dyad, the final sections of Lahu creation myths still identify men and women with essential homogeneity regarding human nature—i.e., the capacity and the willingness to make offerings to Xeul Sha. In other words, men and women are identical to each other—and different from animals and other physical entities—especially in their capacity to recognize the ultimate creator and to produce rice with which to make offerings to that creator. Additionally, heeding the warning from the lesson of the rebellious demigod twins, men and women jointly make moral choices to fulfill their cosmological duties by earnestly seeking blessings from Xeul Sha.

Except during the Cultural Revolution when all religions were prohibited in China, Xeul Sha has constituted the central theme of almost all of the important Lahu rituals, including weddings, funerals, festivals, healing, and the seeking of blessings. A married couple is expected to function as a joint entity to relate to Xeul Sha (Lei and Liu 1999:124), as exemplified by the following verses from a ritual song performed to improve the well-being of the household co-headed by the husband and wife Cal Yawl and Na Meiq (Cal Yawl 1989:184–185).

> Ties the festival string [to his wrist] / It is the ritual of Xeul
> Ties the festival strings [to her wrist] / It is the principle of Sha . . .
> A pair of sticky-rice cakes makes the festival gift / Bring the offering of
>   Cal Yawl
> Seeking blessing seeds from Xeul Sha / Bring blessing seeds to sow in
>   the fields
> Use a pair of beeswax candles as festival flowers / Bring the offering of
>   Na Meiq
> Seeking longevity seeds from Xeul Sha / Planting longevity seeds to hearts.

The absence of inherent and essential differences between men and women in the spiritual arena is also manifested in the Lahu belief in a dangerous and unclean spirit (*tawr*) (see chapter 6). In contrast with many ethnic groups that hold similar beliefs, the Lahu believe the spirit afflicts both sexes rather than women alone.[11] According to folk beliefs in Lancang, the evil spirit not only passes down from parents to offspring but can also pass between husbands and wives. Therefore, a married couple is jointly stigmatized and marginalized for possessing such a spirit even if only one of them was believed by the villagers to have the spirit before marriage.

Consistent with those of the spiritual realm, Lahu ideals of personality and social traits show minimal gender difference. The most important virtue, which is referred to by the word *nud* ('soft,' 'gentle'), is identical for men and for women. As an overarching category for most desirable characteristics, *nud* involves both emotional and rational traits. According to my interviews, Lahu villagers use the term *nud* to refer to a wide range of attributes, including humility and generosity in relating to fellow villagers, respectfulness toward elders, care of children, compassion for the sick and the weak, and the appropriate manner in different social contexts. In the traditional Lahu courting songs, Lahu lovers use *nud* as the highest praise of their partners, addressing each other as "the good (*dar*) and soft (*nud*) young man" or "the good and soft young woman." *Nud* is such high praise that if a family member is considered "nud," other members share the pride. Some of my friends remarked that when one of their relatives was publicly praised as *nud*, they felt as if they were also honored.

As the antithesis to the positive *nud* ('soft,' 'gentle'), the term *hie* ('harsh') describes the most undesirable personality and social traits, including insensitivity, ill manners, boastfulness, aggressiveness, and violence. *Hie* is used to describe the negative characters of both men and women, suggesting no belief in any innate male aggression. Although Lahu oral literature describes the many wars the Lahu ancestors engaged in while defending their territory or rescuing their fellow villagers who had been captured by other ethnic groups, murder is absent both in oral traditions and in social memories of all the village clusters I visited. Specifically, I have never collected a single case of intentional murder although I have noticed several instances of death sentences carried out according to Lahu customary laws as well as a few accidental killings that occurred during fights that often involved drunkards.

Despite the negative perception of harshness in the Lahu culture, violent behavior (including domestic violence) does exist in village life and has been increasing drastically since the 1980s. During my stay in the Qhawqhat village cluster between 1995 and 1996, I witnessed two cases of domestic abuse involving married couples. In the first case, a man who was infamous for being harsh accused his wife of flirting with another man and beat her while he was drunk. I noticed that the man was severely criticized by both his relatives and the village cadres. In the second case, a wife hit her husband and threw firewood and stools at him because he came home too late one night, even though he had merely been discussing some village matters with cadres. Although this was a rare incident in the family, I heard some villagers, while gossiping about the event, criticize her for being harsh. When I asked the husband why he did not fight back, he commented that he did not want to be harsh and set a bad example for their children.

Besides aggression and violence, some behaviors that appear normal for outsiders may be considered harsh by Lahu standards, especially from the perspective of the elders. Lahu sensitivity to the distinction between harsh and gentle can be exemplified by the following episode that occurred in

Qhawqhat village cluster during my fieldwork in 1996. Cal Var, a young man in his early thirties, walked into the household of one of my designated relatives and joined our conversation. After Cal Var left, my designated uncle Cal Lad (about seventy years old) gently suggested that I not be offended by his harshness. Since I had no idea what Car Var had done wrong, Cal Lad explained how he had behaved inappropriately in front of his elders and had talked too much and too loudly. These remarks brought to the surface my subconscious frustrations in talking to many Lahu villagers, especially the elders, who often talked so softly (if they talked at all) that I had to raise my voice to encourage them to speak up. I realized with embarrassment that I must have often acted harshly according to Lahu standards and that my designated relatives were simply too gentle to point it out directly.[12]

Beyond metaphysical, social, and personality traits, Lahu men and women are also measured by nearly identical standards in their physical appearance and attractiveness. To be "good-looking" (*ni sha*), one must first have a well-proportioned body with strong leg and arm muscles. "Your body is as straight as the best tree along the river bank" and "Your calves (and arms) are as thick and solid as the base of a bamboo trunk" are typical analogies used to express the aesthetic appreciation for a strong body build in both sexes (Du 1995). In addition, well-proportioned facial features combined with pleasant expressions are considered attractive for both men and women. Poetic phrases used to describe such physical attractions include "You are brighter than the brightest flower in the world that blossoms for three years and becomes brighter and brighter every night" or "Your skin is as white as silver, as shining as gold."[13] Likewise, "as beautiful as the singing of a cicada" and "as rough as the howling of a wild pig" (or "as rough as the barks of a barking deer") are used to describe, respectively, the attractive and unpleasant voices of men and women alike. Since the same phrases describing physical appearance are used interchangeably for both sexes, one can identify the sex of the person being praised in Lahu courting songs only by the phrases "the good and soft young man" or "the good and soft young woman."

Consistent with the similar beauty standards for men and women, indigenous Lahu costumes tend to play down sex differences. No sex distinction is shown in the traditional head gear—a long black cloth tied around the head as a brim—that is widely shared by Lahu across subgroups and regions. Prior to the 1950s, Lahu men and women in China also wore similar adornments, especially silver bracelets and buttons. Whereas traditional

Lahu clothes bear obvious gender markers—shirts and pants for males and long garments for females—their loose-fitting styles cover most of the secondary features of the sexes. Not only are female body curves concealed, but also middle or even late stages of pregnancy of Lahu women are usually hidden within their loose garments. In the 1990s, many Lahu elders in both China and Thailand still considered clothes that showed female body curves embarrassing, strange, or ugly.[14]

It is worth noting that, whereas Lahu ideals minimize gender difference, they by no means suggest that they cannot distinguish men from women. In fact, the foundation of the Lahu dyadic worldview is the existence of the two distinguishable sexes, although the difference tends to be overridden by their simultaneous submission to a higher entity made of their unity. In accordance with the great ideological emphasis on the unity of men and women, the Lahu language has no word for 'homosexuality.' All of the Lahu I interviewed stated firmly that they had never heard of such behaviors among the people they knew and were therefore unable to offer any moral judgments.[15]

The indigenous Lahu ideals for men and women have been undergoing rapid transformations since the 1980s, mainly because of the impact of the gendered images promoted by the mass media (especially television) and the development of a market economy. For example, Na Mawl, a beautiful young Lahu woman who had had more encounters with urbanites, told me that she felt very embarrassed when older women praised her calves for being as thick and solid as the base of bamboo trunks. She remarked that rural Lahu women did not know that such legs are considered ugly for city girls because they are regarded as masculine. Gender difference in Lahu dress has also become increasingly salient because more and more Lahu villagers (especially the youth) prefer to purchase ready-made clothes from local markets. Replacing the traditional headcloth, Han-style colorful scarves and hats (mainly green and blue) have become fashionable for young Lahu women and men. Except during the period of Lahu festivals, most young and middle-aged Lahu villagers in the 1990s wore dress similar to that of the rural Han Chinese.

In summary, corresponding to dyadic standards in the definitions and evaluations of personhood in the life cycle, which minimize gender differences, Lahu ideals for men and women are identical. Despite the impact of radical social changes, the blending of femininity and masculinity still prevails in rural Lahu life at the beginning of the twenty-first century.

CONCLUSION

Gender unity is coded in the Lahu division of the life cycle and elaborated in mortuary rituals for deaths at different stages. After being simultaneously initiated into adulthood at their wedding, a couple is expected to act in concord throughout life and beyond. Particularly, a husband and wife are to share the responsibility of feeding their household and raising their children to adulthood, an accomplishment that guarantees they will reunite in the world of the dead and receive ritual honors and offerings from their children as parental spirits.

Mapping the life cycle primarily according to marital and parental status, the responsibility, authority, and prestige of men and women are intrinsically intertwined with each other in husband-wife dyads. Such an ideology cherishes gender equality by encouraging a married couple to operate as a single social and spiritual entity throughout the course of life and beyond. The joint identity of husband and wife is so crucial in defining and evaluating personhood that it generates identical ideals for men and women in the realms of cosmology, society, personality, and physical traits. Therefore, from the dyadic perceptions of personhood throughout the life cycle, gender equality is simply a matter of course.

PART 2

JOINT GENDER ROLES

CHAPTER 3

"HUSBAND AND WIFE DO IT TOGETHER": UNIFYING GENDER IN LABOR

I N THE LAST two chapters, I discussed the ways in which the motif of gender dyads prevails in Lahu mythology and life-cycle symbolism, generating as a by-product an ideology that fosters equality between men and women. While the ideal may sound as appealing as many other gender-egalitarian visions, some readers may have begun to question how such an ideology can be applied to social practices in which men and women are usually divided by the roles they play. As I will show in this and the following two chapters, by defining a married couple as a dyadic team, the ideology of gender unity dominates Lahu expectations and practices of gender roles even in such domains as labor allocation and leadership where sex-based division is often considered inevitable.

Since biology has assigned the tasks of pregnancy, childbirth, and lactation exclusively to women, childrearing is often believed to be the natural role only for women, a perception that still prevails both in popular discourse and in academia in the dominant cultures of Euro-American societies.[1] In this chapter, I examine the application of Lahu dyadic ideals to the allocation of reproductive and productive tasks to men and women, as expressed by the common saying "Husband and wife do it together" (*phawd mawd mid ma ted gie te*). A couple's joint responsibility in labor is also symbolically echoed by the joint performance of a pair of chopsticks. In the first three sections of this chapter, I discuss Lahu ideologies and the joint roles of a husband-wife dyad in procreation, as well as in pregnancy, childbirth, and childrearing, activities described by a gender-neutral term (*yad hu*) that means both 'childbearing' and 'childrearing' (Matisoff 1988:369). I then examine the ways in which men and women are unified to "work hard to eat," intermingling both domestic and outdoor activities. To conclude, I argue that by unifying the two sexes in reproductive and productive tasks, the

Lahu allocation of labor shatters the presumed universal link between gender asymmetry and motherhood.

PROCREATION IDEOLOGIES

The Lahu conceptualization of gender unity in child-related roles begins with the cultural perceptions of the joint contribution of both sexes to procreation as expressed by a metaphor that refers to the offspring of a couple as the "bone and marrow–blood and flesh" (*awl xawd-awl nar–awl sif-awf shaf*) of both parties. This procreation ideology contrasts sharply with that found in societies from India to Siberia and throughout China, which links fathers to children's "bone" (essential structure) and mothers to children's "flesh" (supplementary details that fill in the structure) (e.g., Bloch and Parry 1982; Lévi-Strauss 1969:374; Watson 1982).

Lahu perceptions of and attitudes toward fertility and infertility manifest a consistent focus on joint gender roles. Lahu villagers commonly believe that the start of human life results from the joint physical contribution of men and women in the sexual act as tempered by spiritual influences. The cause of pregnancy is explained as what occurs when a man and woman "stay together" (*ted gie chied*). Several Lahu elders told me that, beyond the physical factors, whether or not a couple who "stay together" are able to produce children depends on the blessings of the supreme god Xeul Sha.

Like fertility, infertility is usually explained by the Lahu villagers without noticeable gender bias. While childless couples tend to recognize the possibility of physical causes of their infertility, some of them also pray for Xeul Sha's blessing. According to my interviews and observations, although having abundant children is ideal, infertility brings neither shame nor social pressure to a married couple as a unit. With only two exceptions, my inquiries attempting to identify which member of a couple was held responsible for their infertility were either met with uncertainty or were answered by reference to the god Xeul Sha. In the first exception, the "responsible" party was clearly the husband: he died after more than ten years of a childless marriage, and his widow became pregnant very soon after remarrying. In the second case, the wife was believed to be responsible for the couple's infertility because she had some physical infirmity and was frequently ill.

Lahu perceptions of fertility and infertility contrast sharply with those of most of the neighboring ethnic groups, which have various patrilineal and patriarchal traditions. For instance, asymmetrical pressures for women to produce children (especially sons) and to take the blame for barrenness have been recorded among the Han (e.g., Greenhalgh and Li 1995; Jacka 1997:65), the Hani (e.g., Gan et al. 1991:95; Yang 1992:131), the Wa (e.g., Cheng 1983:39), and the Yi (e.g., Li and Yang 1989:357). Conflicts have arisen over the issue of infertility when Lahu traditions encounter patriarchal ideas. This is demonstrated in the following story:

Na Meiq, a twenty-three-year old Lahu woman from Qhawqhat, married Zheng, a Han man from rural Jiangsu province in eastern China. They lived in Jiangsu for three years, and at the end of 1995, they visited her family for the first time after their marriage. One day in February 1996, right before they returned to Jiangsu after the Lahu New Year Festival, Na Meiq shyly told me that she was pregnant. Then she immediately turned to Zheng, commanding him firmly not to tell this news to his mother when they went back. Shy and quiet, he smiled and said nothing.

"Don't be so shy!" I teased her.

"No! I just don't want *her* to know," she replied firmly.

"Why?!" I was quite surprised because she had previously told me that her mother-in-law was very nice to her, and they seemed to get along well.

Na Meiq replied, "Because she has kept asking me about this. I am still young and have not worried about having a child yet. [Na Meiq explained to me later that even though she and Zheng had not used any contraceptive methods, she was not overly concerned about not having children because she was still young]. She often tells me how miserable and unfortunate a fate she has because I have no children. She even broke into tears several times. *She* cried because *I* don't have a child ?! I could hardly prevent myself from laughing."

"Well," I replied, "many Han do think that it is *very* important to have a child, especially a son. Since Zheng is her eldest son, a grandchild may mean a lot to her."

Na Meiq replied, "I know. But she even believed that I was *sick* [because Na Meiq had not yet conceived], so she concocted some herbal medicine for me to take." She turned to Zheng, "Besides, she did not say that *he* was sick and needed to take any medicine."

I was intrigued. "Did you take it?" I asked.

"I refused to take it the first time she offered it to me—I was *not* sick! She was very upset. Well, Zheng and I discussed it afterwards and found a way to make her feel better: with the excuse that the decoction was too hot, and I would bring the medicine to our room and dump it out without her noticing."

The Han mother-in-law's anxiety and grief contrasted with the Lahu daughter-in-law's perplexity and vexation demonstrate the conflicts between their respective cultural perceptions of fertility and infertility. Na Meiq was irritated by her mother-in-law's oversensitivity to and probing of the couple's fertility; she was further offended by her mother-in-law's stigmatizing her seeming infertility as a "sickness," all the more so since the "sickness" was only ascribed to Na Meiq herself, not to her husband. On the other hand, the Han mother-in-law was frustrated and saddened by Na Meiq's seeming infertility; her anxiety had accumulated over three years of anticipation and had been exacerbated by social pressures. Meanwhile, her grief may also have deepened over what she perceived as Na Meiq's unfeeling disregard for her desperation and ingratitude for her effort to resolve the "problem."

In brief, by regarding the start of human life as a joint physical contribution of men and women through sexuality under spiritual influence, gender roles in procreation are marked by symmetry and unity in Lahu culture. Such a perception serves as a foundation for Lahu expectations concerning joint gender roles in child-related tasks. According to many adult villagers, Lahu principle obligates a couple to join their strength in birthing and rearing their children. The villagers rationalize this principle by saying that "it took the two of them, not one, to conceive the child from the beginning, and they both will eat [depend on] the child's strength in the future." In the following two sections, I discuss how certain typically gender-exclusive tasks—such as pregnancy, childbirth, and childrearing—may be expected to unite Lahu men and women in both ideal and practice.

PREGNANCY AND CHILDBIRTH

As discussed in chapter 1, many versions of Lahu creation myths depict pregnancy and childbirth as tasks that were originally assigned to men and were later taken over by women either by accident or through compassion.

While downplaying sex difference in reproduction roles, this mythological interpretation also implies a moral expectation for a couple to join efforts in pregnancy and childbirth. At the beginning of the twenty-first century, many Qhawqhat villagers still expect a husband to fully participate in all the processes of his wife's pregnancy and childbirth.

Traditional Lahu courting songs aesthetically romanticize the extraordinary care of a husband for his pregnant wife, as shown by the following typical verses sung by a male to his lover:[2]

> When you carry a burden inside you / I am responsible for that burden.
> When we weed the field / you only need to weed
> Three handfuls of grasses at the top of the field,
> Three handfuls of grasses at the end of the field,
> Three handfuls of grasses at the left side of the field,
> Three handfuls of grasses at the right side of the field.
> You may take a rest afterwards / I will finish weeding the rest.
> After the weeding is finished / all the credit will be yours
> Because you have weeded the field / at the top and the end
> At the front and the rear / At the left and the right.
> What I have done is just patching the details in the middle . . . .
> At harvest time / you only need to carry the sickle,
> I will carry the threshing stick and three pieces of mat,
> The mat I have spent three days weaving from bamboo strips.
> You harvest at the top and the end of the field / The left and the right of
>   the field,
> You will harvest with such a little effort / As if you were merely counting
>   the rows.
> On our way home / You only need to carry the light pig food.
> I will carry the grain on my back,
> I will hold the gourd-and-pipe [a musical instrument] in my hands,
> I will play the music while carrying home the grain.

Corresponding to such a committed loving offer, the young woman also assures her lover of her commitment to work together as an inseparable pair even during her future imagined pregnancy:

> I will carry our child within me for ten months / Within these ten months[3]
> I will carry the child up to the mountains / Five months and ninety-nine times,

I will carry the child down to the rivers / Five months and seventy-
   seven times.
But I will not blame you for the arduous task,
The task to carry the child even before its birth.
Although my body will be heavy,
I will be with you all the time / I will not separate from you in
   our work.

The romanticized anticipation in courting songs of husband and wife working together during the wife's pregnancy is closely associated with social expectations for husbands. Several elderly and middle-aged villagers in Qhawqhat offered similar accounts of the demands on a husband during his wife's pregnancy. A husband is expected to carry out a larger proportion of the work that the couple had previously shared. In particular, tasks such as carrying drinking water, firewood, and harvested crops become more of the husband's special province. Since pregnant Lahu women usually continue to work until they feel the pangs of contractions, the husband is expected to increase his duties as the pregnancy progresses. In other words, as the burden the wife carries inside her body increases, so does the husband's burden outside his body. In addition, the extra amount of work that the husband is expected to do is related to the individual experiences of the pregnant woman. For instance, if a woman experiences strong discomfort such as back or leg pains, her husband takes over a larger proportion of work even in the early stage of the pregnancy. A couple's joint role in pregnancy is not only promoted by general social expectations but is also reinforced and guided by the couple's parents. These elders are obliged to instruct the expectant father, especially first-time fathers, to work more during the wife's pregnancy.

In addition to contributing extra work, said my sources, an expectant father is also required to participate in his wife's pregnancy by tracking his wife's bodily changes. In the early stage of a first-time pregnancy, the wife, usually taught by her mother or mother-in-law, imparts such knowledge to the husband. Communication between husband and wife about the pregnancy often continues throughout the entire process. Toward the end of the pregnancy, usually starting with the eighth month, the husband (guided by the couple's parents) is more careful in calculating the date and observing his wife's bodily changes. At this stage, the wife usually works in the fields that are closer to home. Meanwhile, the husband needs to start preparing for childbirth. For instance, he uses a mortar and pestle to pound black pepper and *caoguo* (*Amomum tsao-ko*, a plant of the ginger family) into powder so that they can be mixed into hot water and offered as a drink to the wife immediately after childbirth.

Like pregnancy, childbirth is considered a task that unifies, rather than divides, men and women. According to Lahu elders, it is a Lahu principle that a husband serves as the midwife in order to help his wife bring their children into the world together. While Lahu everyday language makes distinctions between "to give birth" (*baw*) and "to deliver" (*yad tot*), Lahu archaic language recognizes the joint role of a couple in childbirth by using the word *shod* ('to give birth to') to indicate the activities of both parents. For instance, in the antiphonal singing of love songs, "at the time when I was born" is expressed as "at the time when my father and mother gave birth to me on the ground" (*ngal xud phad hawq ma hawq shod ted yad*). In 2002, many Qhawqhat villagers still practice husband-midwifery, a very rare custom also recorded among the Rungus of Borneo (Appell 1991:12) and the Western Bontoc of the Philippines (Bacdayan 1977:286).

Ihad no opportunity to observe childbirth and postpartum practice because none of the Lahu households I was close to experienced childbirth during my stay, and villagers hold a widely shared belief that prohibited outsiders from visiting the newborn (Wang and He 1999:153). The following account of typical procedures is a summary of my intensive interviews with several Qhawqhat men and women who experienced husband-midwifery themselves between the 1950s and the 1990s.

Lahu childbirth usually takes place in the house of the expectant parents. The pregnant woman wears the traditional Lahu female costume consisting of a knee-length garment and a pair of loose-fitting pants. When the expectant mother starts to have contractions, relatives arrive to assist the couple during the birth. Like the expectant father, all four of the couple's parents are obligated to assist in delivering the child. Since the Lahu prefer village endogamy, a couple's parents often live nearby and can arrive immediately at the house after being informed of the contractions even if they occur in the middle of the night. Those grandparents who live too far away to be immediately informed are expected to stay at the couple's house beginning several days before the due date. Any of the couple's married siblings and siblings-in-law who live nearby usually participate in the birth as well. Occasionally, other neighboring relatives also attend, especially when the couple is expecting their first child.

When the wife suffers contractions, the husband and some other assistants hold her hands and comfort her so she can better endure the pains. While there are no particular required positions for other assistants to assume, the husband is ritually expected to support her back while she sits on a stool. Awaiting the birth, especially between contractions, people sit together in front of the hearth, chatting and drinking liquor. Between contractions, the expectant mother can join the group (without drinking alcohol) and can then lie down on her bed or sit on her stool when she suffers contractions. The expectant father can also join the group, but his main task is in the actual delivery.

During the early stages of the contractions, the husband massages his wife's abdomen to examine the position of the fetus. He is usually assisted by one of the most experienced parents of the couple, either male or female. If the fetus is in a transverse or breech position, the husband needs to perform external manipulation, turning it in the proper direction through massage. The method employed is to support the fetus with his left hand, then gently move the baby's head down with his right hand by stroking the wife's abdomen in one direction. If it is their first child, one of the couple's most experienced parents instructs and assists the husband in performing this important procedure.

When the contractions become stronger and the woman seems to be close to delivery, the husband hangs a rope around the crossbeam of the house. The wife holds on to the rope while assuming a squatting position, which helps her to push out the baby. While the laboring woman holds on to the rope, her husband supports her back until the child is born. Although any of the assistants can help support the wife, the husband is obligated to play the major role because it is physically and symbolically required for the couple to join their strength together for childbirth.

The newborn remains in the mother's loose-fitting pants. The husband assists his wife to lay the newborn, still inside the pants, on the ground. After assisting his wife to sit down on the stool to rest, the husband massages his wife's abdomen to speed the discharge of the placenta. The cutting of the umbilical cord, which is also performed by the husband, typically takes place after the placenta is completely expelled. After the cord is cut, the father removes the newborn from the mother's pants and takes his wife to lie on the bed or to sit beside the hearth to rest and drink the hot infusion of pepper and *caoguo* he had prepared earlier. It is the husband's role to be the first to pick up the newborn. He bathes the baby in warm water inside the house. After the bath, the father wraps the newborn in a white cloth and puts him or her into a special bamboo basket that is padded with cloth.

When this delivery procedure is completed, the husband usually sits beside the bed of his wife and the newborn, giving his wife water or tobacco if she requests these. Meanwhile, a ritual meal—rice porridge mixed with a chicken of the opposite sex to that of the newborn—is prepared for all who have attended the delivery. After the meal, the assistants from other households leave, and the husband wraps the placenta and buries it in the dirt floor under the bed where his wife is lying. The final task for the midwife-husband is to wash the bloodstained pajamas, cloths, and bedsheets.

Among the personal stories I collected from Qhawqhat men and women of different ages, the following, told by Cal Lad (male, about seventy) was the most compelling.

I was afraid and did not do well in the birth of Cal Var [his first child], but all the rest of our five children I delivered by my own hands. In her first childbirth, Na Yawl [his wife] suffered a lot from the contractions. I was very afraid, and was constantly worried that there was a severe problem . . . . When I was little, I had seen my mother delivering my younger siblings. She was not in that much pain; she even chatted with me. When I saw Na Yawl in that pain, I was terrified by the thought that she may have difficulty in labor. I was also worried whether she could endure it, if it took too long, and if it was too painful. My mother told me not to worry, because Na Yawl would deliver when the time came. My father had passed away by that time. Only my mother and my wife's parents were present.

My mother asked Na Yawl to lie down on the bed, and then she taught me how to touch my wife's abdomen to see if the position of the baby was right. She showed me where the head and feet were. Yes, the position was right. She also showed me what it would feel like if the baby were not in the proper position. . . . My mother taught me how to support Na Yawl's back while she was delivering.

When Cal Var was born, my mother instructed me how to cut the cord and pick the baby up, but I was too nervous to do so. My mother kept telling me, "This is your child, you must pick him up by yourself. We [the grandparents] are here today, but what if we were not here? Don't be afraid, touch gently. . . . You won't hurt him."

I was still afraid, but I reached out my hand to the baby. He was so tender, so tiny, only a little bigger than the size of my palm! My hands were so rough, and I was afraid of hurting him. My mother finally gave up. She picked up the child herself and asked me to watch carefully so that I could learn. She taught me where and how to cut the cord. She also taught me how to bathe the baby slowly, gently, and softly while she was doing it.

That was my first time. I was just too nervous, and was very afraid that I could have hurt the baby. . . . The next day, my mother let me bathe the baby. Then, I learned to touch babies.

The second time [with the next baby], I made it; I had learned from the firstborn. This time only my mother and my wife's father were present. My wife's parents lived too far away. If they both left even for a couple of days, their home, young children, and animals would have to be left behind, requiring other people to take care of them, so her mother remained behind. My father-in-law came three or four days before my wife delivered. They counted the date, and we did not need to inform them. My older child was there too. My mother showed me again how to touch Na Yawl's abdomen and see the child's position, which I had already learned last time. I knew it was the right position as soon as I touched [my wife's abdomen]. This time, I was not worried and was not afraid. When the child was born, my mother told me to use my right hand first to reach for the child, then pick up with both hands. I picked him up, held him in my own hands. I was very glad. . . . Well, I was still afraid of hurting him and thus very worried and nervous. I was afraid to move my hands, and just let him lie on my palm for quite a while. My mother taught me how to cut and tie the cord. . . .

I was not nervous at all for the other childbirths, Cal Pheud, Cal Xat (who died after eight months), Na Shi, Cal Siq, Na Lawd. I delivered them *all* [Cal Yawl smiles, brightly and proudly].

The following story from Na Var (female, forty-two) provides an example of women's experiences:

I was not nervous at all even during my first pregnancy. My first childbirth was difficult. I felt [labor] pain starting from the afternoon of the day before delivery. My husband, parents, and parents-in-law were all with me. . . . I could not stand the pain, and I did not stay still at home. I walked around. I gave birth to my son while I was walking to our garden.

My mother taught my husband how to cut the cord and pick up the baby. Of course, he was very nervous the first time. But he did as my mother requested. . . . Cutting the cord needs to be done by a husband. If he does not know how to do it, his parents or parents-in-laws will help. My husband buried the placenta and washed the blood-stained clothes and bedding. . . . We were having our own child, of course we had to wash those by ourselves.

Three of our children were all [first] picked up by my husband. . . . We have never asked Wang Yisheng [village health practitioner] for help because I knew I would be fine. Also, my parents and parents-in-law know a lot about delivery, they have delivered all of their children. They all came to help my husband. I was not afraid.

According to many elders of Qhawqhat, without any other options, Lahu villagers in Lancang all practiced childbirth according to the Lahu principles prior to the 1950s. Nevertheless, the practice of husband-midwifery among the Lancang Lahu has undergone various degrees of transformation since the PRC government began to introduce healthcare practitioners, some of whom were trained briefly in Western obstetrical techniques, into Lahu villages.

Depending mainly on the capability and the availability of a practitioner, the frequency with which villagers have sought out rural health practitioners (called "barefoot doctors" during the Cultural Revolution) for midwifery services has varied in different villages and over different periods. In 1961, upper-level officials assigned the Qhawqhat village cluster its first health practitioner, who had received an elementary-school education. Nevertheless, she left the next year after villagers suspected her of possessing the evil spirit (*tawr*). Another health practitioner, a young Han woman, called by the villagers Wang Yisheng, arrived in 1964. Wang was briefly trained in midwifery several years after she arrived in the village. Villagers had been seeking an assistant for severely difficult deliveries since 1969. The traditional way to cope with a difficult delivery is to invite a spiritual specialist (*mawq paf*), who performs the ritual *ned te* to pacify the spirit(s) of the deceased parent(s), if any, of the woman in labor. The health practitioner is often asked for help only if there is still difficulty after the ritual is done. At the beginning of the twenty-first century, most Qhawqhat villagers still rely on their traditional ways of childbirth. According to my letter correspondence with my host family, husbands, elders, and relatives of the laboring women served as midwives for sixteen out of the twenty-seven Qhawqhat infants born in 2000. The female health practitioner, who took office after I left the village cluster, served as midwife for eleven infants. In other words, none of these infants was born in the clinic at the local township.

The increasing significance of health practitioners in Lahu childbirth is beginning to challenge the symbolic and practical unity of a couple during childbirth. In some cases, the activities that help the pregnant woman to bring the infant into the world—examining the position of the fetus, cutting the umbilical cord, and picking up the infant—have shifted from being the responsibility of the husband to being that of the health practitioner. In addition, the change of the wife's position in childbirth to a supine (or lithotomy) position from an upright one renders unnecessary the husband's support of her back.

The elders I talked to uniformly insisted on conducting childbirth according to Lahu principles except in the case of complications. In contrast, many young people, especially members of the younger generation who have received a relatively high level of Han-style education, preferred a health-practitioner midwife. Cal Vol, a thirty-six-year-old primary school teacher who was born in Qhawqhat, argued eloquently for the latter. While he was talking, his wife Na Pheud agreed with nods and smiles. Na Pheud had only a few years of education; nevertheless, her sharing of attitudes with Cal Vol may be related to the fact that her own father is an elementary school teacher.

> Cal Var [his son] and Na Lad [his daughter] were all delivered by Wang Yisheng. I went to her house and invited her to come to our house to deliver when Na Pheud [his wife] began her contractions.
>
> Wang Yisheng's method was different from the Lahu tradition. She asked Na Pheud to lie on the bed to deliver instead of taking a squatting position. The things Wang Yisheng used were all sanitized—she would not use a piece of bamboo to cut the cord. . . . If the contractions lasted too long, she could give the expectant mother a shot [presumably of pitocin], and the delivery would go much faster.
>
> Both of our parents are experienced in midwifery, but we'd like to have Wang Yisheng perform the task. I think that delivery should be done by whoever knows the best. She was trained to deliver babies, and she has medicine and equipment. Many villagers don't understand the significance of science and technology. . . . According to Lahu custom, the family should invite a *mawq paf* [spiritual specialist] to perform superstitious activities if they are having a difficult delivery. Treatment can be seriously delayed. . . .
>
> Of course, husband and wife should join their strength together for the birth of their own children. Our Lahu have the most equality between men and women. . . . But, I think it is dogmatic to refuse to have a doctor de-

liver children because of that. Searching for the best delivery is also a joint effort for the best interests of our children. . . I was there assisting Wang Yisheng during the births of my children. . . . Sure, I washed the blood-stained clothes afterwards.

While the newly introduced system of Western obstetrics has under-mined the core symbolism of the joint roles of a couple in the Lahu tradi-tion of childbirth, it might not necessarily challenge individuals' perceptions of those roles. In the above case, the couple made a joint decision to choose the health practitioner to serve as a midwife for their delivery based on their belief that modern technology would benefit their children. Interestingly, the husband (Cal Vol) criticizes other couples as "dogmatic" if they perceive the Lahu ideology of joint roles of a couple and the use of newly introduced Western-style obstetrics to be incompatible. Cal Vol's argument is backed up by his own action: according to my own observation as well as villagers' comments, he has contributed no less than his wife to childrearing activities.

Despite the impact of biomedicine, Qhawqhat villagers' emphasis on joint gender roles in pregnancy and childbirth is shared at the beginning of the twenty-first century by many Lahu in rural Lancang, especially in the ar-eas where villagers continued to have limited access to biomedical care. Sim-ilar ideals and symbolism were reported among the Lahu who did not prac-tice husband-midwifery. For instance, among the Lahu Nyi of northern Thailand, the expectant father was expected to hang the rope for his wife to grasp in labor, support her back, massage her abdomen to facilitate the de-livery, and wash the blood-stained clothes (Walker 1970:273).

In keeping with Lahu procreation beliefs, Lahu married couples are en-couraged to unite their efforts symbolically and socially in pregnancy and childbirth although these roles are biologically assigned only to women. De-spite the occasional gaps between ideal and practice, as well as the existence of competing ideals and practices, joint gender roles in pregnancy and childbirth persisted in different degrees among the Lahu villagers in Lan-cang at the beginning of the twenty-first century.

CHILDREARING

Gender also serves as a unifier in assigning various tasks of Lahu childrear-ing. According to Qhawqhat villagers, it is a Lahu principle that a married couple join their efforts in childrearing, that they "do not divide you and me" (*nawl kaf ngal kaf mad feof*). Both my observations and interviews in the 1990s suggest that the gender allocation of childrearing tasks among Lahu men and women of Qhawqhat was predominantly marked by unity rather than by division.[4]

According to my interviewees, the joint role of a Lahu couple in childcare starts from the moment the child is born. Qhawqhat women typically enjoy postpartum rest for twelve days (Wang and He 1999:153) while some other Lahu in Yunnan expect more days of rest (Dong et al. 1995:801; Xu 1993:24). During this period when the wife is confined at home with the infant, the husband also stays at home and is expected to take care of both his wife and the newborn. In particular, he is responsible for protecting the infant from the attack of evil spirits (*tawr*) (Wang and He 1999:153) and for doing most of the domestic work that had previously been shared by the couple. During the first few days postpartum, the wife typically lies in bed or on a wooden board close to the hearth, a practice called "roasting" in some Southeast Asian societies (Laderman 1983, 1991). The husband is expected to tend to his wife, for example giving her water to drink and warming a cloth over the hearth for her to massage any painful areas. In addition, the husband prepares special food for his wife, especially killing and cooking a chicken every day because chicken soup is believed to be ideal for women's postpartum recovery.

While the mother breastfeeds the baby and typically serves as the primary caretaker, the father also plays a significant role in taking care of the newborn. The father's tasks usually include bathing the baby as well as cleaning the newborn after urination and defecation. In addition, the father is expected to share with his wife in holding the newborn. Interviewees noted that holding the newborn can be a very challenging task when the newborn refuses to sleep in the cloth-padded basket and cries constantly, which frequently occurs with children born in the winter. In such cases, the husband and wife commonly take turns carrying the infant during the day; at night, it is the parent who is more alert who holds the baby. Because the postpartum woman is frequently exhausted from childbirth and nursing, it is not unusual that the father is more alert at night than the mother and thus takes on this nocturnal responsibility.

Interviewees explained that, during the period of postpartum recovery, the actual number of days that the husband can stay at home full-time to take care of the wife and the newborn varies according to the circumstances of the household. For instance, if the child is born into a household that lacks laborers when it is the busy season for agriculture, the husband has to resume work in the fields as soon as two or three days after the birth. Even so, the husband needs to take care of his wife and their newborn as much as he can when he is at home. In such instances, the husband usually gets up earlier than usual and goes off to work in the field relatively late so that he has time to bathe the infant and prepare the chicken soup. If in a rush, he will kill, pluck, wash, and chop the chicken but leave it raw for his wife to cook. The wife stays home taking care of herself and the newborn, reheating the chicken and rice for lunch. In the late afternoon, the husband comes home earlier than usual, preparing dinner and conducting other household activities such as fetching water and feeding the pigs and chickens.

I observed that when a couple returned to their normal work routine after the postpartum rest period, they continued to play a unified role in childcare. Except for nursing, a Lahu couple was expected to take joint responsibility in all major tasks of childcare, including carrying, bathing, feeding solid foods, playing with, and comforting their child. A typical Lahu strategy to cope with the commonly perceived incompatibility between childcare and many subsistence tasks was for the parents to alternate carrying the child on the way to work and sometimes while they worked.

Indeed, carrying a child to the fields and while working becomes a major task in Lahu childcare. During the first two to three months, an infant is carried in a basket that is very tightly woven with fine bamboo pieces and padded and covered with cloth. The couple often takes turns carrying (on their backs or sides) the infant in the basket on their way to work. Typically, while the couple is working, they place the basket on the ground in the fields in a spot where there is shade in the summer or sun in the winter. Both parents tend to the infant when he/she cries, and the mother nurses him or her when needed. The joint responsibility of a couple to carry and take care of their children at this stage is vividly expressed in some conventional Lahu courting songs. For example, one can praise his or her partner by phrases such as "You are as beautiful as *a vawd shawd vet* [a kind of white flower of a particular tree] because your parents have known how to take good care of you ever since you were born. They placed you in the finest basket under the prettiest white-flower tree while they were working." To heighten the praise due to the lover, the singer may also debase himself or herself according to convention: "I am as ugly as a deformed tree because my parents did not know how to take good care of me after I was born. They placed me in a shabby basket in the fields while they were working. Ants and mosquitoes dined on me; thus I became the leftovers."

From the age of about four months, when the child's neck muscles are strong enough to support its head, he or she is carried in a cloth baby carrier (*pi khawd*). Compared to a basket, it is much more convenient to carry a child in the baby carrier while working because it takes less space and is more flexible. Children up to five years old are occasionally carried in the cloth baby carrier, especially when they are sick or when they need to walk a very long distance to the fields. As a child grows, especially after he or she can walk and has a younger sibling, the frequency of being carried decreases drastically. Young Lahu children often walk with their parents to the work site, only being carried when the road is too long or too steep. While the parents are working, young children usually entertain themselves nearby or play with their older siblings. When a child is sleepy or clingy, whichever parent the child goes to will carry the child until he or she falls asleep. Once asleep, the child is often placed in bed while the parents are doing domestic work or on a wooden board in a nearby field shelter when they are working outside. If the weather is cold and there is no shelter near the work site, the child is often carried in the carrier in turn by both parents for the duration of the nap.

While such a dual parent-child bond is highly emphasized socially and symbolically, the child-related roles of a couple at all stages are often taken over by many other family members in order to attain the optimal use of labor. Nonparental childcare is especially significant during the segment of the agricultural season when a strict work schedule must be maintained in order to obtain the best yields. Married couples receive supplementary childcare on a regular basis from a variety of resources including the couple's parents and older children, other relatives, and neighbors. In contrast to most societies in which substitute childcare is practiced so that mothers can keep working after childbirth (e.g., Clark 1999:725; Weisner and Galimore 1977), the caretakers in the Lahu culture are of both sexes rather than being predominantly female.

The ideal of joint gender roles in childcare is socialized throughout childhood both by playing and by assuming responsibilities. Playing piggyback or "baby-holding" (*yad yied pud*) is one of the most popular games for boys and girls between the ages of one and four. Upon the request of a child, an adult makes a "baby doll" out of cloth and ties it around the child's back with a scarf. The child usually pats the baby doll, which is often beyond the reach of his or her hands, and pretends to hum the "baby" to sleep while rocking and walking. When tired of the game, the child may try to untie the

FIGURE 6 A male relative (arms raised) joins a couple threshing wheat in their field while their children play nearby. Photograph by Shanshan Du

FIGURE 7 A Lahu man, carrying his young daughter on his back, aims at a bird perched in a tree. Photograph by Shanshan Du

scarf and often screams for help when unsuccessful. I observed a one-year-old boy making loud noises and eventually crying to get the attention of his parents, then pointing to his back to indicate that he wanted to play "baby-holding." Older toddlers sometimes find their own cloths and wrap them up as a doll in a scarf, asking their parents to tie the dolls to their backs and un-tie them when they finish the game. When children are between five and six years old, childcare is gradually transformed from a game to the responsi-bility of babysitting younger siblings.

While children are socialized into childrearing through playing or taking on some responsibilities, adolescents romanticize the task in courting. Po-etically, yet realistically, the lovers may express their commitments to future childrearing by singing interchangeable verses such as:

When you carry grain / I will carry the baby.
I will not mind / If I have to carry the baby on my back while working,
I will not mind / If the child messes up my clothes.

The Lahu childcare practices I observed differ drastically from those in some of the neighboring ethnic groups, especially the Han Chinese. Al-though urban Han practices (Jankowiak 1992) have largely transformed the traditional "strict father / kind mother" dichotomy (Ho 1987:231), domestic work, especially childcare, continues to be conducted almost entirely by Han women in rural areas (Jacka 1997:103). Many Lahu villagers I inter-viewed tended to assume, when they compared their practice to the Han, that the Lahu principle of childcare was the natural one. For example, Na Thid (female, twenty-eight) expressed her puzzlement that Han fathers could be so irresponsible in childcare that they acted "as if the children were not theirs," and she expressed surprise and sympathy over Han mothers' handling childcare on their own. Beyond the discursive arena, encounters between the Lahu and the Han traditions have given rise to daily conflicts in certain cases of intermarriage. For instance, a Qhawqhat woman named Na Vol married a Han peasant named Zhao and migrated to a rural Han area. According to Na Vol's relatives, when Na Vol and Zhao visited Qhawqhat in the early 1990s, they constantly quarreled over childcare matters such as who was supposed to clean up the mess when their two-year-old son turned over his rice bowl in the middle of a family meal. The conflicts seemed to re-flect their fundamental and irresolvable disagreement over roles that were defined quite differently by the two distinct traditions. While the Han husband believed that childcare was exclusively a woman's task—an attitude that prevails throughout the rural Han population in China—his Lahu wife insisted that they should share childcare equally because the child belonged to them both. Nevertheless, I neither observed nor heard such remarkable behavior differences in parenting among the few Han-Lahu marriages in Qhawqhat. This might be because those Han men have grown up in Lahu villages and have thus adopted local childrearing traditions.

In summary, the ideal of "unity," coexisting with competing principles and practices, still predominantly governs the gender allocation of most child-related tasks among the Qhawqhat Lahu at the beginning of the twenty-first century. By encouraging a married couple to take joint responsibility for their child as if they were a single social entity, this social ideal naturalizes a dual-sex "parent-child" bond.

"WORK HARD TO EAT"

In addition to childrearing, the ideal of "husband and wife do it together" also includes the concept "work hard to eat" (*kheor cad*, or *kheor cad meol cad*). This phrase connotes all the tasks involved in feeding a household, from planting to weeding, harvesting, storing, pounding (rice), cooking, fetching water and firewood, raising pigs and chickens, and gardening. These tasks apparently blur the boundaries between food production, which is commonly viewed in the anthropological literature as subsistence work and is often linked to males, and food preparation, which is typically classified as reproductive work and is usually associated with females. In other words, this ideal unites a husband and a wife as a single labor team to jointly perform both productive and reproductive tasks.

Lahu villagers cannot overemphasize the importance of "working hard to eat." Almost all of the villagers I asked regarded being "capable of working hard to eat" (*kheor cad meol cad peuq*) as the most important criterion for choosing a husband or a wife. My observations in the Qhawqhat village cluster and many other Lahu villages in China and Thailand indicated that the ideal that married couples jointly "work hard to eat" was widely realized in practice, a phenomenon supported by the household surveys I conducted in the Abo village (sixty-three households in 1996) of Qhawqhat. According to my surveys, fifty-one out of the sixty-three head couples of these households (81 percent) had an equal share of labor, both inside and outside

FIGURE 8 A Lahu couple performs domestic work together. The husband carries a sleeping baby in a cloth baby carrier while sharpening a knife to prepare dinner. The wife chops the trunk of a banana tree to feed to pigs. Photograph by Shanshan Du

the house. The remaining twelve pairs of household head couples were considered as exceptions because of idiosyncratic conditions.

A spouse could be excused from doing an equal share of household-related work through both physical and social circumstances. Eight of the twelve cases of uneven labor sharing could be classified as belonging to this "excusable" category. Chronic disease often physically hinders a spouse from contributing to the household as a normal adult laborer. Two of the above twelve cases belonged to this category: in one case, the wife suffered from severe back pains; in the other case, the husband suffered from arthritis.

Another valid reason for unequal workloads between spouses was that one person was occupied with other work that prevented him or her from full participation in household-related work. Six of the above twelve cases belonged to this category. It is worthwhile to notice that the work that prevented these couples from participating fully in household-related tasks was all related to recent social transformations—either state-assigned tasks or tasks resulting from recent economic reforms. In the first case, the husband served as the health worker for the village. In the second case, the husband worked under contract for the local factory that processed tea. In the third case, the husband was often on the road because he drove a truck to earn a living. In the fourth case, the husband frequently offered his labor for hire to other Qhawqhat villagers and often ate at the hiring household(s). In the fifth case, the husband often stayed at the household's field shelter, which was far from the village, to tend the cattle and raise chickens. In the sixth case, the wife, a leader of the village cluster, had to attend meetings frequently, especially prior to the dissolution of the commune in Lancang in 1984.

Among the twelve cases in which head couples shared labor unequally, the final four cases were caused by "inexcusable" personal problems. One case involved an alcoholic wife. In the other three cases, "laziness" (*bawl*) was counted as the crux of the couples' uneven sharing of labor. The husband in one case and the wife in another were considered extremely lazy, and their households were consequently impoverished. The negative impact of "laziness" both on one's spouse and on one's household at large can help us to understand why local wisdom ranks being "capable of working hard to eat" the top quality in selecting spouses.

Breaking down the twelve cases of the couples' uneven sharing of labor tasks by gender, there seems to be a huge gender difference: in only three out of the twelve cases was the woman the party that did less work while men accounted for nine such cases. Nevertheless, if we exclude the six excusable cases in which one spouse was involved in extra workloads resulting from significant social transformations in recent decades, there were left three males and three females who did less than their share of work. Judging by this, we may presume that there was a much smaller proportion of Lahu couples who had unequal sharing of household work prior to the radical social transformations that have occurred in Lahu village life since the 1950s.

Along with the ideal of gender unity, the practical necessity for making the maximum use of available labor also contributes to the overlapping of gender roles in Lahu village life. In order to achieve the optimal use of a household's labor pool, Lahu villagers generally focus on the availability of and demands for labor instead of emphasizing fixed criteria such as sex and age. Accordingly, rather than being constrained by a strict sexual division, the division of labor in a Lahu household tends to be flexible, varying according to daily circumstances as well as to the developmental cycle of the household. Such contingent logistics for managing the entire pool of household labor can enhance the efficiency of production—although at the cost of having to repeatedly recalculate solutions.

The arrangement of herding in a Qhawqhat household related to my host family (a home I visited frequently) exemplifies how optimal use of household laborers defies sex or age differences in task assignment. In 1996, the household consisted of the head couple, Cal Thid (about seventy years old) and his wife Na Var (also about seventy years old), their youngest daughter, Na Meiq (in her early twenties), and son-in-law, Cal Lawd (in his early twenties), as well as their baby granddaughter, Na Xeul (ten months old). During the last few months before I left the village, the task of herding had shifted among all the adults of the household. Since herding was a relatively light task, Cal Thid and Na Var, the eldest members of the household, often took turns at the job. During a couple of days in the rainy season, the baby Na Xeul was not feeling well. Therefore, the young mother, Na Meiq, took over herding so that she could spend more time with the baby, staying in a shelter longer and going home earlier to keep the baby out of the cold. The cattle were also taken away by the son-in-law, Cal Lawd, to a remote field shelter where he plowed. A neighboring teenage relative also helped tend the cattle during the harvest season. According to Cal Thid, their household's arrangement of labor in herding, which was then basically an adult's task, was different from what it had been fifteen years earlier, when the household had three six- to ten-year-old children. At that time, the ten-year-old boy—who did not attend school so he could stay home and herd—often took the six-year-old and the family's cattle to the mountains. During school vacations, however, the eight-year-old girl, who attended school, took over herding, allowing her brother to be shifted to other agricultural tasks.

The ideal of the gender-blind sharing of labor in both domestic and outdoor work is socialized in childhood and often starts with playing and then gradually involves auxiliary responsibilities. Typically, little children from two to six years old are socialized without gender distinction to play both domestic and outdoor roles through games. Besides childcare, another significant domestic role—cooking—is intensively socialized in a gender-blind manner through games. The game is called "playing cooking" (*awf ted cad geud*) and is most popular among young children between three and six years old. Lacking commercially made toys, Lahu children find leaves to roll into "bowls" and "woks," taking some ashes to use as "rice," breaking some leaves as "vegetables" or "dishes," and using some small sticks as "chopsticks." Cooking is typically played in a collective context. Two to three children, sometimes as many as eight, usually play cooking games together. They often "cook" their own food and then carry it to the "table" on the ground in the front yard to share. Sometimes they hold their own "dishes" to offer others a taste of their delicious "food." As explained by adults, a child will not play at cooking alone, because that makes it boring. The cooperative aspects of cooking games prepare boys and girls alike for entrance into the Lahu social reality that defines cooking as a cooperative effort by all household members, especially by a couple. There are sometimes so many children in a play group that parents may halfheartedly complain that "when a bunch of children are into 'playing cooking' in your front yard, you can never keep your yard clean because there are broken leaves and sticks everywhere."

Both boys and girls between three and five also like to imitate work in the fields. "Hoeing" is most commonly played at because of children's access to real tools that they can carry. Boys and girls both like to play at digging using the small-size hoes that their parents use for weeding. Nevertheless, digging games are often discouraged by parents (who may hide the small hoes) to prevent the mud-padded ground of their front yards from being destroyed.

Typically from age six to age eight, little children begin to apply their games to real-life situations or to play at enacting joint gender roles in work. More specifically, Lahu boys and girls start to assist their parents in performing domestic work such as babysitting, carrying water, and washing their own clothes. Encouraged by their parents, children at this stage are usually eager to try out their imitation of working games in real life. For instance, the parents may encourage children when they are willing to wash their own clothes—although the parents may later rewash the laundry if it is not clean. Thus, from six to eight, little children's imitative activities, often supervised by adults, mainly serve as a transition between play and work.

From the ages of about eight to twelve, children start to take supplementary responsibilities in domestic and outdoor work, especially in childcare and cooking. In fact, these children provide one of the major sources for assistance in childcare, especially when the parents are busy working in the fields. The older children may stay at home taking care of their younger siblings, feeding chickens and pigs, carrying water, and cooking rice while waiting for their parents to come home from the fields. However, they are often discouraged from cooking dishes because many Lahu parents feel that these children cannot wash the vegetables carefully enough and because the dishes will not remain fresh until the parents come back from the fields. They may also go to the field in which their parents are working to take care of their younger siblings, collect firewood, and cut grasses to feed the pigs. Boys and girls of this age are also starting to herd cattle in the fields without the presence of adults. Nowadays, however, more children attend public school, so such work is perfomed after school.

Despite the seamless gender unity suggested by the ideal that "Husband and wife do it together," not all tasks performed by Qhawqhat men and women are identical in practice. In fact, clear division of labor by sex in Qhawqhat is observable in a few tasks, conforming to predominant patterns of the sex-based division of labor across almost all cultures (Mordock and Provost 1993). For instance, hunting, blacksmithing, and tasks in the fields that require intense strength (such as plowing and cutting trees), are typically men's work. In addition, weaving cloth is typically a woman's task. Similar patterns in the division of labor have also been reported among Lahu elsewhere (e.g., Zhang and Peng 1982:48; Zhang et al. 1996:119). Gender difference, which seems to slightly favor girls, is manifest in rural schooling. For example, only twenty-one out of the fifty-four graduates (39 percent) of the Qhawqhat Elementary School in 2001 were boys, and the four students who successfully entered junior high school were all girls. In brief, while the focus of Lahu villagers on optimal use of labor fosters great overlapping of gender roles in task assignments, it only minimizes, rather than completely eliminating, the impact of sex difference.

It is interesting that the dominant Lahu gender ideology, which focuses on unity, largely ignores the existence of a sex-based division of labor. The rich Lahu mythology and the folk songs provide no rationale for any division of tasks by sex. Not only is gender division invisible in the myths regarding the origin of agriculture, but men and women are also sometimes depicted hunting large game together (Hu 1996; Wang and He 1999:68–69). The denial of any division of labor between the sexes is most salient in ritual songs. "Chasing bees," one of the classic themes in Lahu oral literature, tells how a couple chases bees in order to make beeswax candles to offer Xeul Sha; it vividly describes a husband-wife team performing all tasks, including cutting bamboo and trees, reaching the honeycomb, blacksmithing, and hunting. Typically, two lovers sing such songs antiphonally to each other in anticipation of their future marriage, depicting their imagined spiritual journey to attain ritual materials and to perform rituals to seek blessings from Xeul Sha. The following verses are some extracts from a version of "chasing bees" in which the couple acts as a team in all tasks described in the nearly five hundred verses (Cal Yawl 1989:235–246).

FIGURE 9 A Lahu boy (eight years old) tends to a cooking fire while taking care of his younger sister (two years old). Photograph by Shanshan Du

FIGURE 10 A group of Lahu boys and girls play "house-building" while tending cattle. Photograph by Shanshan Du

Two of us join heart and strength / high mountains and steep rocks cannot
  deter us.
You hold a long knife in your right hand / I hold a chopping knife in my
  left hand,
Fell silver bamboo at one end of the valley basin,
Fell golden bamboo at the other end of the valley basin.
The silver pole is as long as seventy-seven joints
The golden pole is as high as seventy-seven joints.
You raise a hand to take the honeycomb / I raise a hand to reach the
  beeswax. . . .
You use a steel knife / I hold a steel axe,
Cutting trees in a pair / Felling a tree to make drums. . . .
We arrive at the place where many rivers converge / Begin to chop the tree.
Each stands on each side / Each chops one at a time. . . .
Tasks of blacksmith and carpeting / You and I learn to do,
[Learning] the skills of blacksmith / [Learning] the craft of carpeting. . . .
It took three nights to make the male drum / It took three nights to make
  the female drum,
Finished the male-female drums / [We] need to get animal skins to cover
  the drums. . . .
You led a yellow dog / I led a black dog. . . .
With hard bows and arrows in hands / Go to hunt barking deer and red deer.
You shoot an arrow / Kill a barking deer,
I shoot an arrow / Kill a red deer.
Stretch the skin of the red deer on the male drum,
Stretch the skin of the barking deer on the female drum.

Furthermore, the emphasis on the teamwork of men and women as ide-
alized by the Lahu phrase "husband and wife do it together" can transform
some of the scholarly conceptualization of the sexual division of labor into
the ideal of gender unity. For instance, all of the Lahu villagers I talked to
considered it to be a perfect example of, rather than counterevidence for,
"husband and wife do it together" if a husband was plowing while his wife
was seeding. In contrast, a couple was considered to be divided by their tasks
if they had to work in separate fields—which frequently occurs due to the
intensive labor exchange among relative households—even if they were performing the same task (such as harvesting). Furthermore, none of the tasks
marked by sex division was accorded differential value, and many of them

FIGURE 11 A young couple sits with a relative, making balls of spun cotton. The wife carries their baby on her back. Photograph by Shanshan Du

were not even gender-exclusive in everyday life. For instance, I observed some men participating in supplementary tasks involving cloth weaving, such as rolling thread, while a family was sitting together and chatting.

While the dominant Lahu gender ideology generally ignores the impact of sex difference in labor organization, individual villagers do recognize such an impact. For instance, the general advantage of men in physical strength was the common answer to my persistent inquiries concerning the reasons for the clear gender-based division of a few tasks. However, the villagers also acknowledged individual diversity in strength among members of the same sex. Many people gave me examples of some women in the village who were physically stronger than their husbands and performed heavy tasks such as plowing and woodcutting. Na Lad, a woman in her forties, proudly told me (in her husband's presence) that she was stronger than her husband and therefore performed all the heavy work in the household that was usually done by men. Ethnographic studies have also recorded that some Lahu wives plow and hunt together with their husbands although males typically perform tasks that require more strength (Lei and Liu

1999:142). Accordingly, while most Lahu villagers recognized the general sex difference in strength as responsible for some task allocation, neither individual strength nor related productive tasks were strictly coded by sex.

In summary, the ideal that married couples jointly "work hard to eat" promotes a motif of gender *unity* in Lahu organization of labor in both the domestic arena and beyond. While gender serves mainly as a unifier, rather than a divider, of roles, spaces, and values regarding task allocation, the "sexual division of labor" still applies to a few tasks in practice. According to my letter correspondence with my host family, the same pattern of labor allocation is still practiced in the village cluster of Qhawqhat in 2002.

CONCLUSION

Lahu allocation of labor tends to revolve around the principle of gender unity, which defines a married couple as a single labor team that performs a variety of tasks, ideally functioning together as smoothly as a pair of chopsticks. According to this principle, both productive and reproductive tasks are oriented towards the couple's common goal of sustaining their household, submerging the productivity of the husband and wife within the duty of the couple as a whole. The Lahu ideal of gender unity and the pragmatic focus on optimal labor usage minimizes rather than eliminates the impact of sex difference. Such a correlation between the social emphasis on husband-wife teams and a minimal division of labor by sex has also been found in some other societies, for example, among the Aka Pygmies (Hewlett 1991) and in the Ecuadorean Andes (Hamilton 1998).

The biological fact of the long-term dependency of human infants is often used to explain gender asymmetry by positing a universal link between the female role and reproductive activities (e.g. Ortner 1996[1974]; Mukhopadhyay and Higgins 1988). Instead of constructing a strong mother-infant bond to cope with biological constraints, the Lahu people have established a dual-sex, parent-child bond. When the child-related role is shifted from "motherhood" to "parenthood," the presumed universal link between women and domestic work is expanded to include men. Meanwhile, women are also considered an integral part of the productive labor force of both household and society. While the tasks that unify men and women leave little room to develop gender asymmetry, Lahu symbolism places no value differentiation on the few gender-specific tasks in the society.

CHAPTER 4

"MALE-FEMALE MASTERS":
HUSBAND-WIFE DYADS IN LEADERSHIP

BEYOND EXPECTING married couples to join their efforts to feed the household and raise children, indigenous Lahu ideologies also promote joint leadership of husband-wife dyads. Conforming to the cosmological power structures represented in mythology, Lahu principle (*awl lid*) suggests that households and villages are manageable only when "a pair of male-female masters rules together" (*shief phad shief ma qha cir qawr kuad xad*). In this chapter, I first discuss the institution of *yiel shief phad-yiel shief ma* ('male-female masters of the household'), focusing on the joint authority and responsibility of household co-heads in making consensus decisions. Then, in the historical context of increasingly direct control by the central Chinese government, I examine the forms and transformations of some indigenous Lahu institutions that require married couples to hold social and spiritual posts in the village and the village cluster.

"MALE-FEMALE MASTERS OF THE HOUSEHOLD"

The Lahu use the term *yiel* to represent 'house', 'household', and 'home.' As among the Lahu in northern Thailand (Hill 1985), the household serves as the basic economic, social, and spiritual unit of Lahu village life in Lancang. Those who reside in the same house typically have close genealogical relationships, and they form the core members of the Lahu kinship category "one family" or "members of one household" (*ted yiel chaw*). The average size of a household in Qhawqhat was 4.2 persons in 1995. Conventionally, a household is headed by a couple who is collectively called *yiel shief phad*, which means 'the master(s) of the household', 'head couple', or 'household co-heads.' When further distinction is necessary, the male and female co-heads are respectively called *yiel shief phad* and *yiel shief ma* (Gen 1997:85; Lei and Liu 1999:246; Wang and He 1999:114). In accordance with the connotations of these terms, Lahu head couples typically enjoy a great degree of unity in managing their households.

Just as a couple is simultaneously initiated into adulthood, a man and a woman jointly go through the process of becoming household co-heads. Except for some Lahu Shi who practice matrilocality, the postmarital residence pattern among the Lancang Lahu is predominantly bilocal (Gen 1997:76–86; Wang and He 1999:113–118). According to the bilocal principle, a young couple resides first in the household of the bride's parents for three years and then in that of the groom's parents for two or three years. Afterwards, they may build their own house near the parents of either the husband or the wife. In practice, the principle is applied with great flexibility, shaped mainly by the labor needs of the couple's families.[1]

A young couple in Qhawqhat typically takes one of two paths to become household co-heads. The most common way is to establish an independent household two years after building a house close to the set of parents from whom they have inherited their houseland. Normally, after they finish their obligation to serve both sets of parents, the couple can establish a house adjacent to the household of the parents from whom they will inherit their farmland and houseland. The newly established house has only two rooms and has no altar for making offerings to the paired guardian deity of the household. During this period, which typically lasts two to three years, the couple remains in a liminal status. On the one hand, they have built their own house and have gained economic autonomy, particularly the authority to manage production on their inherited land. On the other hand, since they are not formally recognized as household heads, the couple is still ritually and socially affiliated with the household from which they inherit their house site. The spiritual dependence of such a household is symbolized by the house's physical differences from a fully established house, which contains three rooms with an altar for the household's guardian deity pair in the middle room. When both sets of parents agree that the couple have fulfilled their obligation and are ready to establish their own household, the dependent house is expanded to three rooms. During a ritual feast attended by the two sets of the couple's parents and other senior relatives on the first day of the Lahu New Year, an altar is built in the middle room. When the paired beeswax candle is lit on the altar, the couple is presented as co-heads, ritually and symbolically, to Xeul Sha and the guardian deity pair of their own independent household.

The second way of becoming household co-heads is to inherit a house directly from one set of the couple's parents. An elder couple passes on their house and household to only one of their children by means of an agreement that is often reached before the wedding. If a young couple is to inherit the house from the parents of the wife, they will reside in the house of the bride's parents after their wedding and will inherit the house and household in three years; the same norms apply to inheritance from the husband's parents. The transition of household co-headship also takes place at the beginning of the Lahu New Year, and the new head couple will start serving the household guardian deities afterwards. In this case, no formal rituals are performed because the guardian deities remain unchanged.

After being recognized as household co-heads, the couple jointly owns the material property of their household—including the house, land, and livestock—regardless of the origin of that inheritance. In addition, they jointly hold complete authority over the household and are expected to share its managerial responsibilities throughout their entire tenure of headship. The joint ownership, authority, and responsibility of a head couple is well expressed by their title "male-female masters of the household."

The joint ownership and authority of a head couple is represented by the name of their household, which is typically a combination of the personal names of the couple. For instance, if a household is co-headed by a couple named Cal Lie (male) and Na Xeul (female), the villagers would most often refer to it as Cal Lie Na Xeul *tiel* ('the household of Cal Lie and Na Xeul'). Villagers most frequently use such joint names in daily life to refer to corresponding households. As I found out in my fieldwork, it was much easier for an outsider to get immediate directions to a house if he or she asked about the house by using the names of both co-heads, rather than using only one name. The name of a household is subject to changes corresponding to the shift of co-headship through the developmental cycle of the household. For instance, when a senior couple retires from the position of household co-heads, the household will gradually come to be referred to by the joint names of their successors. Likewise, if one co-head of a household is deceased, the household often retains its old joint name until the household is co-headed by a new couple, either when the surviving spouse remarries or when one of their children and his or her spouse inherit the household and become the new co-heads.

While household names typically confirm the joint authority of Lahu head couples, they may also reflect the unbalanced contribution of the spouses to the management of the household. When one spouse rarely participates in making plans and decisions for the household, villagers tend to refer to the household by the name of the spouse who is actually in charge. For example, I found the household of the couple Cal Mud and Na Thid was named only after the wife and was called Na Thid *tiel* ('Na Thid's household'). Villagers explained to me that the husband, Cal Mud, was infamous for his inadequacy in making plans, leaving all the responsibility of decision-making to his wife, although he had a strong ability to "work hard to eat" and took good care of his children. While praising Na Thid for her strength and competence in maintaining their household in a relatively well-off position, villagers were sympathetic to her having to make plans for the household all by herself. As one of her relatives commented, "Na Thid's life is hard. [Beside working hard to eat], she alone has to plan for production, feeding and clothing the children, buying things for the household." The tendency to name a household by the dominant partner of a couple while still focusing on their union is also found among the Lahu Nyi of northern Thailand (Anthony Walker, 2000, personal communication).

The joint naming system has been undermined by official documentation of the central Chinese government. For example, on standardized household census forms in the 1990s, the space left for the household head (*huzhu* in Mandarin) was designed for only one person's name, which was conventionally that of the eldest male in the household, as in the Han tradition. Many village records cadres (*wenshu*) conformed to the standards by singling out the male co-head of a household as "the household head." Nevertheless, some cadres still insisted on the joint authority of Lahu head couples. For instance, I found that the Lahu records cadre of Qhawqhat managed to squeeze the names of both co-heads into the small box on the standard forms provided by the government. The cadre responded to my curiosity by claiming that it was simply her duty to record the facts despite the inconvenience. However, Lahu villagers have gradually accepted in their household naming system the unbalanced significance of one member of the head couple, whose status is elevated by the state-introduced cadre system. In Qhawqhat, villagers commonly refer to a certain household by the name, together with the title, of a male spouse who serves as a major cadre. For instance, the household of Cal Pheud and Na Lad is referred to as "the household of the party secretary Cal Pheud" (Cal Pheud *zhishu tiel*).

The joint authority of household co-heads is intrinsically intertwined with their shared responsibilities in managing the household. According to Lahu principle, a household "can only be managed when a male and female leader rule together," and a head couple is defined as a dyadic team in managing and leading their household. This general principle manifests itself as a widely shared expectation that a head couple will discuss their household matters and make consensus decisions, as expressed in the metaphor "A single chopstick cannot pick up food."

The authority and responsibility of most Lahu head couples in rural Lancang reside in their daily decisions concerning production and consumption. Because of the complex ecological and agricultural conditions and the heavy reliance of most Lahu villagers on their self-sustaining system, the importance of the management of household production cannot be overemphasized.

As discussed in the previous chapter, instead of following a fixed pattern of labor division depending on such factors as age and gender, Lahu labor management focuses on the availability of and demand for labor in each household on a daily basis. While this flexible pattern of labor management can enhance the efficiency of production, it operates at the expense of household head couples, who have to recalculate solutions to labor allocations every day in order to optimize the outcome.

Except during the collectivization period, households have constituted the basic unit for production and consumption among the rural Lahu in Lancang, rendering decision-making concerning such matters the substantial responsibility of a head couple. Household head couples usually discuss their labor allocation informally on various occasions, especially during evening meals. Such discussions occur mainly between the two co-heads, but other adult members may also participate. The head couple of a household is also expected to jointly make consensus decisions over their consumption, which is crucial to the well-being of Lahu households because of the constant threat of food shortages. Such decisions mainly include budgeting the daily consumption of grain so that the household can be fed throughout the year, selling and purchasing grain and livestock (if a household has extra grain), and purchasing tools, clothes, and large items (such as televisions). As is the case with labor management, decisions concerning household consumption are also typically made through a series of casual discussions between the husband and wife.

The following episode provides an example of the decision-making process in many Lahu households. In April 1996, Cal Pheud and Na Nud, the head couple of my host family, began to exchange their concerns about the lack of grain to feed their livestock (three pigs and more than a dozen chickens). These discussions took place mostly over meals and after feeding the animals. Cal Pheud proposed selling one or two of their pigs, but Na Nud was concerned that none of their pigs were large enough to sell for a good price. Cal Pheud agreed with the concerns yet suggested asking the owner of the Qhawqhat grocery shop about current pig prices in the local market; these turned out to be disappointing. The couple therefore agreed to borrow some grain from relatives to feed the livestock. One evening in June, Na Nud proposed selling all the young chickens and keeping only the hens to lay eggs and a single good rooster to breed. This idea occurred to her because one of their female relatives had invited her to go to a nearby market the next day, where she knew that she could sell the young chickens. Cal Pheud expressed his concern that they would have hardly any meat in their meals for a few months, but in the end he agreed to the proposal because the young chickens indeed demanded too much food. After reaching the agreement with her husband, Na Nud brought the young chickens to the market early next morning and sold most of them.

In general, the management of production and consumption in a household means that more responsibility than authority is granted to a Lahu head couple. Since the core responsibility of a head couple is to lead the household to "work hard to eat," the impoverishment of the household is often attributed to their poor management, including their inability to reach agreement through effective discussions. When I asked about the sharing of labor between husbands and wives in Qhawqhat, several informants disparaged three individuals (two males and one female) who worked hard yet left all household management to their spouses because of their inability to plan.

When their children begin to marry and establish their own households, a head couple needs to make consensus decisions regarding inheritance. In most Lahu Na areas of Lancang, the property of a head couple typically undergoes sequential divisions when their children and children-in-law establish their own households, a process that ends only when they retire as household co-heads. This process is called *yiel piel*, which means 'household divisions.' According to many Qhawqhat elders, it is the Lahu principle that a head couple divides their farmland equally among all their children except for their primary heir, who additionally inherits the couple's share. More specifically, the land of a household is potentially divided into a number of equal shares equivalent to the number of their offspring plus two shares (usually the best share) for the head couple. These two shares will be given to the heir couple as a reward for their support and care of the retired co-heads until their deaths.

The normative principles of household division are practiced with great flexibility, depending on the labor and land situations of the child-in-law's family. Thus, a head couple plays a significant role in decisions about each division and actively negotiates with their children's parents-in-law. According to the Qhawqhat elders, prior to the collectivization period, the authority of a head couple in their household division was so high that the children had no say about their shares even if the divisions were very uneven. In some extreme cases, the head couple could withhold a child's share of household property if the child insisted on a marriage in spite of the parents' strong objection. While collectivization completely deprived Lahu head couples of their authority over land ownership, such authority was restored to a certain degree after state polices granted households the right of land usage in the 1980s. In the 1990s, the authority of a head couple in land inheritance decisions declined greatly; withholding land from certain children is no longer possible since the children can now request the cadres of the village or village cluster to claim their share for them.

In contrast to the drastic decline in their control over their land and its division, Lahu head couples have retained great authority in the choice of heirs for their household. When they retire from being co-heads, they pass on the co-headship as well as the house and its furniture and utensils, together with grain and small livestock such as pigs and chickens, to one of their children and his or her spouse. This process is called in Lahu Na *yiel pif tid-iel* ('to fill in the old household'), and it has a significant impact on the retirement life of the old co-heads. Factors that shape heir selection include the labor and age configuration of the household members, the personal characteristics of the child and child-in-law (especially "gentleness" and the capacity to "work hard to eat"), and the couple's relationship with the child and child-in-law. When the head couple reach a consensus, they often propose their selection of the heir to the parents of their prospective child-in-law. Although a head couple tends to decide on an heir couple prior to the latter's wedding, they can reverse their decision if they are disappointed prior to their retirement. I heard of two such cases in Qhawqhat, both involving tensions between the senior couples and their heir's spouse.

Beyond managing their own household, a head couple is expected to act as joint representatives of their household when participating in village-wide activities, including ritual reciprocity among their kin-set and political activities in the village. According to Qhawqhat elders I interviewed, prior to 1949, the village head couple used to be elected by household co-heads through the ritual called "dropping in the corn kernels" (sha ma shil keo). The election traditionally started at noon, when evil spirits were said to be the most inactive. Meeting in the house of the previous head couple, each voter picked up one corn kernel, which served as a ballot, from the basket on the table. They put the kernel back into the empty basket to vote for the couple or made only a gesture of dropping it to vote against the candidate couple. Although every qualified voter received a corn kernel, each pair of household co-heads was expected to agree on whom they would vote for. After the vote, the kernels were counted in front of the crowd, and the number was announced. If the vote did not exceed half of the total voters, the election was declared null and void. If they had received the support of the majority, the newly elected co-heads of Qhawqhat distributed corn liquor to all the voters, a ritual called qhat shief lar meud cad ('feasting from the hands of village co-heads').

In summary, as "male-female masters of household," a head couple is symbolically and socially combined into a single entity, jointly sharing the household's ownership, authority, and responsibility. Despite regional differences and historical transformations that have severely disrupted the traditional Lahu village structure, the degree of unity among most household co-heads has generally remained high at the turn of the twenty-first century (Lei and Liu 1999:124; Wang and He 1999:292).

DYADIC LEADERSHIP IN VILLAGES AND VILLAGE CLUSTERS

Whereas the Lahu people formed temporary regional religious-military organizations during their revolts against state control between the late 1700s and the early 1900s (Chen 1986:29–40; Wang and He 1999:22–32), the indigenous institutions that were constantly maintained at the highest level were the village and the village cluster. Lahu villagers commonly use qhat to refer to both 'village' and 'village cluster', although they may distinguish the two as qhat yied ('small village') and qhat luq ('large village'). The residential nucleus of a Lahu village usually consists of a group of houses located close to each other on the same side of a terraced mountain. In the late 1940s, the number of houses in a typical Lancang village ranged from twenty to forty, a number that had nearly doubled in many villages in the 1990s. In principle, each village possesses its own ceremonial center and altar for village guardian spirits as well as its own farming territory whose boundaries are usually marked by natural features such as streams.[2] A village cluster often consists of four to ten villages which have, over generations, typically been segmented from a founder's village and are located on the same mountainside. Since the farmland is beyond the residential nucleus, the distance between two households within a village cluster is usually less than that between a household and its farmland. Typically, the ceremonial centers of the founder's village also often serve as the center for the village cluster for special ceremonies and festivals.

The Lahu ideal of dyadic village leadership is manifested in such expressions as "The village (cluster) head is a pair" (*qhat shie ted cie*) and "A single person cannot be a village (cluster) head" (*chaw tif qhat shie te mad phier*). The cultural indifference to sex difference in village headship is further clarified by another common saying, "Village (cluster) heads are selected by men and women, but not because they are men or women" (Wang and He 1999:292). Some elders remarked that before the "liberation" (1949), it was considered an ill omen for a village (or village cluster) not to be headed by a married couple because this was interpreted as a hopeless decline of population. Whereas elders in many village clusters of Lancang still shared similar dyadic ideals regarding village leadership in the 1990s, the gap between ideal and practice has widened greatly during the twentieth century, mainly as a result of the drastic intensification of state control. Therefore, the indigenous village leadership can only be understood in the historical context of the encounters between the Lahu people and the central Chinese government, as I will explain briefly below.

The Lahu first appeared in Chinese imperial records as a distinct ethnic group during the eighteenth century (Chen and Li 1986:6; Lei and Liu 1999:24). During the next two centuries, the Lahu were recorded as being involved in more than twenty incidents of revolt against state control (Chen and Li 1986; Wang and He 1999:22–32). Although some Lahu stayed in the areas conquered by the imperial military forces, most migrated south to the more marginal and mountainous regions after major suppressions. During the series of large-scale migrations, most Lahu settled on the China side of the current China-Myanmar (Burma) frontier (west of the Lancang River), while others migrated farther to Myanmar, northern Thailand, Laos, and Vietnam. The Lahu who resided west of the Lancang River maintained a high degree of political autonomy at the levels of the village and the village cluster throughout the end of the Qing Dynasty (1644–1911), more than six hundred years after the central Chinese government had inaugurated direct control over most of Yunnan Province. A combination of natural features (such as geographic barriers, climatic extremes, and malaria) and Lahu military and cultural resistance contributed to the lasting local autonomy.

Since the middle of the GMD (Guomindang) regime (1912–1949), however, Lahu village autonomy in these areas began to be fundamentally challenged by the implementation of a strict local control system (called the *lü-lin* or *baojia* system) (Gen 1997:117–119), which was also applied elsewhere in China. In some cases, the regional officials requested indigenous Lahu village heads to function also as the heads of *lü* or *lin* (later *bao* and *jia*) to collect taxes and direct conscription (Zhang et al. 1996:464). In other cases, indigenous heads of villages and village clusters existed parallel to the state-appointed heads of *lü* or *lin*, who were selected from Lahu villagers based primarily on their fluency in local dialects of Han Chinese and their smooth interethnic relationships. By the end of the 1940s, the significance of the roles played by indigenous institutions in village sociopolitical lives varied greatly in rural Lahu areas in Lancang.

Although Confucianism no longer served as state orthodoxy after the fall of imperial China, patriarchal hegemony dominated the social and political structures of the GMD regime. As was true elsewhere in rural China, the GMD government-appointed officials at all levels in Lancang County were exclusively male. Not only were the female co-leaders of Lahu villages unrecognized in state appointments, but they were also often subjected to gender discrimination during the involuntary encounters with upper-level non-Lahu officials. Because of the visibility of their roles, some female co-leaders of Lahu villages came into conflict with the externally imposed gender hierarchy and the newly introduced notion of female subordination in the 1940s. As I will show later in this section, while some female co-leaders were victimized by patriarchal prejudice in dramatic encounters between the Lahu and Han ideologies, others succeeded to varying degrees in negotiating their rights within the framework of Lahu gender ideology.

Since 1949, the CCP has fundamentally dismantled Lahu indigenous political organization at the village level. As it did with other ethnic minorities in China (Harrell 2001b; Heberer 1989), the party achieved complete control mainly through the implementation of the minority cadre system, which appoints indigenous leaders at different administrative levels. Together with cadres of the Han and other ethnic identities in Lahu autonomous areas, Lahu cadres implemented state policies, and Lahu villagers experienced the nation-wide upheavals during the Mao era, including the doomed Great Leap Forward Campaign (1958) and the catastrophe of the Cultural Revolution (1966–1976). Under more relaxed state policies during the post-Mao era, a few village clusters in Lancang restored indigenous Lahu village organization, which has become one of the most successful arenas during the large-scale revivals of Lahu traditions since the 1980s.

The ideal of equality between men and women (*nannü pingdeng* in Mandarin) promoted by the socialist state echoes the Lahu tradition that "men and women are the same [in value]" (*yad mid hawq qhat qhe yol*), although the concepts derive from different ideological roots. While repudiating the explicit ideology of female subordination as part of the feudalist tradition and generating such well-known rhetoric as "Times have changed; men and women are equal" and "Women hold up half the sky" (Jacka 1997:37), the Chinese Communist Party has reconstructed gender in China based on the ideologies of Marxism and nationalism.[3] The state has begun to incorporate women into its administrative apparatus (Jacka 1997:84–89) although their advancement is often limited in any positions beyond those in charge of "women's work" and family planning (Judd 1994:86–87).[4] In sharp contrast to the Guomindang officials, non-Lahu officials of the CCP are prohibited from imposing explicit discrimination on Lahu women through administrative power even if some of them may personally believe in gender hierarchy.

While the cadre system has greatly enhanced the overall status of Lahu women in state politics in contrast to their position under the GMD regime, it has inadvertently undermined their political authority at the levels of village and village clusters by serving as a substitute for the indigenous male-female co-leadership. Specifically, except for the office of "women's work"—which is exclusively reserved for women—and records cadres, all of the major offices tend to be held by males. Take the village cluster of Qhawqhat as an example: During the period between 1948 and 1996, out of fifty-five total positions in forty-eight years, women held only three positions aside from "women's work" and records cadre. Meanwhile, all seven cadres who served as heads of Qhawqhat during this period were males. In fact, during my fieldwork in Lancang County, I did not hear a single case in which the state-appointed village head was a woman.

In the remainder of this section, I highlight the transformations of the Lahu dyadic leadership in different historical contexts by examining the cases of Qhawqhat and Fulqhat, representing the village clusters in Lancang that have been exposed, respectively, to the medium and the mildest impact of direct state control. I first discuss the impact of the state administrative institutions on Lahu village co-headship in the 1940s by exploring some social memories in Qhawqhat. Then I examine the structures of Lahu village co-leadership of the Fulqhat village cluster, one of the handful of village clusters where indigenous village organization has revived since the 1980s.

QHAWQHAT LEADERSHIP IN THE 1940S

As in most Lahu village clusters in Lancang, male-femal co-leadership was practiced in Qhawqhat with a large degree of incoherence in the decade before its abolishment in 1949. With very few exceptions, all of the younger Qhawqhat villagers I interviewed in the mid-1990s were unaware of such a tradition in their recent history because it existed only in the memories of the elders. While providing me overviews of their leadership structures in the 1940s, the recollections of some Qhawqhat elders offered many dramatic anecdotes regarding the intense encounters between the indigenous gender ideology and the externally imposed patriarchy during the period.

At the village level, indigenous dyadic leadership remained, requiring a married couple to jointly hold the office of village head (*qhat shie*). All of the household co-heads elected their village co-heads according to criteria such as gentle personality, leadership capability, and long-term residence in the village (more than three generations). The major duties of the village co-heads included settling disputes, organizing ritual activities and festivals, giving permission for new settlers, and symbolically approving marriages. The head couple was also responsible for collecting grains and financial contributions for their villagers' participation in the major festivals and rituals of the entire village cluster. Beginning in the early 1940s, upper officials of the GMD regime assigned the office of *jiazhang* to the male co-heads of the six villages in Qhawqhat, expanding their duties to include tax collection, conscription, and hosting upper-level officials when they visited the village.

At the village cluster level, there were three important offices in Qhawqhat—the indigenous village head, the state-assigned official (*baozhang*), and the chief Buddhist monk. The position of head of the village cluster (*qhat shie* or *qhat shie luq*) was the most prestigious and respected among these three, and the Lahu principle that required a married couple to hold the office continued to be followed. Some elders recalled that villagers then believed that it was crucial to their well-being that Qhawqhat and its affiliated villages be headed by married couples with desirable characteristics and leadership capability. Qhawqhat elders still held revered memories of the head couple Cal Thawd and Na Yawl, who jointly acted as the head of the village cluster of Qhawqhat throughout the 1940s. According to the elders, they were both capable in management and were gentle by nature, but Na Yawl (female) was less smooth in social interactions. Therefore, she had been reluctant to take office after the election until elders assured her that her manner could be improved while holding the office because she was warm-hearted and "soft" (*nud*). The major duties of the head couple of the village cluster included organizing festivals and rituals on behalf of the entire cluster, dealing with village affairs according to conventions, and settling disputes that involved members of different villages as well as those involving Qhawqhat villagers and members of neighboring clusters. Before the GMD government appointed a *baozhang* in Qhawqhat in the early 1940s, the head couple also represented Qhawqhat in interactions with outsiders regarding matters that involved the interests of the village cluster.

The elderly villagers I interviewed all insisted that they held the same respect for both the husbands and the wives of their paired leaders at the levels of both village and village cluster. While enjoying shared prestige among fellow villagers, however, the co-heads appeared to play unbalanced gender roles. For example, the male co-heads tended to play a much more dominant role in settling disputes and some other village affairs, and the male co-head alone actually interacted with outsiders. In addition, the four to six regular assistants (*zi yad*) of the co-heads of the village cluster were all males; they served mainly as errand-runners.

Paralleling the indigenous head of the village cluster, the second major official in Qhawqhat was the *baozhang*, an administrator appointed directly by officials of the GMD government at the township level. First established in Qhawqhat in the early 1940s, the office of the *baozhang* was responsible for implementing orders from upper-level offices, especially tax collection and conscription, and for policing the village cluster. Like other GMD administrative officeholders, *baozhang* were exclusively male. Some elders remarked that the upper-level officials did not appoint Cal Thawd (the male co-head of Qhawqhat) as *baozhang* because he was not fluent in Chinese

(Yunnan dialect with Lancang accent), and, most important, because he sometimes refused to listen to orders from above. The last *baozhang* of Qhawqhat was Cal Xat, one of the few Qhawqhat villagers who spoke the Yunnan dialect fluently and who was very experienced in interacting with the Han Chinese. Holding a powerful and profitable position, Cal Xat was both feared and despised by fellow villagers, who secretly complained that he had bribed upper-level officials in order to attain the position and that he cheated the villagers when collecting taxes.

The third office of the Qhawqhat village cluster was was held by the chief Buddhist monk (*phaf*), who was required to be a single and celibate male. Qhawqhat villagers adopted Mahayana Buddhism several generations before the 1940s, and their Buddhist temple was larger than that in any of the surrounding village clusters and was one of the most influential Buddhist centers in Lancang. In the early 1940s, the side buildings of the temple housed four monks, a chief monk named Cal Pul Phaf, and his three apprentices, who studied under him while conducting service work such as cleaning and cooking. The monks in Qhawqhat all lived a single and celibate life style. A married male villager served as a an additional assistant, sending messages and collecting offerings. The chief monk's major duties included chanting every day to seek blessings on behalf of Qhawqhat, performing rituals in the event of natural disasters, and hosting rituals for major festivals, especially the Lahu New Year and the celebration of the fifteenth day of the eighth month of the lunar calendar.[5]

Like that in most Buddhist centers in Lancang, Qhawqhat Buddhist practice restricted the monk's position exclusively to males, and gender bias also existed in temple rituals. For instance, women between fifteen and fifty years old were prohibited from entering the temple and were constrained to stay only in the gathering house of the temple compound during ritual services. All of the elders I interviewed claimed that such restrictions came from *ful lid* ('Buddhist principles'), yet they were unfamiliar with the underlying notion of pollution in the menstruation taboo observed in some Buddhist practice. Nevertheless, the male advantage in office was greatly undermined by conflicts between Buddhist doctrines and Lahu dyadic ideals. Despite the high prestige of the chief monk, the office was undesirable to Qhawqhat villagers because it required a single and celibate lifestyle. According to some elders I interviewed, boredom led Cal Pul to become heavily addicted to opium in his thirties. Being sympathetic to his unmarried status, Qhawqhat villagers willingly made extra donations for his opium consumption, thereby helping to pacify him and prevent him from quitting the position. In addition, villagers sent only orphans to study with Cal Pul, who was himself an orphan, hoping that the lack of kinship support would prevent them from changing their minds and returning to secular life. Unfortunately, one after another, all of his apprentices ran away with long-distance traders once they became teenagers or young adults. From the early 1950s, Cal Pul lived in the temple alone, and he died in the 1960s.

The drastic increase of direct state control in Lahu village life in the 1940s brought about confrontations between the Han patriarchy and the dyadic ideals of the Lahu people. As the following anecdote shows, some female Lahu leaders have had traumatic experiences of externally imposed gender inequality during their direct encounters with Han officials. Specifically, although villagers recognized Na Lieq as the female co-head of Aq Pul Qhat (one of the villages of Qhawqhat), upper-level officials appointed only her husband, Cal Siq, to the office of *jiazhang*. When taking the responsibility for hosting Han officials on their occasional visits, Na Lieq was expected to serve her husband and the Han officials rather than sitting and dining with them at the same table. Most dramatically, she was even unexpectedly punished for an assumed offense to a male Han official. Na Nud, who was in her late fifties, described the incident, which is well-known to Qhawqhat elders:

> You Han people really look down on women. I learned that when I was very little, before the liberation [1949]. The Han men from "above" [officials above the level of the village cluster] could be offended by women for many ridiculous reasons. The household of Cal Siq and Na Lieq was once heavily fined just because Na Lieq stepped on the frame of the bed in which the Han man had slept the night before. Cal Siq and Na Lieq were *qhat shie* [village heads] of Aq Pul Qhat, so they needed to host some Han men who were higher officials. Once there was a Han official who could not make his way back to Yong Ping [the nearest township] so he stayed overnight in their house. Treating him nicely as a guest from afar, they let him sleep in their best bed. The next morning, they made him breakfast, specially killing a chicken to make soup for him. While the chicken was boiling, Na Lieq made some sauce for the chicken and found that they had run out of dried chili peppers. So Na Lieq stepped on the

frame of the bed to reach peppers from the attic. . . [with exaggerated facial expressions] "My father and mother!!" [a Lahu interjection]. The Han man was furious, he yelled at Na Lieq, called her names, and threatened to beat her up. He also scolded Cal Siq for allowing his wife to humiliate him. He said that a woman should be punished if she stepped on a man's bed. He was some kind of higher official, and he fined Cal Siq and Na Lieq. I forget the amount [of the fine], but it was really high. Yes, Cal Siq and Na Lieq paid the fine eventually. It was so unfair and humiliating for them. Cal Thawd *qhat shie* [the male co-head of the Qhawqhat village cluster with which Cal Siq and Na Lieq's village was affiliated] went to different Han places, and he said that the Han man had not lied about their principles—a Han man would indeed be insulted if a woman stepped on his bed. Cal Thawd *qhat shie* was sympathetic to Cal Siq and Na Lieq, but he could not help them. . . . If they refused to pay the fine, more troubles could have come as a result. The entire Qhawqhat village cluster heard of this soon. Almost everybody was shocked and confused. The elders were talking about how weird and harsh the Han principles were—they knew the Han looked down on women but still could not understand why they made such a fuss. Although I heard the elders complaining and ridiculing the Han principles, they all seriously taught us girls to stay away from Han men to avoid trouble if we ever saw them coming to the village. We were scared whenever Han men came and have stayed far away from them ever since because you never knew what they would say women must not do. All your relatives had to help you pay the fine if you offended them.

In the 1940s, beyond the strong discrimination against Lahu women by Han officials during their direct encounters, the increasing exposure of male village heads to the patriarchal Han culture also challenged the Lahu dyadic ideals for their co-leaders. Patriarchal Han practices often provided the husband with new opportunities that could directly threaten the interests of the wife, as shown by the following story of the co-heads of Qhawqhat. Not having their own children, Cal Thawd was for a while tempted by polygyny, a custom practiced by leaders of the Han and some other ethnic groups in the 1940s. Because it conflicted fundamentally with the Lahu dyadic ideal, the idea of taking a concubine greatly offended his wife, Na Yawl, who negotiated her rights successfully in an extreme manner. The texts below are taken from my conversation with a Lahu couple (both in their early sixties) when we sat and chatted under a mango tree in their yard one humid summer afternoon in 1996. Cal Thawd, the male co-head of Qhawqhat in the 1940s, was the uncle (mother's brother) of the wife in the conversation. I use "W" to represent the wife, "H" to represent the husband, and SD to represent myself.

W: [Let me] tell you a funny story, Shanshan. My uncle Cal Thawd was once beaten up by his wife Na Yawl [*giggles*]. I was only about fifteen then [in the early 1940s]. . . . Cal Thawd once asked Na Yawl whether she would allow him to marry another woman [concubine] as many Han headmen did. Of course, Na Yawl ridiculed and scolded him. He explained that he was just teasing her. I heard my parents and other elders gossiping that Cal Thawd probably wanted to take a concubine so that he could have his own children because Han men laughed at him for having only adopted children.

Cal Thawd did not raise the issue any more, but he probably was still thinking about it. He seemed to be interested in a young widow in Boqhat [one village of Qhawqhat]. That woman made corn liquor and sold it at her home. For a period, he often went with a couple of his peers to her house to drink. Since Cal Thawd had made that ambiguous "joke" not very long before, Na Yawl thought that he still had that bad idea in his mind. So, she warned him to stop going to that woman's house even if accompanied by his peers, and he agreed. But he still went there one day, thinking that she would not know. . . . That was probably his peers' fault. They invited him to go because he always paid for the drinks. Anyway, they went there again, and someone told Na Yawl the news immediately. Na Yawl waited for him on his way home outside the village, with a thick stick in hand. When Cal Thawd and his peers passed in front of her, she jumped up and started beating Cal Thawd with the stick [*laughs*].

H: [*turns his head aside, expressing dissatisfaction*] Humph! I am tired of listening to the story of your harsh aunt Na Yawl.

SD: [*laughs with W*]: Why didn't he run away when he saw her with a stick in hand?

W: [*smile*] You know, our Lahu women's clothes are similar. She sat under a tree by the road, head bowed, and her face was partially covered by her headcloth. She was sitting there quietly, just like a woman resting after work until they walked in front of her.

SD: Was Cal Thawd beaten hard?

W: Yes, black and blue over his shoulders and back. My parents went to see them. Well, she did not beat him on his head and other parts that might have hurt his internal organs. Just to give him a lesson.

H: [*frowning*]: Your aunt was harsh. She was like a chili pepper, and the elders commented on her short temper even before she became *qhat shie ma* (female village co-head). They probably would not have elected her if they had known that she was that harsh.

W: Beating people is indeed not good; it is harsh. But Cal Thawd went too far, he even thought of getting a concubine, and what he had in mind may have been just that woman. He himself must have felt guilty and embarrassed, otherwise he would have invited the elders to discuss the matter and criticized Na Yawl. Qhawqhat people joked and laughed about Cal Thawd. If he had not been a village head, they might have done so in front of him. . . . But Cal Thawd and Na Yawl got along well again [after the event].

SD: I still can't understand how he could have been beaten up so severely. Couldn't he defend himself with his peers?

W: I heard that Cal Thawd only used his arms to protect his head and then ran, chased by Na Yawl. His peers did not defend him because they knew Cal Thawd was at fault; they themselves were probably afraid of being beaten up by Na Yawl, because they had prodded him to drink at the widow's. . . . Also, Cal Thawd would lose even if they fought, because Na Yawl was stronger; she used to carry more grain than Cal Thawd at harvest. I told you before, Na Yawl was very strong, and she could do the same heavy work as any man.

H: [*makes a noise, while shaking his head*] Come on! A man will never lose to a woman in a fight if he is serious about fighting, because "a man does not fight with a woman." Cal Thawd was a tender man and he just tolerated Na Yawl and avoided a fight.

W: [*holds her laughter; winks at SD; speaks in a funny tone*]: Oh yes, oh yes. . . no woman can win a fight with a man. Cal Thawd was just too nice to fight back.

SD: [*tries to hold her laughter; turns to H*] Well, you Lahu people are not like the Han. Wife-beating is still common in many rural areas of the Han.

H: I know that. Our Lahu have the most equality between men and women. Wife-beating is *mad dar* ('bad'), but so is husband-beating! A couple's conflicts can always be solved through discussions.

W AND SD: [*nod in silence, appreciatively*].

This story demonstrates that, while the male co-head was empowered by the state in the 1940s, he could negotiate his potential advantages with his wife only within the framework of Lahu gender unity rather than that of Han hierarchy. Tempted by polygyny, Cal Thawd presented the idea only cautiously to Na Yawl to seek agreement and quickly dismissed it as a joke when he was rebuked. Even though Cal Thawd's further ambiguous transgression was punished by Na Yawl in an extreme manner, Cal Thawd did not fight back and later initiated their reconciliation. Interestingly, although the means Na Yawl used to negotiate her rights transgressed Lahu social expectations, she did not suffer from social criticism for her extreme behavior, as might have occurred in other social contexts. In this sense, Qhawqhat public opinion seemed to have excused an internal violation of the gender ideal (through husband battering) when such a violation occurred as a means of resisting external challenges to the Lahu ideal (through the possibility of taking a concubine).

Although the ideal of husband-wife co-leadership in the village and in the village cluster has been out of practice in Qhawqhat since 1949, the indigenous practices were still alive in the memories of many elders. The disruptions of indigenous village leadership in many Lahu village clusters in Lancang County were similar to those of the Qhawqhat village cluster.

FULQHAT LEADERSHIP IN THE 1990S

With some of its farmland adjacent to that of Burmese villagers, Fulqhat village cluster is located on the outermost margins of Lancang and is one of the most remote village clusters, where there was still no electricity in the mid-1990s. Because of this remoteness, Lahu indigenous social institutions remained far more coherent in Fulqhat than in other clusters until they were abolished by the CCP in 1949. Most impressively, as soon as the state policies began to relax in the early 1980s, Fulqhat became one of the handful of village clusters in Lancang where indigenous village organization immediately revived. Since the late 1980s, the power structure of Fulqhat has operated at two levels—the traditional village and the village cluster.

Both the state and the indigenous administrative centers in Fulqhat are located in the same village—the founders' village (called "the old village of Fulqhat"), from which other villages in the cluster have sprung—with the state center located at the west end of the village. Nevertheless, villagers set up a "gate" made of two wooden posts that symbolically separates these two administrative centers. The village gate in Lahu tradition marks the boundary of a village. In 1995 and 1996, there were about a dozen houses situated outside the gate, including the official administrative center (*cungongsuo* in Mandarin), one state-owned local shop (*gongxiaoshe* in Mandarin), and two small private shops. Even though the closest houses located on the two sides of the gate were only a few meters apart, many Fulqhat elders claimed that their residents were ruled by different principles. Those who lived outside the gate abided only by "the principles of the state" (*guo jia ve awl lid*, a phrase that is a combination of Lahu and Mandarin). In contrast, while also abiding by "the principles of the state," those who were within the gate were characterized as "incense burners," i.e., keepers of Lahu traditions in the broad sense. The "incense burners" were expected to obey Lahu principles and were believed to be protected by the village guardian spirits and by Xeul Sha. By building the gate to separate the two kinds of residents, many elders hoped to prevent the offenses committed by the cadres and other outsiders against Xeul Sha and many spirits from bringing disaster for the villagers.

Gender configurations in the leadership of the two administrative centers differ drastically. While the state administration appoints individuals (mostly males) to cadre posts, married couples held all of the traditional Lahu posts. In the remainder of this subsection, I focus on the structures

FIGURE 12 The spiritual specialist couple of Fulqhat prepares a ceremonial post for the Gourd Festival. Photograph by Shanshan Du

and norms of the traditional village leadership that were practiced in Fulqhat during my fieldwork between 1995 and 1996.

At the village level, there are three pairs of leaders—*qhat shie* ('village head'), *cawl paf* ('leading spiritual specialist'), and *cal lieq* ('leading blacksmith', who is called *ca liq* in Lahu Na). Each term can refer either to the head couple as a unit or to one of the couple's constituent individuals, depending on the linguistic contexts. When clearer distinction is necessary, a suffix is used to specify each individual post-holder—*qhat shie paf /qhat shie ma* ('male/female village head'), *cawl pal paf/cawl paf ma* ('male/female leading spiritual specialist'), and *cal lieq paf/cal lieq ma* ('male/female leading blacksmith').[6]

The three pairs of village leaders are in charge of different domains of village life. The village head couple is mainly responsible for maintaining social order both within and beyond the village and especially for the enforcement of customary laws. The head couple of spiritual specialists mainly represent the villagers in serving village guardian spirits, especially performing rituals at "the temple of village guardian spirit(s)." "Leading blacksmiths" perform rituals to assure spiritual security for a village's agricultural production, which is also symbolized by tool-making for the village. In other words, whereas the village heads focus on social affairs and customary laws, spiritual specialists and the leading blacksmiths are in charge of the spiritual aspects of village life.

While each couple has certain specialized duties, the three leading couples also cooperatively organize major village rituals and activities. On such occasions, all of the leaders are equally respected, especially in ritual symbolism. For instance, during the Lahu New Year festival, villagers play gourd-pipe instruments and dance for the households of all three pairs of leaders, offering on each household altar two pairs of beeswax candles, two bundles of incense, and one pair of sticky-rice cakes. Since the Lahu New Year Festival is focused on the "Master of the Year" (*qhawr shief phad*, i.e., Xeul Sha), spiritual co-leaders have more responsibility, and the first stop of the dancing villagers is at the leading spiritual specialists' house.

At the level of village cluster, traditional Lahu posts are also held by husband-wife dyads. The locus of the power structure of the Fulqhat village cluster is in the founders' village, called "the Old Village," from which other villages have segmented over several generations. Besides the triple posts set up for an ordinary village, the Old Village possesses two additional posts—the head of the village cluster and a Buddhist "monk-couple"—representing not only the village but also the entire village cluster.

The head couple of a village and a village cluster are often called by the same term, *qhat shie* ('village head'), which can also be distinguished as *qhat shie yied* ('the head of large village' or 'the head of village cluster') and *qhat shie luq* ('the head of small village' or 'the head of village'). The duty of the head couple of the village cluster focuses on legal and social relations between the villages and neighboring village clusters. Those who are dissatisfied with the settlement of a dispute at the village level, especially a dispute involving members from more than one village, can appeal to the heads of the village cluster.

The most interesting post in Fulqhat is that of the Buddhist monk-couple. While the Mahayana Buddhism practiced elsewhere in China requires celibacy of monks, Fulqhat villagers have transformed the monk position to a dyadic unit reserved only for a married couple. The Buddhist monk-couple is called *ful yiel*. *Ful yiel* is a Mandarin loanword meaning 'Buddhist monk who is a celibate senior male.'[7] Ironically, this Han term is used by Fulqhat villagers to refer both to the married couple who holds the post and to either individual member of the couple, just like the gender-neutral terms used for other village-cluster posts. Modified by gendered suffixes, this term can also be transformed into two gender-specific terms—*ful yiel paf* ('male Buddhist monk') and *ful yiel ma* ('female Buddhist monk')—in order to distinguish the individuals in the post when necessary. The most significant duty of a Buddhist monk-couple is to represent the entire village cluster when worshiping and making offerings to Xeul Sha (a Lahu translation of Buddha) at the pair of Buddhist temples, which are adjacent to each other but of different sizes. The large temple (female) is called *hawq yiel* and the small one (male) is called *ful yiel.*

The leaders of the entire village cluster of Fulqhat also work cooperatively in major village-cluster activities, especially during rituals. For instance, at the beginning of the Lahu New Year, all of the leading couples jointly represent the village cluster, followed by many villagers, at a ritual site at the top of the mountain (*yal meo*) where they dance and make offerings to welcome Xeul Sha to Fulqhat. Afterwards, the group stops at the village dancing center to make offerings and to let Xeul Sha have a little rest; then, with music and dance, they send Xeul Sha to stay at the paired Buddhist temples, assuming that they will stay there during the entire festival (fifteen days). At the end of the Lahu New Year, the same ritual is held, although in a reverse direction, to send Xeul Sha back to the ritual site at the top of the mountain.

At the levels of both village and village cluster, the traditional leaders of Fulqhat are elected by communal consensus based mainly on a combination of personality and competence. Insisting that a husband-wife team holds each post, the criteria for leadership candidates focus on the gentleness, fairness, and leadership capability of both members. The head couple of Fulqhat indeed exemplifies Lahu ideals; they have impressed me by their soft speech, gentle manner, humble attitudes, and organizational skills since I first met them in 1987. The elders I talked to insisted that they measured their leadership candidates by the overall strengths of each couple considered as a unit, a statement that was confirmed by their consistent answers to some hypothetical scenarios I proposed.[8]

The traditional Lahu leaders of Fulqhat are characterized more by their community service than by their authority. None of the indigenous leading couples are exempt from labor, although villagers do provide some voluntary labor services to compensate for the time and materials the leading couples dedicate to the community. In addition, the prestige and authority of the leading couples are informal and impermanent, derived from and maintained by generosity, competence, persuasiveness, job performance, and good fortune. Elders may call a reelection to replace a leading couple if they perform their job unsatisfactorily or if the village or village cluster suffers any misfortune within the year or two following their undertaking the position. Such a situation occurs most frequently for the position of spiritual specialist and leading blacksmith when there are natural disasters and bad harvests. Because of the general expectation that the leading couples are to set moral examples and provide selfless service to the community and because of the high risk of being blamed for the village's misfortunes, some qualified couples are reluctant to take such offices. Nevertheless, if they have been elected, refusing to take the office would be taken as an offense to norms or principles. Therefore, some head couples take on the responsibility with a certain reluctance, a tendency that has been intensified by the increasing influence of the market economy. For instance, Zhang Bao temporarily left Fulqhat to live elsewhere with his relatives in the early 1990s, soon after he and his wife had been elected the leading blacksmith. His departure sent the subtle message that the couple was unwilling to take the office, but elders still succeeded in saddling them with the responsibility upon his return.

Adhering to the dyadic principle, leadership shifting occurs when one co-leader is unable to perform the task. The death of one member of a leading couple requires the surviving spouse to resign from the position even if he or she remarries soon. For example, when the male monk of Fulqhat died in 1990, a new leading couple was quickly elected and took over the position. A couple may request permission to resign as a leading team due to old age or the failing health of one member of the dyad. In addition, the moral misconduct or negligence of duty of one co-head normally results in the impeachment of both leaders. For example, in a village cluster that is a neighbor to Fulqhat, the head couple of a village was removed from the post in the mid 1980s when the male co-head was found to be involved in an extramarital relationship.

Despite villagers' great emphasis on gender unity and communal consensus in selecting Fulqhat leadership, I still observed manifestations of unequal opportunities for village leadership that were based on kinship relations and gender. The posts of village-cluster head tend to be reserved for a kinship set called *qhat shie ceol* that consists of the descendents of the founders of the village cluster. For instance, in 1995, the male head of the Fulqhat village cluster was the son of his predecessor, and the male Buddhist monk was one of the grandsons of his predecessor. According to some Lahu elders, the inability to find qualified candidates from *qhat shie ceol* suggests a decline of the founders' kin-set—a phenomenon that is taken as a bad omen for the entire village. Although the election of new leaders strongly emphasizes the overall characteristics and competence of a husband-wife team, potential male candidates tend to be relatives of the current male leaders.

Besides patrilateral skewing in leadership selection, the roles of male and female co-leaders, except for the leading spiritual specialists, also tend to be unbalanced in favor of males. For instance, it is usually the male village head who is more active in settling disputes and organizing social activities, while the female village head mainly substitutes for the male co-head when he is out of the village or occupied by other matters. Likewise, it is the male monk who performs most rituals at the Buddhist temple while the female monk typically substitutes for him when he is unavailable. The most unbalanced gender roles are manifested in the taboo that prohibits women, including the leading female blacksmith, from participating in blacksmithing. In this sense, the leading female blacksmith plays mainly symbolic and ritual roles in the village power structure, i.e., achieving the completion of the post in order to maintain the sacred social and spiritual order. The Fulqhat villagers I interviewed were unable to provide a systematic account for the above-mentioned gender bias.

The gap between the ideals and the practice of gender-unified leadership has been greatly increased during the interactions between traditional Lahu leaders and local cadres of the administrative village. Between the mid-1980s and the mid-1990s, the official head of the Fulqhat village cluster was Cal Lawd, an unmarried young Lahu man. Although Cal Lawd was brought up in Fulqhat and was fully aware of the traditional system of male-female co-leadership, he typically, if not exclusively, turned only to Cal Mawl, the male co-head of the village cluster, to inform and mobilize villagers to implement certain state policies. Cal Mawl submitted the matters to the traditional male-female co-leaders of the village cluster for deliberation and then transmitted the collective decision to Cal Lawd. For instance, in 1995, Lancang County decided to build a primary school in Fulqhat with the condition that the villagers contribute free labor and partial financing. Cal Lawd was informed of the county's decision, and he passed it on only to Cal Mawl. The traditional Lahu leaders—both males and females—then held a meeting and reached a consensus to accept the proposal.

While traditional Lahu female leaders of Fulqhat tend to be ignored by local cadres, higher officials have rarely known of their very existence, often inadvertently empowering only the male Lahu co-leaders. For example, benefiting from the relaxed state policies on religion since 1982, the male co-head of the village cluster (Cal Mawl) was recognized as an "minority religious leader" (*minzu zongjiaotouren* in Mandarin) and appointed to the office of "people's representative of the county" to attend annual meetings at the county seat.[9] Cal Mawl was also sponsored by the state for two trips to "visit-and-learn" with the farther trip reaching as far as the capital of the province (Kunming). Such opportunities were very special because Fulqhat was still so isolated that many villagers had never been to the county seat of Menglangba in the 1990s. When Cal Mawl recalled his travel experiences with excitement, he sighed that his wife had never had a chance to visit even the county seat and wished that both of them could be sponsored if there were another chance.

Beyond the absence of official recognition by the government, the female co-heads of Fulqhat have also been invisible to scholars. I myself noticed that the wives of Fulqhat traditional leaders participated in rituals together with their husbands during my first visit in 1987. Nevertheless, I had interpreted the phenomenon merely as another manifestation of the high status of Lahu women until my third visit in 1995, when one villager shocked me with the remark that Fulqhat leaders must be in pairs.

The de facto unbalanced roles of the leading village couples form a sharp contrast to the joint leadership of household co-heads, who typically contribute jointly and equally to household decision-making and to activities beyond the household. Nevertheless, the tendency toward differentiated gender roles among the village's leading couples, especially those who represent the village cluster, does not exempt male co-heads from their household responsibilities. When simultaneously playing the role of household co-heads, the leading couples typically make major decisions for the household with mutual agreement and hold joint roles in both domestic and farm work.

Two ordinary events that occurred during the celebration of the Gourd Festival in 1995 may illustrate the joint nature of the domestic work of head couples even while their leadership roles at the village level are sometimes unbalanced or divided. The first occurred in the morning ritual dance in which all the leading couples of Fulqhat danced around the festival post (*qhawr ciel*). When villagers started joining the dancing circle and the village

FIGURE 13 The head couple of the village cluster of Fulqhat prepares vegetables for pickling on their raised patio. Photograph by Shanshan Du

heads were no longer obliged to participate, the female village head quietly left the crowd and went to the raised balcony of her house to prepare vegetables for making pickles. Since the house is located right beside the dancing center, I noticed her shifting roles from the public to the domestic. A few minutes later, the male village head also withdrew from the crowd, went to the balcony, and performed the same task with his wife (see figure 13). Afterwards, they both went into their house to perform other household chores. The second event occurred on the same day in the late afternoon. I was talking to the Buddhist monk-couple in their household while they were making sticky-rice cakes (see figure 14). The male monk said that he had to leave the house to burn incense at the temple before sunset. As soon as he returned from the temple, he rejoined his wife to pound sticky rice in the mortar.

In summary, the revived traditional leadership in Fulqhat realizes the Lahu dyadic ideology by assigning posts exclusively to married couples as co-leaders. Nevertheless, the degree of gender unity tends to diminish as one moves from the configurations of leadership positions to leadership roles—a tendency that has been intensified by the the interactions between tradi-

FIGURE 14 The Buddhist monk-couple of Fulqhat
makes rice cakes together at their home. Photograph
by Shanshan Du

tional leades and state-appointed cadres. In contrast to the case of 1940s
Qhawqhat, however, the village leadership of Fulqhat in the 1990s demonstrated a greater structural consistency in terms of gender unity and fewer
patriarchal pressures imposed by state officials.

Hints of husband-wife leadership at the village level and beyond can also
be found among the Lahu people outside the Lancang County. As excep-
tional cases, two female Lahu village heads—Na Ye Ma of the present-day
Meng Lien County and Na Thid of the present-day Jing Gu County—were

noted for their outstanding reputation in dealing with regional and interethnic matters in the early twentieth century (Wang and He 1999:292). It seems to me that the administrative and diplomatic capabilities of the two Lahu women were so extraordinary that the co-headship of their husbands simply became invisible to outsiders. Traces of the dyadic ideal in Lahu leadership traditions are also manifested in the social lives of many Lahu in northern Thailand. For example, both the office of village head and the office of ritual specialist among the Lahu Nyi demand a married couple although the formal leader is the male spouse (Anthony Walker 2000, personal communication). Ethnographers also observed the particular significance of the wife of the official village head among both the Lahu Nyi (Walker 1992 [1982]) and Lahu Shehleh (Jacquetta Hill 1999, personal communications).

CONCLUSION

The Lahu ideal of gender dyads is manifested in the ideology and practice of male-female co-leadership. In 2002, Lahu household head couples in rural Lancang still enjoy a high degree of unity in ownership and leadership despite the varying degrees of patrilateral skewing in different areas. In contrast, great variation and inconsistency existed in the practice of gender unity in village leadership in Lancang even in the 1940s, resulting mainly from the drastic expansion of state control. Whereas the ideal of dyadic leadership at the village and village-cluster levels has been fundamentally disrupted or even eliminated in most Lahu areas since 1949, it has been restored and practiced with great consistency in a few village clusters since the state policy relaxed in the late 1980s.

PART 3

STRUCTURE AND ANTISTRUCTURE

CHAPTER 5

UNIFYING GENDER IN KINSHIP AND INTERHOUSEHOLD ORGANIZATION

THE LAST four chapters discussed the dyadic ideology and the application of such ideals in gender roles. In the chapters in part 3, I explore the dyadic principles underlying social structures and the tensions and conflicts within such structures. In this chapter, I examine gender unity in social structures by exploring how married couples serve as building blocks for kinship relations and interhousehold networks. I first examine the ways in which Lahu kinship terminology calculates kin relations from the perspective of a married couple (dyadic ego), which parallel the reference point of an individual ego. Then I discuss how kinship principles govern the ways the head couple of a household relates to other household co-heads, forming concentric circles of social relations accompanied by different rights, duties, and obligations. I conclude that the dyadic principle embedded in the Lahu kinship system, as well as its applications to interhousehold organization, fosters gender equality in social structures.

By designating membership in a kin group exclusively through either the male or the female line, unilineal societies are fundamentally based upon, and in turn reinforce, the principle of gender division.[1] In contrast, tracing kinship relations through both male and female, bilateral kinship systems reduce the potential for built-in gender divisions in social structures.[2] Such systems also tend to blur the impact of dichotomous principles beyond gender that are built into unilineal kinship structures, such as alliance/descent, and endogamy/exogamy (Lévi-Strauss 1982 [1975]; Carsten and Hugh-Jones 1995). The Lahu kinship system is predominantly bilateral, although varying degrees of matrilineal or patrilineal skewing can be found among certain subgroups in certain regions (Gen 1997:75–95; Wang and He 1999:113–120). While sharing with some other societies the bilateral principles that undermine gender discrimination, the Lahu kinship system goes a step further by structurally promoting the principle of gender unity, which is rooted in the orientation toward the dyadic ego (paired ego) in the kinship terminology.

DYADIC EGO IN KINSHIP TERMINOLOGY

As is true in all known cultures, the individual serves among the Lahu as the reference point ("ego") from which kinship relations are categorized. Beyond the ego-oriented principle, however, Lahu kinship terminology also uses the married couple, which I term the "dyadic ego," as a reference point for the classification of kin categories. In the process, all married relatives of the couple are also categorized as joint entities, in principle occupying only one genealogical position. Although kinship relationships are traced predominantly by individuals in daily lives—thus appearing to be oriented exclusively toward an individual ego—the dyadic ego tends to serve invisibly as a parallel reference point at a higher level. For example, Na Nud, a married woman, usually operates as an individual ("ego") when she relates to her mother's sister's daughter and her husband's mother's sister's son's wife. Meanwhile, the principle of dyadic kin calculation decides that the genealogical distances between Na Nud and the two women are identical. This is because the two married couples in the latter case (Na Nud and her husband as well as Na Nud's husband's mother's sister's son and his wife) occupy only two relational spaces. Therefore, Na Nud not only addresses the two women by the same kin term, but she is also expected to fulfill the same level of social and ritual obligations in regard to them.

Since "dyadic ego" is an alien concept even to anthropologists, it seems necessary to first explain its origin rather than using it as a given. I began to study Lahu kinship terminology and recorded the primary kinship categories during my first field trip to Lancang in 1987. Nevertheless, the bilateral and generation-based kin terms were so inclusive that every time I revisited the issue, my list of kin relations for each key category kept expanding in a seemingly endless and chaotic way. Both my anthropological training and my empirical experiences finally led me to conclude that Lahu kin categories are too elastic and fuzzy to define and that their kinship structures, if they exist at all, are too fluid and elusive to grasp.

My misconception about Lahu kinship terminology remained unchallenged until I was struck by a casual incident in 1996, only a few months before I ended my latest fieldwork. I was talking with Cal Lad one evening when he excused himself to leave to attend the wake of a woman named Li Lan, who was the mother of the wife of one of his grandsons. I was amazed when Cal Lad explained to me that because Li Lan and he were related as *haw mawd lawd mawd*, villagers would have considered him to be "abandoning principles" (*awl lid mad cawl*) if he did not attend her wake. According to my understanding, in its definable usage, *haw mawd lawd mawd* was a term referring to the two sets of the parents of a married couple. Although I was aware that villagers also used the term to refer to numerous kinds of affinal relations, I believed that the over-broadened connotations were incapable of identifying specific relationships. Given such a distant kin relation and the size of the crowd at a wake (usually over a hundred people), it seemed to me that most villagers could not possibly notice Cal Lad's absence, let along judge him for neglecting his ritual obligation. Responding to my astonishment, Cal Lad added that his sister Na Mud had the same obligation to attend the wake because she and Li Lan were also *haw mawd lawd mawd*. In other words, villagers would consider Na Mud neglecting her kin obligation if she did not attend the wake of Li Lan, who was the mother of the wife of a grandson of one of her brothers.

The incident revealed to me that the boundaries of many Lahu kinship categories were crystal clear to Qhawqhat villagers while being vague and fuzzy to me. Both inspired and frustrated (by my own ignorance), I immediately returned to kinship terminology, rigorously searching for the underlying principles that I had given up on several years before. However, I became further confused during the next few weeks; as I recorded even more relatives under each major kin term, the boundaries of these terms became even more blurry. My confusion also frustrated my Lahu informants: although they could easily disprove my various hypotheses regarding the way they drew lines around the major kin terms, they were unable to explain their defining principles.

My investigation made a quick turn when it occurred to me one day that villagers might be using "pair," or a married couple, as a single unit to define kinship relations. Testing this hypothesis became a most rewarding fieldwork experience in which my informants shared my level of excitement over my new understanding of their lives. As Cal Lad remarked with smiles,

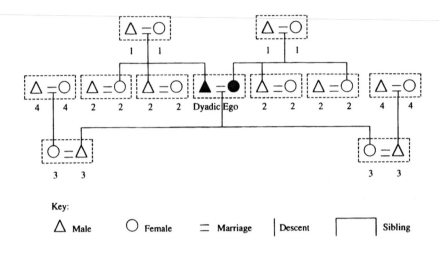

Key:

△ Male   ○ Female   = Marriage | Descent   ⌐¬ Sibling

CHART 1: *CORE RELATIVES OF THE DYADIC EGO*

NOTE Individuals marked with the same number belong to the same primary kinship category (1, 2, 3, and 4 represent the dyadic ego's *chaw mawd, awl viq awl ni,
awl yad,* and *haw mawd lawd mawd,* respectively). Chart by Monica Cable

"See, our Lahu principle is not confusing!" Indeed, the relations included
in a given kin term no longer appeared boundless and chaotic at all once I
understood that, when taking married couples as joint entities, a marriage
adds relatives as if each person occupied the same status as his or her spouse.
My new comprehension of generalized kin categories helped me to find a
long-missing piece of a giant jigsaw puzzle that finally allowed me to make
connections between these categories and the "chaotic webs" of interhousehold relations. In brief, the crux of my previous confusion lay in my perception that the individual ego is the only and exclusive reference point; this
resulted in my failing to record many affinal relatives who I had considered
too distant to be included in my questionnaires.

In the following discussions, I explore the dyadic ego orientation used in
the kinship terminology of Qhawqhat villagers. I demonstrate that, not only
are kinship relations reckoned equally through both male and female, but
kin terms tend to be referenced by and, in turn, refer to, combined hus-

band-wife dyads (see chart 1). I will focus on the primary kinship categories, which are generalized terms, while embracing secondary kin terms within each primary category. Abbreviated kinship references follow the conventional anthropological system of notation: F=father; M=mother; S=son; D=daughter; B=brother; Z=sister; H=husband; W=wife.

CHAW MAWD

As a term in the Lahu life cycle, *chaw mawd* refers to adulthood and its several substages (see chapter 2). As a kin term, it refers to a couple's senior generational relatives and is used only in reference (*chaw* means 'person' or 'people'; *mawd* means 'old' or 'elder'). In other words, when a man and a woman marry, both sides' senior generational relatives (both consanguineous and affinal) are categorized as this couple's *chaw mawd*.

The core relationships of a couple's *chaw mawd* include their two sets of parents, as indicated by the individuals marked as "1" on the kinship chart. Both husband and wife refer to and address their own father and mother as *awl pa/ngal pa* and *awl-e/ngal-e* respectively. In contrast, they refer to and address their spouse's father and mother as *awl pul/ngal pul* and *awl pi/ngal pi* (the same as the terms for 'grandparents'), respectively. While a couple does not appear to share the same kin terms, they are still categorized as a dyadic ego in this case because in addressing each other's parents as "grandparents," they are representing their (future) children as a joint unity.

The peripheral relationships of a couple's *chaw mawd* include the following:

1) the couple's parents' siblings and their spouses (i.e., FB, FBW, FZ, FZH, MB, MBW, MZ, MZH);
2) the couple's parents' first generational cousins (cross and parallel) and those cousins' spouses (i.e., FFBS, FFBSW, FFBD, FFBDH, FFZS, FFZSW, FFZD, FFZDH, FMBS, FMBSW, FMBD, FMBDH, FMZS, FMZSW, FMZD, FMZDH, MFBS, MFBSW, MFBD, MFBDH, MFZS, MFZSW, MFZD, MMZDH, MMBS, MMBSW, MMBD, MMBDH, MMZS, MMZSW, MMZD, MMZDH).

The above two sets of relations refer to relatives from a couple's parents' generation. There are several subcategories among these relations. The couples'

MB and MBW form a special set of subcategories who are referred to and addressed as *awl-o phad/ngal-o phad* and *awl-o ma/ngal-o ma*, respectively. Besides MB, males of the couple's ascending generation who are older than the couple's linking parent are referred to or addressed by the couple as *awl pa loq/ngal pa loq* (*loq* means 'older' or 'big').[3] Besides MBW, females of the couple's ascending generation who are older than the couple's linking parent are referred to or addressed by the couple as *awl-e/ngal-e*, the same as the term for 'mother.' Those who are younger than the couple's linking parent are referred to or addressed by the couple as *awl pa yied/ngal pa yied* (male) and *awl e yied/ngal e yied* (female).

3) the eight grandparents of the couple;
4) the couple's grandparents' siblings and their spouses (i.e., FFB, FFBW, FFZ, FFZH, FMB, FMBW, FMZ, FMZH, MFB, MFBW, MFZ, MFZH, MMB, MMBW, MMZ, MMZH).

The relations included in 3) and 4) are relatives of the couple who are two generations above their own. In turn, these two sets of relatives can be broken down into two gender-specific subcategories—*awl pul/ngal pul* (male) and *awl pi/ngal pi* (female).

AWL VIQ AWL NI

Awl is a prefix for many Lahu reference kin terms; *viq* means 'older,' and *ni* means 'younger.' Used exclusively as a term of reference, *awl viq awl ni* refers to relatives of a couple's own generation. In other words, when a man and a woman marry, both the consanguineous and the affinal relatives of their own generation on both sides combine into this category.

The core relationships of a couple's *awl viq awl ni* include their siblings and their siblings' spouses (B, BW, Z, ZH), as indicated by the individuals marked as "2" on the kinship chart.

The peripheral relationships of a couple's *awl viq awl ni* include:

1) all of the couple's first generational cousins and all those cousins' spouses (i.e., FBS, FBSW, FBD, FBDH, FZS, FZSW, FZD, FZDH, MBS, MBSW, MBD, MBDH, MZS, MZSW, MZD, MZDH).

2) all of the couple's second-generational cousins and all those cousins' spouses (i.e., FFBSS, FFBSSW, FFBSD, FFBSDH, FFBDS, FFBDSW, FF-BDD, FFBDDH, FMBSS, FMBSSW, FMBSD, FMBSDH, FMBDS, FMBDSW, FMBDD, FMBDDH, MFBSS, MFBSSW, MFBSD, MFBSDH, MFBDS, MFBDSW, MFBDD, MFBDDH, MMBSS, MMBSSW, MMB-SD, MMBSDH, MMBDS, MMBDSW, MMBDD, MMBDDH).

Awl viq awl ni can be transformed into age- and gender-specific terms. Separating *awl viq awl ni* into two parts—*awl viq* ('the older') and *awl ni* ('the younger')—produces two age-specific subcategories, which can also be modified to address forms (*ngal viq* and *ngal ni*)—by replacing *awl* with *ngal*. For instance, referring to one's older brother or sister as *awl viq*, one will address them as *ngal viq* or *ngal viq-al* (an intimate term of address). In subsequent discussions, unless otherwise noted, I include two sets of terms, with the first in the reference form and the second in the address form. Interestingly, age difference here can be a relative criterion if the husband and wife of the referential couple are of different ages. On such occasions, a couple share the kin term, which is the one used by the genealogically linked spouse, to refer to and address a sibling or sibling-in-law. For instance, even if a husband is older than his wife's elder brother or sister, he will follow his wife to refer to him or her as his *awl viq* ('older sibling'). The subcategories *awl viq* and *awl ni* can be further modified to make gender-specific terms (*awl viq paf, awl viq ma, awl ni paf,* and *awl ni ma*) by adding a suffix as a gender marker (*paf,* 'male' or *ma,* 'female'). For example, one can specify an older sister's gender by referring to her as *awl viq ma* or by addressing her as *ngal viq ma* or *ngal viq ma-al*. Thus, by completely adopting the terms by which one's spouse referred to his/her relatives of his/her own generation before marriage, a husband and wife maintain this shared terminology to refer to or address the relatives of their own generation even in these age-specific terms.

The connotations of the kin category *awl viq awl ni* are commonly shared among the Lahu in both Lancang and Menglian County (Wang and He 1999:122–123). In some Lancang villages, Mandarin terms such as *xiongdi jiemei* ('siblings') and *yijiaren* ('family members') are sometimes used in certain contexts, especially in interactions with Mandarin speakers. In addition, *awl viq awl ni* resembles the Thai term *phi rong*—meaning 'siblings', 'kin of same generation', and 'friends' (*phi* means 'older'; *rong* means 'younger')—which can be used both in reference and address.[4]

AWL YAD

Awl yad (*yad* means 'child') refers to a couple's consanguineous and affinal relatives in the first generation below their own. By substituting *ngal* for *awl*, this term can also be used as a term of address, *ngal yad*. *Awl/ngal yad* can be modified into two gender-specific subcategories—*awl/ngal yad paf* (male) and *awl/ngal yad mid* (female).

The core relationships of a couple's *awl yad* include their children and their children's spouses (i.e., S, SW, D, DH), as indicated by the individuals marked "3" on the kinship chart. Among these core relationships, children-in-law can form specified categories. One's son-in-law is referred to as *awl maq paf* and addressed as *ngal maq paf*, and one's daughter-in-law is referred to as *awl kheud ma* and addressed as *ngal kheud ma*. Members of kin within this category are most commonly addressed by their names in daily life.

The peripheral relationships of a couple's *awl yad* include their siblings' children and those children's spouses, the couple's first cousins' children, and those children's spouses (i.e., BS, BSW, BD, BDH, ZS, ZSW, ZD, ZDH, FBS, FBSW, FBD, FBDH, FZS, FZSW, FZD, FZDH, MBS, MBSW, MBD, MBDH, MZS, MZSW, MZD, MSDH).

HAW MAWD LAWD MAWD

Haw mawd lawd mawd means 'affinal elders'—both *haw* and *lawd* refer to 'affinal' and 'closely related'; *mawd* means 'old' or 'elderly.' When a child of a couple marries, all relatives of their child-in-law's senior generations are classified as this couple's *haw mawd lawd mawd*.

A couple's core *haw mawd lawd mawd* includes their children's spouses' parents (i.e., their SWF, SWM, DHF, and DHM), as indicated by the individuals marked as "4" on the kinship chart. There is no subcategory to specify this set of core relations, yet they are highly recognized in kinship-based social activities.

Acouple's peripheral *haw mawd lawd mawd* includes:

1) the grandparents of a couple's children-in-law (i.e. the couple's SWFF, SWFM, SWMF, SWMM, DHFF, DHFM, DHMF, DHMM);

2) the couple's children's parents-in-laws' siblings and those siblings' spouses (i.e., the couple's SWFB, SWFBW, SWFZ, SWFZH, SWMB, SWMBW, SWMZ, SWMZH, DHFB, DHFBW, DHFZ, DHFZH, DHMB, DHMBW, DHMZ, DHMZH);

3) the couple's children's grandparents-in-laws' siblings and these siblings' spouses (i.e., the couple's SWFFB, SWFFZ, SWFMB, SWFMZ, SWMFB, SWMFZ, SWMMB, SWMMZ, DHFFB, DHFFZ, DHFMB, DHFMZ, DHMFB, DHMFZ, DHMMB, DHMMZ).

Haw mawd lawd mawd is completely gender-neutral and is used only in reference, never address. Since members of *haw mawd lawd mawd* often belong to different generations, there is not a uniform term that is used for them to address each other. People within this category usually address each other according to the relevant individuals' generational and age relations.

TED YIEL CHAW ('CORE RELATIVES')

Ted yiel chaw—ted means 'one'; *yiel* means 'house', 'household', and 'family'; *chaw* means 'person' or 'people'—is completely gender-neutral and is used only in reference, never in address. The Lancang Lahu typically translate the term into Han Chinese as "family members" (*yijiaren*). Different from the commonly accepted academic distinction between "family" and "household" (Yanagisako 1979), the term *ted yiel chaw* defines "family" according to both common residence and kinship relations (Harrell 1997). In the narrow sense, *ted yiel chaw* refers to the members living within the same physical boundary of a house, forming a basic economic, social, and ritual unit. In its broad sense, *ted yiel chaw* includes members both within and beyond the physical boundary of a house and beyond the social boundary of an economically independent household. I use the term "core kin-set" to represent *ted yiel chaw* in its broad sense.[5] For the sake of convenience, I use the phrase "core relatives" to refer to the members of a core kin-set.

Among the Qhawqhat Lahu, a married couple's *ted yiel chaw* includes their core relations in the above-described four primary kinship categories (*chaw mawd, awl viq awl ni, awl yad,* and *haw mawd lawd mawd*), i.e., all of the numbered individuals included in chart 1. The members referred to by this term include the married couple's parents, their siblings and siblings-in-law, their children and their children-in-law, and their children-in-laws' parents. Thus, *ted yiel chaw* consists in its narrow sense of the members of a household and in its broad sense of the core members of an unmarried single's or of a married couple's bilateral kin. In contrast to Qhawqhat, some other Lahu village clusters in Lancang use *ted yiel chaw* only in its narrow sense, i.e., household members.

TED CEOL TED QHAD ('PERIPHERAL RELATIVES')

Ted ceol ted qhad means 'the peripheral kin-set' or 'peripheral relatives'—*ceol* means 'category', 'type', and 'kind', and *qhad* means 'line' and 'reckoning.' When talking to Han Chinese, the Lancang Lahu often translate the term as *qinqinqiqi* ('relatives') or *huaqinhuaqi* ('distant relatives') in the Yunnanese dialect of Chinese with Lancang accent. Like *ted yiel chaw, ted ceol ted qhad* is completely gender-neutral and is used only in reference, never in address. *Ted ceol ted qhad* includes a couple's peripheral relations of the four primary categories, i.e., their peripheral members of *chaw mawd, awl viq awl ni, awl yad*, and *haw mawd lawd mawd*. In other words, a couple's *ted ceol ted qhad* consists of those who are recognized to have kinship relations to the couple consanguineously or affinally yet are not close enough to be counted as the members of their *ted yiel chaw* ('core relatives', 'one family').

Ted yiel chaw and *ted ceol ted qhat* are used frequently by both the Lahu Na and the Lahu Shi in Lancang County although the relations suggested vary between the two branches of the Lahu, as well as within the same branch in different locations. Like other Lahu kin terms, *ted yiel chaw* and *ted ceol ted qhad* are also fundamentally oriented toward married couples although they are convertible to a single-ego orientation.

As is demonstrated by the primary kin terms, the principle of Qhawqhat kinship terminology is enormously gender-unified. The method of reckoning kinship relations is completely bilateral, using the married couple as the reference point for classifications. Such a terminology system unifies a married couple as a single social category (a dyadic ego) that reckons kinship relations with other paired social units (other married couples). Specifically, when any married individual reckons his or her relatives, each major category of relatives will end up including their own relatives and those of their spouse. It is important to point out that such a dyadic-ego orientation coexists with individual-ego orientation; while the former offers the governing principle for defining the boundaries of primary kin categories, the latter is used to identify specific relations between individuals in particular sociolinguistic contexts.

The gender-unitary principles, especially those that classify certain consanguineous and affinal relatives into the same categories, are also implied by the kin terms recorded in many Lahu documents across subgroups and regions despite their enormous diversity in details (Wang and He 1999: 121–123; Lei and Liu 1999:138–139). Nevertheless, Lahu kinship terminology also varies in details across subgroups and regions. The diverse adoptions of Han loan kin-terms in different Lahu villages of Lancang demonstrate increases in kin categories and patrilateral skewing.

HOUSEHOLD CO-HEADS AND INTERHOUSEHOLD INTERACTIONS

In keeping with anthropological appeals for a close examination of the connections between kinship terminology and kinship relations, we may ask, "To what extent does the dyadic principle of Lahu kinship terminology apply to their social organization and everyday interactions?"[6] As is true in many other societies in Southeast Asia (e.g., Cunningham 1964; Carsten and Hugh-Jones 1995), households serve as the building blocks of Lahu social organization. Lahu household interactions are typically organized according to kinship principles. Specifically, a head couple maps their kinship relationships with other households into three concentric circles—those co-headed by "core relatives" (see chart 1), "peripheral relatives," and "nonrelatives"—and is expected to interact with those households with different levels of rights, duties, and obligations. In Qhawqhat and among most Lahu in rural Lancang, the close association between kinship principles and interhousehold reciprocity is elaborated in labor cooperation, food shortage assistance, and ritual obligations.

LABOR COOPERATION

Except during the period of collectivization, when production and distribution were organized at the village level, the household has always been the basic production unit of Qhawqhat as it has been for the Lahu elsewhere. Despite their economic autonomy, individual households often engage in intensive labor cooperation with each other. Interhousehold labor cooperation is particularly critical at times such as rice planting and harvesting, when a strict work schedule must be maintained in order to obtain the best yields, thus requiring extra human laborers and sometimes more cattle. The intensive and pervasive labor cooperation is brought about mainly by the different labor bottlenecks of individual households that are caused by the great variety of crops, altitudes, and prevailing weather patterns of different fields. Additionally, households' different auspicious days for planting further diversify the urgent periods for accomplishing particular tasks.

As is true in most Lahu villages in Lancang, labor cooperation in Qhawqhat takes the forms of generalized reciprocity ("mutual help"), balanced reciprocity ("exchanging laborers"), and commoditized exchange ("hiring laborers"). In principle, these three categories are practiced, respectively, among households whose co-heads are core relatives, peripheral relatives, and nonrelatives. At the times for planting and harvesting, a household often engages simultaneously in two, or sometimes all three, forms of labor cooperation with other households in order to cope with labor shortages related to rice cultivation.

The first type of labor cooperation, called *ga dar* ('mutual help'), is practiced among households whose co-heads are core relatives. According to social norms, these households are obligated to offer each other labor assistance as if they were working for their own household, as expressed by the common expression "household members doing their own things within the household" (*yiel qhaw ve siq, yiel qhaw aq shu awlmid-awlqhat te*). Ideally, households engaged in "mutual help" should "not calculate or remember" (*mad phut mad shawf*) discrepancies in the number of laborers used to help each other. Therefore, the principle of "mutual help" is that of generalized labor reciprocity in which the number of laborers involved should not be carefully calculated for possible future returns.[7]

Whereas the overall principle requires households of core relatives to engage in "mutual help" with undifferentiated commitment, the priority of a household's obligation changes according to the significance of particular kin relationships during different stages of the life cycle. When none of their children is married, a head couple is usually most obligated to help the households co-headed by both sets of their parents and by some of the couple's siblings and siblings-in-law. When their children begin to marry, the head couple becomes most obligated to help the households that are co-headed by the parents of their children-in-law; this labor cooperation is especially important between the head couples whose married children reside in the household of either side. Intense labor cooperation between such in-law households is expected regardless of their differences in labor and economic resources, and any unwillingness to cooperate would be considered "abandoning principles." Additionally, the poor affinal household is not obligated to repay the unbalanced labor exchange when their labor conditions have improved years later. During my stay in Qhawqhat, I even noticed several occasions when the co-heads of the better-off household hired labor to help their closest affines when they themselves were too busy to offer labor. In these cases, villagers praise the better-off head couples. The obligation of intensive labor cooperation between the households co-headed by a couple's parents bears structural significance in the principle of gender unity in marriage and kinship. Particularly, rather than one set of parents losing the labor of their married son or daughter, both sets of the parents of a young couple jointly share the couple's labor through intensive labor cooperation (James Wilkerson 2000, personal communication).[8]

The second type of interhousehold cooperation is called *xad jaw dar* ('exchanging laborers') and applies to the households co-headed by peripheral relatives. When a household has received labor assistance through "mutual help" yet still needs more laborers, the head couple's household usually initiates "exchanging laborers" with more distant relatives who generally offer assistance according to convenience rather than obligation. "Exchanging laborers" is a typical form of balanced reciprocity, i.e., cooperators keep a tally of laborers involved, and they expect this to be returned, although not immediately. Qhawqhat villagers generally expect the loaned laborers to be repaid within a year, but some labor debts can last longer if the household that has offered labor assistance is not in need. At the end of any given year, a Qhawqhat household with an average amount of labor and economic resources typically owes four to seven laborers to households with whom they engage in "exchanging laborers."

Qhawqhat social norms expect the initiator of labor exchange to directly express his or her willingness to repay the labor whenever the lender's household is in need. Usually, the evening before the planned workday, one member of the household that lacks sufficient labor visits the closest household that is co-headed by their peripheral relatives and requests assistance with a promise to repay. Without obligation to offer help, the host household tends to offer laborers according to its own convenience. If the household cannot offer labor assistance or cannot offer enough, the petitioner goes to another household that is co-headed by members of his or her peripheral relatives. The next morning, all helpers go directly to plot(s) of the visitor's field, bringing their own lunch to eat during the day.

Compared to the initiation of a reciprocal labor process, the subsequent exchanges are much subtler. Members of the initiating household often search actively for a chance to repay its labor debt, paying close attention to the agricultural activities of the household that has offered them help. As soon as they notice signs of a labor shortage, they offer labor assistance as long as they can manage their own production activities. Occasionally, a household that loaned laborers to other households may request labor assistance. In such a situation, the household that owes laborers is obligated to offer as many laborers as requested, no matter how busy they are themselves. Although both sides are clear about the laborers owed, neither the debtor nor the lender explicitly mentions the debt when returning the payment.

The third type of productive cooperation between households is called *xad ca* ('looking for laborers' or 'hiring laborers'), and is typically practiced among households co-headed by nonrelatives. Hiring labor requires immediate payment. The payment is usually made at the end of each day, mostly in the form of rice or, occasionally, cash. In addition, the household that hires laborers is obligated to bring lunch for the laborers to eat together in the field. Except during the collectivization period, the lack of grain or cattle (and of land prior to the 1950s) has meant that a typical Lahu village has usually had several households that depend heavily on offering hired labor to other households.

Depending on which side makes the initial move, labor hiring typically takes two forms in household production interactions. If a household lacks hands at a particularly busy season after receiving assistance through "mutual help" and "exchanging laborers," the members of the household may visit some nonrelatives' households to "look for laborers." The fact of hiring labor as a commodity is softened by the norms of politeness on the part of the visitor. Typically, the petitioner politely inquires the availability of host and hostess for a couple of days' help for their labor shortage, gently mentioning that either rice or cash is available as payment. Either way, the payment will be offered immediately after the day's work is completed. This type of labor hiring is practiced exclusively among households co-headed by nonrelatives.

Sometimes "labor hiring" is initiated by a member of a household lacking food, who visits some nonrelatives' households, asking for grain with the promise of offering laborers in exchange. The petitioner usually tells the host directly that he or she will offer labor assistance when the host's household is short of hands. According to the amount of grain offered, the household that loaned the grain will later visit the borrower's household to "look for laborers" whenever they find themselves in need. Some households that are co-headed by distant relatives may occasionally engage in this type of labor hiring, expecting relatives to interact subtly and never mention immediate payment. When the lending household is short of hands, they will visit the borrower's household, expressing a request for labor assistance as if they were engaging in "exchange of laborers," the form of labor cooperation appropriate to their kinship relations.

COPING WITH FOOD SHORTAGES

The dyadic kinship principles also provide a structural basis for households to assist each other in coping with crises, particularly food shortages. As is the case with labor cooperation, gender distinctions are irrelevant in arranging for crisis-support networks. A household has the right to solicit assistance from, and is obligated to offer help to, members of its head couples' bilateral kin who are household co-heads. Additionally, the intensity of obligation between households is defined by the closeness of kin relations between their head couples and decreases from core relatives to peripheral relatives to nonrelatives.

Food shortages are a common phenomenon in most Lahu villages, which are usually located in mountainous areas with impoverished soil, erratic weather conditions, and minimal transportation and infrastructure. Although the living standards of Qhawqhat were above average among Lahu villagers in Lancang because of the village's success in growing tea, food shortages still haunted many villagers, as suggested by my survey results in the village of Abo in the cluster of Qhawqhat. In 1995, only forty-one of the total sixty-three households (65 percent) in the village had enough grain to last the entire year. The remaining twenty-two households (35 percent) suffered from varying degrees of food shortages. Among these households, thirteen lacked food for one month, eight for two months, and one for three months. Coping with food shortages still constitutes an important arena in Qhawqhat interhousehold interactions in 2002.

A household experiencing a food shortage seeks help from households that produce extra grain. The extra grain of a household is counted as the sum total of the year's yields after deducting state taxes paid in grain, the yearly household consumption, and seeds kept in reserve for the next year. In principle, depending on their relationships with the head couples of the households having extra grain, Qhawqhat villagers have three options for receiving assistance: they can "look for [food] to eat" from core relatives, "borrow to eat" from peripheral relatives, or "borrow to eat" from nonrelatives.

Households co-headed by relatives are all obligated to support each other in coping with food shortages. Ideally, core relatives ought to offer such support under the principle of generalized reciprocity, never expecting a return. Therefore, seeking grain from core relatives is called "look for [food] to eat" (*ca cad*), and the request is for the host or hostess to "give," rather than to "lend." In practice, however, considerate receivers would return, at least partially, the rice "given" to them. In fact, a receiver would usually feel too embarrassed to revisit the giver's household to "look for [food] to eat" if they have received such assistance for three years running while failing to make any return. Despite the discrepancy between ideal and practice, however, offering grain to help core relatives is usually a sacrifice. First, the food given to core relatives may never be returned if the receivers are unable to recover from a food shortage and requesting any payback in such a case would be considered "abandoning principles" (*awl lid mad heut* or *awl lid mad ca*). Therefore, when a household has given to the same household for several years in a row, the host or hostess usually declines further requests with the excuse that they themselves have just enough to eat. Furthermore, even if the receivers can overcome a food shortage in a few years and return the same amount of grain, the giver still bears a small amount of "storage loss" (*sheor haoq*) due to dehydration.[9]

If the households co-headed by a villager's core relatives cannot offer enough food assistance, the villager suffering a food shortage usually turns to households co-headed by peripheral relatives "to borrow to eat" (*chid cad*). Consistent with the connotation of the term "borrow," the receiver is expected to return the grain, typically within one to five years. Before the five years are up, any hints from the lender to request repayment are considered inappropriate or degrading to the relationship. In contrast to assisting core relatives, helping peripheral relatives to cope with a food shortage is much less costly because it is, in principle, a balanced reciprocity. However, whereas peripheral relatives risk very little in lending grain, they do still have to bear the weight deduction of the grain during storage.

Villagers borrow food from nonrelatives when they have to. In contrast to relatives, who usually lend food with varying degrees of sacrifice, nonrelatives often demand interest in return, typically under the name of compensating "storage loss."[10] In the late 1940s, several rich villagers of Qhawqhat adopted the practice of lending grain at high rates of interest. According to elders, if the borrower could not return the loan until the third year, the accumulated interest would require the household to return over twice the amount of grain originally borrowed. If the borrower still could not pay back the debt within three years, the impoverished household sometimes had to sell its land to repay the ever-mounting debt. The CCP has outlawed high-interest grain loans in the Lancang area since 1956, and the practice was abandoned during the period of collectivism. Nevertheless, since the 1980s, borrowing grain from nonrelatives has again required a return with interest, which is implicitly covered under "storage loss" but is no longer cumulative.

RITUAL RECIPROCITY

Echoing its efficacy in defining interhousehold economic relationships, the dyadic kinship principle also provides a structural base for interhousehold ritual reciprocity. As is true in situations of economic reciprocity, households co-headed by nonrelatives in a village have no ritual obligations except for elders' funerals, which are considered a village-wide event. Among the relatives, the intensity of ritual obligation decreases slightly from core to peripheral relatives.

The most important Lahu rituals are those celebrating three major life-cycle transitions—birth, marriage, and death (of elders)—which all the relative households in a village are obliged to attend. The only difference between the two circles of relatives on those occasions is that core relatives are further obligated to attend each others' rituals even if they live in different village clusters. At the weddings and funerals I attended in Qhawqhat, I observed many visitors from neighboring village clusters that were within a day's walking distance; some even came from as far away as the county seat. As the most important rituals, funerals for elders are the only ones that extend reciprocal obligation to the households of nonrelatives whose houses are located in the same village of the Qhawqhat village cluster. Interestingly, life-cycle rituals even bring together those relatives whose conflicts are so intense that they barely talk to each other, let along have any economic reciprocity. The strong moral significance attached to such rituals explains the episode I discussed at the beginning of the chapter, in which Cal Lad was obliged to attend the funeral of his very distant relative Li Lan, whose household had few reciprocal relations with Cal Lad's in daily activities.

Beyond reciprocal obligations in life-cycle rituals, three important propitiation rituals also require the participation of all Qhawqhat households co-headed by relatives. The most important is called "praying for blessings from the place of Xeul Sha" (*Xeul Sha mud mil bo lawl-shiq lawl*), which is held to rescue the household from a cycle of constant misfortunes that have not been stopped by other rituals. Another ritual is called "looking for blessing from Xeul Sha's Place" (*Xeul Sha mud mil bo ca shiq ca*), which is held by a household to improve its general well-being. The third ritual that involves intensive household reciprocity at the level of the village cluster is "calling souls from the place of the deceased parents and parents-in-law"(*chaw mawd hawq ha qho*), which is the highest level of all soul-calling rituals.[11]

Related households in Qhawqhat are also obligated in a series of annual ritual feasts, held during the Lahu New Year Festival (*qhawr*), the New Rice Tasting Festival (*cal siq cad*), and the Grave Repairing Ritual (*lier piel gu*, or *tuf phu gu*). In contrast to those of life-cycle rituals, reciprocal obligations to attend the annual rituals are less intense for households co-headed by peripheral relatives. Within the scope of the Qhawqhat village cluster, all households co-headed by core relatives are obligated to each other in those rituals. In contrast, the households co-headed by peripheral relatives are obligated to attend each other's annual rituals only if they live in the same village of the cluster. Most obligations to attend the ritual feasts can be fulfilled because the entire Lahu New Year Festival lasts for fifteen days, and the dates of the New Rice Tasting Festival and the Grave Repairing Rituals are decided by each household.

It is important to note that Lahu ritual obligations focus on participation and moral support, demanding minimal material contribution. Even some large-scale rituals expect each household representative to contribute only a bowl of rice, which relieves the host household from the risk of later food shortage as a result of feeding the large crowd. The other objects required from guests are usually symbolic, causing little economic burden to the givers. For instance, each pair of head couples attending a "calling souls from the place of the deceased parents and parents-in-law" needs to contribute a string of "soul thread," which is blended from pieces of black and white threads. Believed capable of imparting the blessings from the contributing households, the "soul thread" will be put on the wrist of the sick person at the end of the ritual after his or her soul is presumably called back.

FLEXIBILITY AND TRANSFORMATION

According to my observations in Qhawqhat, while the bilateral kinship relations between household co-heads clearly define the principles of interhousehold reciprocity, the interactions between head couples in everyday life show varying degrees of flexibility. At one extreme, ritual obligations are usually associated with the strongest social expectation and failing to conform to the norms tends to incur criticisms that harm one's reputation. At the other end of the spectrum of reciprocities, labor cooperation seems to offer individual head couples the greatest flexibility in choosing cooperative partners, as I will examine in more detail in the remainder of this section.

From a large pool of bilateral relatives defined by the extreme inclusiveness of Lahu kin categories, a household head couple tends to establish long-term labor reciprocity with only a few other households, based on the closeness between the head couples as well as the proximity of their houses or fields. Occasionally, personal relations between the head couples may even override kinship relations, as shown by the following two examples I observed in the 1990s. In the first case, two married brothers lived next door to each other but had not engaged in labor cooperation since they had serious land disputes stemming from the village's contracting the communal land to households in the early 1980s. In the second case, two female coheads had been close friends since childhood, and their friendship resulted in the two unrelated households' intensive labor exchanges despite the availability of many of their relatives' households in the same village. While Qhawqhat villagers I interviewed commented negatively on the former case for breaking the relationships between core relatives, no one criticized the latter for establishing intense reciprocity with nonrelatives.

The great flexibility in labor cooperation also manifests itself in the gap between ideal and practice in "mutual help" (*ga dar*), which expects the households co-headed by core relatives to enthusiastically help each other without any expectations in return. While all of the villagers I interviewed denied that they themselves had ever calculated the discrepancy of labor input in their "mutual help" with their core relatives, most pointed out that some other villagers did calculate such discrepancies. Na Nud, an outspoken woman in her late forties, even told me once that real *ga dar* never existed because no household would keep helping another household if the latter returned too little for too long. Interestingly, she had firmly stated on another occasion that her household had a true *ga dar* relationship with the impoverished household of her daughter as a result of offering many years of labor assistance to the latter. According to my observations, based on comments expressed subtly in private contexts, many Qhawqhat villagers indeed expected returns when engaging in "mutual help" with their core relatives' households. For example, when a head couple logistically planned their labor cooperation with other households on a daily basis, they sometimes also discussed how many labor days they had helped core relatives, as shown by the following observations.[12]

The episode occurred in the household of Cal Thid and Na Var one evening in June 1996 when it was near the end of the season for transplanting rice seedlings. The head couple lived together with their youngest daughter, Na Meiq, their son-in-law Cal Lawd, and their granddaughter Na Xeul. While the head couple sat by the hearth waiting for the rice to be done, Na Var began to express her concerns about whether or not they could finish planting two of their plots in time. The majority of their labors had been spent assisting their reciprocal households for the last several days. During that day, Na Meiq and Cal Lawd had assisted Cal Lawd's parents in transplanting wet rice; Na Var had assisted the household of her second son and his wife in weeding their dry land; Cal Thid had fertilized one plot of their planted wet rice while taking care of the baby, Na Xeul. The head couple casually chatted on and off about the matter throughout dinner and a little afterwards. They finally decided to keep assisting their relatives for two more days until two of their close reciprocal households finished their planting so that the head couple could receive the most assistance in return. On the third day, all the adults of the household indeed started to plant their own wet-rice land, assisted by laborers from households of both core relatives (Cal Lawd's parents, Cal Thid's sister and brother-in-law, and Cal Thid and Na Var's second son) and a few peripheral relatives. With more than ten adult laborers transplanting each day, the two plots of the household of Cal Thid and Na Var were completed within two days.

Lahu villagers' increasing involvement in the market economy has greatly intensified the flexibility in interhousehold reciprocities and has widened the gap between ideal and practice, especially regarding the principle of generalized reciprocity among core relatives. For example, the rapid expansion of cash crops, especially tea and sugarcane, has directly challenged the principle of "mutual help" since the late 1980s. The strong commercial ambitions of an entrepreneur household often lead to a great labor shortage, and generously assisting such core relatives will be an endless drain of laborers from the helpers' households.

Despite the strong impact of commercialization, however, the Lahu principles that govern interhousehold interactions are still appealing to many villagers, some of whom are even willing to pay high economic prices in order to conform to the indigenous ideals. Some villagers' choice of generalized principle over profit-making can be exemplified by my conversation with a Qhawqhat couple, my designated Lahu relatives, who were in their late thirties in 1995. I use "W" to represent the wife, "H" to represent the husband, and SD to represent myself.

SD: Things have changed so much in Qhawqhat since I last visited [1989]. There was only one private shop then. Look how many you've got now [eight]!

H: Yes, many people prefer it over farming. Running a shop demands no hard [manual] work and can bring you more money. . . . We opened one a few years ago, too. She [his wife] ran it.

SD: Really?! What happened with it?

W: It ran out of business. We lost money.

SD: How come? There were far fewer shops in Qhawqhat then. You should have at least made some money.

W: No, we lost all. You know, we have so many relatives in Qhawqhat.

H: She often gave away things to them.

W: I gave away only small [inexpensive] things. How could you take money from your own *awl viq awl niq* and *awl ceol awl qhad* ('relatives') when they just came for a box of matches or a scoop of soy sauce? Many of them are our *ted yiel chaw* [they had about two dozen core relatives in Qhawqhat].

SD: But village shops sell almost nothing else but small things!

H: It was indeed too embarrassing to accept money from [close] relatives when they came to our shop for small things. When in lack, we always visit each other's households to look for salt, chili pepper, and rice [without expectations for returns].

SD: What about those successful shops [in Qhawqhat]?

W: [Naming several shop owners], they have few relatives in Qhawqhat! Some people [several other owners] care for nothing but money. They are not embarrassed to take money from relatives for even smallest things they sell. We do not want to abandon principles like they do.

H: It's very difficult for Lahu people to do business unless you abandon Lahu principles [regarding how to treat relatives]. The rice-noodle restaurant Na Mawl opened last year in Menglangba [the county seat where her husband worked for the government]] ran out of business in just a few months. They did not expect that so many of their rural relatives would come to Menglangba and visit their restaurant during market days. How could she charge relatives for meals?

In summary, according to the dyadic principle of Lahu kinship terminology, a head couple categorizes their relationships with other households as core relatives, peripheral relatives, and nonrelatives. Such circles of relations provide structural bases for households to prioritize their economic and ritual rights and duties with each other. In this sense, the dyadic orientation in kinship terminology and the central role of head couples in interhousehold interactions reinforce each other. Despite the flexibility in traditional practice and the impact of the commodity economy, the social norms that govern household interactions among the Lahu of Qhawqhat and other rural areas in Lancang are still predominantly based on the dyadic kinship principles in 2002.

CONCLUSION

The Lahu kinship system suggests that, while the principle of gender division tends to lay foundations for clearly defined kinship structures in unilineal societies, the blurring of gender divisions in bilateral societies may not necessarily predicate the lack of structural principles in their kinship organization. The dyadic orientation of Lahu kinship terminology provides a married couple with circles of kin relations that structurally connect them with other husband-wife dyads as well as with single individuals. Consequently, the bilateral kinship networks between household head couples regulate the forms and intensity of interhousehold reciprocity in both economic and ritual activities. Such an interhousehold organization empowers men and women jointly as household head couples, laying a structural foundation for the unitary ideals in both cosmology and gender roles. In other words, by unifying a husband and wife into a single social entity, the Lahu kinship system structurally eliminates the common tendency to use gender as an institutional marker to induce asymmetrical structures and social orders.

CHAPTER 6

THE DYSFUNCTION AND COLLAPSE OF
GENDER DYADS: DIVORCE, ELOPEMENT, AND
LOVE-PACT SUICIDE

WHILE THE preeminence of the Lahu dyadic worldview in social institutions and practice effectively promotes symbiotic and symmetrical relations between males and females, it has by no means created a paradise. In this chapter, I focus on the gaps between the dyadic gender ideal and social practice, especially the dysfunction and collapse of marriages. I first discuss the major personal and social factors that are recognized by Lahu villagers as severe threats to marital quality and stability. I then examine some typical causes of the break-up of a marriage—decisions that shatter even the minimal requirements of the gender-dyadic principle—including events as tragic and dramatic as love-pact suicide. I conclude the chapter by exploring the institutionalized gender equality embedded even in Lahu responses to the dysfunction and collapse of marriages.

MAJOR THREATS TO HUSBAND-WIFE DYADS

As discussed in the preceding chapters, Lahu gender ideology and institutions are based on the solidarity and endurance of monogamous marriages in which a husband-wife dyad is expected to function as jointly and harmoniously as a pair of chopsticks. However, even in the Lahu rural areas where indigenous ideology and institutions have been preserved most systematically, such as the Qhawqhat village cluster, the degrees to which individual couples live up to the dyadic social expectations vary from exemplary harmony to intense conflict. The ideals of harmonious marriage are also systematically challenged both by indigenous sociocultural factors and by the radical social changes introduced by state policies and intercultural encounters. In the remainder of this section, I discuss three major factors identified by Lahu villagers as significant threats to their marital ideals: social deviance, parental intervention in the choice of mates, and extramarital affairs.

BEING "UNLIKE OTHERS" OR "PECULIAR"

Similar to many Lahu elsewhere, Qhawqhat villagers use the phrase "unlike others" or "peculiar" (*shu mad qhe*) to categorize the individuals who deviate from social expectations for a spouse, thereby constituting fundamental threats to the normal functions and even the stability of their marriages. Although some acquire the stigma from their family backgrounds, most individuals are classified by villagers as being "peculiar" because some of their own characteristics or behaviors are opposed to gender ideals.

One of the most important features that makes people "peculiar" is their failure to fulfill the joint responsibility with their spouses of providing for the household. Contrary to the expectation for each spouse to "work hard to eat" [feed the household], some villagers are considered "lazy." In contrast to those who are lazy, some are physically incapable of performing heavy tasks because of poor heath conditions, especially chronic diseases. Although villagers are sympathetic to the latter, such people are still considered "peculiar" and, therefore, failures as spouses. The households co-headed by a spouse of this kind tend to be particularly poor and are most vulnerable to food shortages. Such couples are also prone to marital conflicts because one spouse is overloaded with responsibilities. Therefore, parents often warn their children with the Lahu saying "Beauty is inedible"(*ni sha kaf mad cad phier*), cautioning them against being attracted to potential mates because of their appearance while ignoring their capacity to "work hard to eat."

While the ability to share working responsibility with one's spouse may determine the material well-being of the family, the characteristic of *nud* ('softness')—which includes tenderness, care, and humility—is central to the harmony of a marriage and to the couples' inter-household relationships. Therefore, "peculiar" is inevitably associated with the trait of *hie* ('harshness'), which includes aggressiveness, arrogance, lack of consideration for others, a hot temperament, and rudeness. Not surprisingly, tensions and conflicts tend to mark the marriages in which one or both spouses are harsh. I witnessed two incidents of domestic violence in Qhawqhat, one involving wife-beating and the other husband-beating (see chapter 2). While criticizing both actions as being harsh, villagers agreed that the wife-beater (Cal Hie) was harsh in nature because he tended to quarrel and initiate fights with other villagers as well. Villagers I interviewed were all sympathetic to the two victims of domestic violence. Nevertheless, some commented that the victimized wife was suffering from her own choice because she had insisted on marrying Cal Hie, who was handsome and capable of "working hard to eat" but was known to be harsh even before their marriage.

Social disapproval of harsh personalities is so strong that the entire household is disgraced if villagers consider one of their members to be such a person. In the 1990s, many Qhawqhat villagers still talked about two households as being outrageously harsh, mainly because of what had happened twenty years ago. In the first case, the household members frequently quarreled and fought. In one especially vicious fight, the mother bit off a piece of her eldest daughter's ear. In the second case, a woman mistreated her blind mother-in-law, who was once seen eating the pigs' food during the food shortages of the 1970s. Consequently, all of the children of these two households had to marry out of Qhawqhat because no one in the village cluster would allow their children to marry them.

In addition to personality flaws and the inability to "work hard to eat," individuals are also stigmatized as being "peculiar" because of their habitual engagement in destructive activities, particularly addictions to alcohol, opium, and gambling. Qhawqhat men and women, old and young alike, commonly consume homemade corn liquor during festivals and many rituals, but alcohol addiction was rare until the booming of private shops in the village in the late 1980s. These shops sell large amounts of extremely low-quality alcohol, which they even sell by the dram. I noticed a drastic increase in the number of drunkards in Lahu villages between my first visit to Lancang in 1987 and 1996. During my stay in Qhawqhat in the 1990s, I often saw children, many of whom were less then ten years old, passing around alcohol bought with their pocket money while they gathered around the counters of local shops to watch television.

The consumption of opium has a long history in many Lahu villages. During the decades of the 1930s and 1940s (the GMD regime), many Lancang Lahu grew opium to cope with inflated taxes, to purchase waivers from military service, and to purchase guns to protect the villages from organized robbers. The CCP outlawed opium growing in the early 1950s, and opium addiction was no longer a problem during the collectivist period because of the lack of supply. Since the 1980s, however, Lahu villagers have been reintroduced to opium as a result of the increasing trade between Myanmar (Burma) and China. Lancang's location has allowed it to participate in normal trade but has also made it one of the first stops for international drug infiltration into China, and many young people in the county seat (including the daughter of one of my best friends) even became addicted to heroin. In 1996, Qhawqhat had eleven opium addicts, which was a very mild situation compared to that in some other villages. Nevertheless, opium addiction among the Lancang Lahu in the 1990s seemed less severe than in some Lahu villages in northern Thailand (Sanit 1989; Walker 1992).

The Lahu also have a long history of exposure to gambling as a result of their social and economic ties to the Dai, whose gambling houses in local markets often attract highlanders (e.g., Colquhoun 1970:296; Milne 1970:119). Nevertheless, gambling did not constitute a severe social problem in the Lahu villages of Lancang until recently. Qhawqhat villagers can identify the year (1991) when some young men began to gamble in the village cluster, and many have become addicted since then. In the years following 1991, Qhawqhat cadres and public security officials from the district organized several campaigns against gambling. According to the villagers, a few people still gathered secretly at night to gamble out in the mountains during the time of my stay in Qhawqhat.

While neglecting their responsibility to join with their spouses to provide for their households through hard work, those addicted to opium, alcohol, and gambling often secretly took away grain and other things from their households and sold them to satisfy their addictions or to pay debts. Not only do the addicts bring harm to their marriages and households, but they have also caused the number of village thefts to soar since the 1980s.

In addition to the personal problems that often lead to marriage conflicts, certain family backgrounds can also lead villagers to consider individuals "peculiar" or undesirable spouses. The worst of all is belonging to a household whose members are believed to possess a dangerous spirit (*tawr*), an overwhelming fear of which is widely shared by the Lahu and neighboring ethnic groups (Sang 1983). Sometimes a cluster of households co-headed by a core kin-set may be collectively considered "unlike others" to varying degrees because of the high proportion of problematic individuals among their members or because of their noticeably high rate of marital conflicts, divorces, or suicides. In addition, some Lahu households were classified as "landlords" during the land reform of the mid 1950s, and their members underwent humiliating criticisms and even violent physical abuse during the period of the Cultural Revolution (1966–1976). Consequently, those households were stigmatized until the early 1980s as "peculiar" for political reasons. Although most individuals in stigmatized families are both hardworking and easygoing, their family backgrounds often bring shadows to their marriages, and their choice of mates tends to be objected to by the parents on the other side.

In summary, whether because of character flaws or marginalized family backgrounds, individuals who are perceived as being "peculiar" are usually predisposed to fail social expectations for a normal marriage, challenging the gender-dyadic ideals. The extremely unsuccessful marriages in a village often involve "peculiar" spouses, reinforcing the popular perception of "peculiarity" as the major threat to marriage. It is important to note that no gender distinctions exist in either the measurements of or the discrimination against the social deviants.

PARENTAL INTERVENTIONS IN MATE CHOICE

In order to ensure successful marriages for their children, many Lahu parents tend to interfere to varying degrees in their children's choice of a mate. On the one hand, parents may offer their wisdom to prevent their children from marrying "peculiar" individuals, thus reducing the risk of failure of their children's future marriages. On the other hand, some forceful parental intervention may result in emotional trauma for their children, thus inadvertently sowing the seeds of discord and instability in their future marriages.

Supported by the ideology that promotes the authority of parents as being comparable to that of the parental god (Xeul Sha), Lahu parents are usually very influential in their children's lives, especially in their choices of mates. Qhawqhat villagers classify the intensity of parental interventions in a child's choice of mate into three categories: "finding one's own spouse," "parental guidance," and "parental arrangement." According to my survey of three villages of Qhawqhat in 1996, out of the 148 household head couples, 120 married according to their own choice (81.1 percent), 16 married according to parental suggestions (10.8 percent), and 12 married by compulsory parental arrangements (8.1 percent). The percentage of arranged marriages did not include three cases occurring between 1986 and 1992 in which the women ran away from their arranged marriages to other provinces and were therefore no longer counted as Qhawqhat residents.

As the statistics show, most Qhawqhat villagers found their own spouses. Typically between the ages of thirteen and sixteen in the 1990s and between fifteen and eighteen prior to the 1980s, Lahu youth started to "play with boys" or "play with girls" (*yad mid geud* or *chaw haq geud*), activities serving as a prelude to finding a spouse. In a normal setting of "play with boys/ girls," a group of girls and boys gather at night, sitting on opposite sides of a bonfire or standing on village roads. Prior to the 1990s, the most popular activities on such occasions were listening to a courting couple sing love songs in an antiphonal manner (Du 1995). Since the 1990s, Lahu courtship singing has been replaced by watching Gongfu (Kung Fu) videos as well as soap operas and movies on TV, and the folk-song tradition has declined dramatically in rural Lancang. A traditional courtship ritual that was still widely practiced by rural Lahu youth of Lancang in 1996 is "snatching the headcloth or hat" from a member of the opposite sex and running away from the group in a joking manner. Through such a ritual, a boy or girl initiates a semiprivate conversation with someone he or she is interested in or attracted to. In addition, when a boy and girl confirm their mutual affection for each other, they still follow tradition by asking their peers to talk to the two sets of parents, waiting for their approval so that a wedding can be held. If the parents on either side veto the proposal—usually because the individual or the family involved is considered "peculiar" or because deep conflicts exist between the parents—there is little hope they can marry each other.

Most young people obey their parents and give up their own choice of mates. Nevertheless, the impact of the decision on the emotions of the young people varies greatly according to the mutual affection of each couple. If the young couple are only lightly attracted to each other, they tend to accept their parents' rejection easily. For instance, the parents of Cal Yawl (male, forty-six) refused to propose to the parents of his first love for him when he was eighteen because the family of the girl was widely suspected in the village of possessing the evil spirit (*tawr*). According to Cal Yawl, he accepted his parents' decision without any difficulty because he and the girl did not know each other very well, and he changed his mind when he heard about the dangerous background of her family. If the young lovers are emotionally devoted to each other, however, they tend to be traumatized, and the consequent emotional scars are often carried into their future marriages, as shown by the example of Cal Lie and Na Mawl, who married in the early 1980s. While commenting sympathetically on some love-pact suicides of his peers, Cal Lie once confided that he himself was also a victim because his parents had vetoed his proposed marriage with his first love. The consequent emotional despair, combined with many other coincidental events, led him to marry Na Mawl, the young woman who had been teased since childhood about "becoming one family" with him. Cal Lie's emotional trauma was at least partially responsible for the couple's poor relationship and the difficulties they faced constantly in maintaining their marriage, which was finally dissolved in 2001.

Rather than obeying their parents' decisions silently, a few devoted young lovers decide to "become one family" at the cost of suffering social ostracism throughout their lives. I collected two such radical cases in Qhawqhat. In the late 1940s, a young man insisted on marrying a young widow with two children whose family was widely believed to possess the evil spirit. Consequently, his parents disowned him and denied him his share of land. The couple was marginalized in the community, and their children were also believed to have the evil spirit. In fact, the couple would have been unable to survive in the village if they had not had the fortunate support of the widow's family and later inherited land from them. In 1994, a girl insisted on marrying a boy from a neighboring village whom she met at the village video room and whose family was believed to have the evil spirit. She was also disowned by her family after she ran away to live with the boy's family and had an incomplete and thus awkward wedding held only at the house of the boy's parents.

In some extreme cases, the young lovers may resist their parents' decisions by committing love-pact suicide, believing that they will be able to marry in the world of the dead. I recorded two such cases in Qhawqhat. In 1985, a girl's parents turned down a marriage proposal to their daughter because her boyfriend was infamous in Qhawqhat for being lazy. Near the Lahu New Year Festival in 1986, the girl married a man chosen by her parents. Three days after her wedding, however, the bride committed suicide together with her former boyfriend on a mountain near their village. Similar to the plot described in Lahu love-pact suicide stories, the girl's parents cried loudly while burying her, deeply regretting having forced their will on her, wishing that they had understood her determination. Unfortunately, not all parents learned from this lesson. In 1994, the parents of an eighteen-year-old girl firmly rejected the marriage proposal of her twenty-year-old lover and soon arranged for her to marry another young man of Qhawqhat. The night before the scheduled wedding, the lovers committed suicide together.

While parents may veto their children's choices when they try to "find their own spouses," two sets of parents may encourage or even force their children to marry each other. Such parents are typically close relatives (often cross-siblings) whose emotional and social bonds are so strong that they desire the bonds to be retained and renewed in the next generation. Many Lancang Lahu prefer both cross-cousin and parallel-cousin marriages yet prohibit marriages between the children of male siblings. Such a marriage is especially desirable if one set of parents has only one child (or one set has all sons and the other has all daughters) because it will bring each family the "son" or "daughter" whom they have loved and helped raise. According to the villagers I interviewed, not only can such marriages protect the families from the risk of relating to "peculiar" families, but it also brings close relatives even closer. Parallel to their own pragmatic considerations, these parents tend to believe that they are making the wise choice for their children, who, in the parents' eyes, are making a perfect match.

Among the marriages resulting mainly from the will of both sets of parents, some are considered "guided by parents" (*awl pa-awl e jut maf* or *awl pa-awl-e bet maf*), who tend to offer suggestions with no binding obligations. In such cases, parents simultaneously express their will to the boy and the girl and encourage them to court each other ritually, but they usually respect their children's will if one or both of them reject this advice. Such parental interference involves no apparent emotional costs. Nevertheless, since such marriages are suggested when the children enter puberty, they rarely participate in "playing with boys/girls" and may thus be deprived of romantic experiences. Consequently, some of these spouses become more prone to temptation by extramarital romance in the future, as suggested by the confidences of the personal experiences of some villagers.

In contrast, some parents arrange marriages for their children regardless of the latter's desires, and such marriages are called "matched (arranged) by parents" (*awl pa-awl-e maf ka*). Prior to the 1950s, parents in such cases used to hold the wedding for their children when they were as young as eleven or twelve years old, preventing them from being attracted to someone else when they reached puberty. Although Lahu tradition discourages arranged marriages, there were few socially approved means to prevent such activities. The CCP government has outlawed arranged marriage in the Lancang area since 1950. I have recorded that, since the late 1950s, no Qhawqhat parents have forced their children to marry before reaching puberty. Nevertheless, I heard that such arranged marriages still sporadically occurred in some other villages until the 1980s, when the strict implementation of family-planning policies required a couple to reach minimal ages before they could marry.

Some parents still occasionally forced their wills on their children in the 1990s. Nevertheless, they often made the decision based upon idiosyncratic conditions such as a labor shortage or the poor health of a youth. The Qhawqhat couple Cal Wuq and Laf Meiq, who married in the early 1990s, provide a typical example. Cal Wuq fell into unrequited love with Laf Meiq when they were at the stage of "playing with boys/girls." Despite Laf Meiq's disinterest after some "headcloth" chatting, Cal Wuq signaled to his parents that he wished them to propose a marriage to her parents. Laf Meiq's parents accepted the proposal and arranged the marriage despite Laf Meiq's reluctance. They made the decision because they appreciated Cal Wuq's capacity to "work hard to eat," his physical strength, his "soft" temperament, and his enchantment with Laf Meiq—all of which were particularly significant in the case of Laf Meiq, who was born relatively weak for some heavy tasks.

In most cases, young people accept the marriages arranged by their parents with varying degrees of reluctance. The marital lives of these young people are usually very difficult. Some arranged marriages remain unconsummated for a long time after the wedding. A newly married person may "not listen to parents' teaching" and refuse to "get along" with the unwanted partner, even claiming to be "tired of seeing" (*ni bawl*) his or her spouse. According to Lahu informants, if a couple does not get along, they cannot "stay close to each other," let alone "stay together" (a euphemism for having sex).

According to the personal stories of arranged marriages I heard in Qhawqhat, the parties who refused sexual relations in marriages were all females. The explanation I was given was that boys tend to be more obedient to their parents concerning the matter. These young wives shared some similar experiences at the beginning of their marriages. At first, the wife stayed up all night over the hearth weaving cloth in order to avoid going to bed. Scolded by her parents, she would finally agree to go to bed at night, but she tended to bind herself up tightly in her own blanket. In most cases, these women gradually accepted their husbands, and their relationships usually improved after they had children.

Nevertheless, some of these women refused their husbands for a long time, even two or three years. When the rejection lasted for about a month, the woman's mother sometimes sewed the two quilts of the newlyweds together. In response, the woman might find a piece of wooden board on which to sleep beside the hearth, where she covered herself with her headcloth. Usually, the woman refused to talk to her husband or even to sit with the family around the table during meals, taking her own bowl of rice and walking away. Unsurprisingly, such couples could not fulfill the social expectation that "husband and wife do it together" with "one strength and one breath" and be filled with "happiness in their hearts." Whereas the parents often intentionally arranged for the couple to work alone together in the fields or herding, the woman often chose to work on the other side of the field.

The denouement of the lasting tension between poorly matched newlyweds was sometimes dramatic, as suggested by the following cases of Qhawqhat couples. The ice was broken between San Meiq and A Zhe by a romantic accident. In the 1950s, the couple were returning home late one evening when a leopard suddenly jumped onto the mountain road and attacked their cattle. San Meiq, who was behind the cattle keeping the usual distance from A Zhe, was frightened when the cattle were startled. She cried out the name of A Zhe, who ran back and held her in his arms. From this dramatic incident, the two developed a lasting romantic attachment.[1] In the second case (from the 1970s), the woman, Na Qi, gradually accepted her husband due to the kindness and consideration she received from him and his family once they moved to his parents' house three years after their marriage. In the third case (from the 1940s), the woman's parents asked for a divorce on her behalf, apologized for her disobedience (she had slept by the hearth since the wedding), and paid a large amount of compensation. In the fourth case (from the 1950s), the woman's parents suggested that the couple move to the house of the man's parents before their three-year obligation to live with them was over, expecting that they might get along afterwards. Nevertheless, a few months later, the woman had an extramarital affair with another young man in the village and committed love-pact suicide with him. In the other three cases I recorded (1986, 1987, and 1991), the unhappy young wives ran away to Han areas (Jiangsu, Hunan, and Guangdong Provinces, respectively).

In brief, while deviant individuals ("the peculiar") tend to generate dysfunctional marriages, parental intervention in their children's choice of mate may, contrary to the intentions of the parents, also result in marriages of disharmony and instability. While the social deviants obviously challenge the social expectations for a normal marriage, the emotional discord of many couples in arranged marriages subtly threatens the dyadic gender ideals. Regarding the social inequality involved in forced parental interventions in children's marital choices, it is interesting that both the authorities and the victims tend to constitute male-female pairs, reflecting a generational, rather than a gender-based, hierarchy.

EXTRAMARITAL RELATIONS

Violating the legitimate sexual relations approved by Xeul Sha in marriage, extramarital affairs (*haq chawd te*, or *haq chawd meul*) constitute one of the worst sins in Lahu culture. It is widely believed among the Lancang Lahu that illicit relations incur defilement for a village, resulting in disasters such as a house catching fire or pigs or cattle being stolen from the village by tigers or leopards. In general, different from Lahu Shi traditions, extramarital (including premarital) relations are strictly prohibited in most Lahu Na villages in Lancang. Until the 1950s, extramarital affairs were rare among the Lancang Lahu because of the overall coherence between moral expectations, social structures, and sanctions of customary law. According to my interviews with many Qhawqhat elders, there were only two cases of illicit sexual relations between the 1920s and the 1940s. The scarcity of extramarital affairs resulted mainly from the institutional encouragement of the bonds between married couples and from severe sanctions on illicit relations by customary law, which is gender-blind both in social restrictions on extramarital relations and in the punishment of transgressors.

The radical social transformations introduced by the socialist state since 1949 have greatly undermined the solidarity and cohesion of Lahu husband-wife dyads, which used to effectively prevent illicit sexual relations. This disruption reached its peak during the period of collectivism when Lahu villages were transformed from a household-based community to a socialist unit in which the husband-wife dyads were broken down in many social arenas into two individual members of a production team.

During the period of collectivism, a Lahu couple was no longer able to "work hard to eat" together, resulting in a radical erosion of the traditional cohesive bond between a husband and wife. The cadres of production teams organized daily labor according to the local agricultural and political needs as well as by age, gender, class labels, and physical strength. As a result, a couple was often separated from each other and from other members of their household in productive activities on a daily basis. Moreover, a couple was also constantly separated in the evening, engaging in activities organized by the work team and the brigade, such as attending political meetings, criticizing landlords, receiving militia training, and patrolling the village. Exhausted by the work in the field during the daytime and pressured by many demanding domestic tasks in the evening, most families considered the politically required tasks a painful burden. Thus they often fulfilled the minimal requirement by sending only one member out in the evenings. Since the elders needed more rest, and singles were not considered "adults," one member of the young couple of the family tended to represent the household at such meetings and other activities. Therefore, a couple became separated most of time in their daily lives.

A Lahu couple also underwent separations beyond daily village life. For instance, during the Great Leap Forward Campaign (1958–1959), about two hundred Qhawqhat laborers, together with other peasants from Lancang County, were organized to work for several months in a coal mine and an iron plant several hundred kilometers away from Lancang. In the 1970s, each household was frequently obligated to provide a young laborer to clear new farmland in the forest and to build reservoirs and roads. Some of these locations were so far from the village that the laborers had to camp on the sites. Consequently, emotional attachments and even sexual liaisons developed among many of those young people who worked and lived collectively for weeks and even months at a time separated from other members of their villages, including their spouses if they were married. Since the implementation of agricultural reforms in the early 1980s, Lahu society has shifted back to its household-oriented economy. This has resulted in a partial restoration of the cohesion of Lahu couples in productive activities. At the same time, the dyadic bond of a couple has been weakened by many other factors, such as the impact of the commodity economy, the increasing mobility of the population, and increasing exposure to mass media.

Severe punishment of extramarital relationships by customary laws is common to Lahu in many areas (Lie and Liu 1999:142–143; Wang and He 1999:291). While social changes have drastically weakened Lahu institutions that promote marital solidarity, Lahu customary sanctions on extramarital affairs were strengthened in many Lancang areas during the Mao era. Take the example of a couple convicted of extramarital relations in Qhawqhat village at the beginning of the 1970s. The couple was sanctioned with a modified version of the most severe punishment in the customary law of the village. As decided upon by village cadres, who applied the local tradition, the couple was ordered to kill a pig and cook it unskinned, with its bristles on—symbolizing that they were as shameless as a pig. In this case, it was the man's household who offered the pig because this married man was involved with a single woman, so he was considered guiltier than she. They then cut the meat into small pieces and strung the pork slices together on bamboo sticks. The couple was required to take a string of the pork to each household, bearing submissively any scorn, spit, and even attacks by dogs. To add to their humiliation, they were required to take the meat only before breakfast, and the task of taking a portion to each household was counted as valid only when they were let into the house and their meat was accepted by one of the co-heads. Therefore, the process took almost ten days. In the end, the couple had to take rotten meat, which incurred even more scorn and scolding. In addition, the couple was also punished by some methods that were common Cultural Revolution practices, such as being required to beat a broken tin basin with a stick as if it were a drum when they were on their way to each household.[2]

The weakening of indigenous institutions that promote cohesion in husband-wife dyads was compounded by more restrictions on divorce and the increased punishment of extramarital affairs during the Mao era. As I will show in the following section, the clash between Lahu traditions and radical social changes trapped many Lahu youth in a fatal dilemma, triggering an outbreak of love-pact suicides.

THE COLLAPSE OF MARRIAGES

While dysfunctional marriages challenge the harmony and solidarity promised by the gender-dyadic ideal, their dissolution completely shatters the ideal. The collapse of a marriage breaks the couple's sacred commitment to Xeul Sha, destroys their joint identity and corresponding social obligations, and tears apart the close affinal networks built around their unity. Nevertheless, some Lahu marriages still fall apart, even in places such as Qhawqhat where the social pressure to maintain marriage stability is particularly strong. In Qhawqhat, as well as in many other Lancang Lahu villages, marriages break down mainly through divorce, elopement, or love-pact suicide.

DIVORCE

The moral discourses of the Lahu across regions tend to be against divorce (*bal dar*) because it conflicts fundamentally with the dominant ideology of gender unity manifested in the cosmological order, the social structure, and the core ethics. As discussed in chapter 2, the conventional wedding speeches among the Lahu in many areas teach the newlyweds the expectation for life-long commitment to marriage, using metaphors to indicate the impossibility of divorce.

Some local interpretations of the CCP policies have reinforced the discursive prohibition of divorce among many Lahu in China. At the very beginning of its regime (1950), the CCP passed a Marriage Law that promoted women's right to divorce (Johnson 1983; Stacey 1983). Nevertheless, the party soon softened its enforcement of the Marriage Law, in particular abandoning its policy of making divorces easy to obtain because it undermined the party's primary goal of class struggle.[3] Most Lahu in Lancang encountered the state policies on marriage and divorce mainly after 1956, when the state had clearly discouraged divorce in its reinterpretations of the Marriage Law. Detached from the previous implementations of state policies on marriage and divorce, most Lahu understood the state's policies as conforming to and reinforcing the Lahu principles that prohibited divorce.

State policies and conventional Lahu discourse tend to blend in a wedding speech, jointly claiming the prohibition of divorce. During the Mao era, local cadres used to propagate the state policy against divorce to Lahu villagers by offering moral teachings at weddings. Since all large means of production, such as cattle, belonged to the production team, the traditional expressions that used impossible numbers of cattle to compensate one's spouse in exchange for the right to ask for divorce no longer applied. In many Lancang areas, local cadres shared a saying that the one who asked for divorce would be fined ninety-nine *jin* (one *jin* is equal to 0.5 kilograms) of *piaozi*, which is a colloquial Chinese generic term for Chinese paper currency (*renminbi*). Ninety-nine *jin* of *piaozi*, which leaves the denomination of the bills unspecified, represented an infinite amount of money to Lahu villagers, who barely had enough food, let alone hard cash, during the period. During the post-Mao era, the eldest brothers of the mothers of the bride and groom regained their dominant role of offering moral teachings at a wedding and using old analogies to state the virtual impossibility of divorce. Nevertheless, they sometimes also blend their understandings of state policies regarding divorce with Lahu tradition. In one Lahu wedding I attended, the elder's wedding speech included: "Divorce is not allowed, . . . state law says so, our Lahu principles say so."

While conventional Lahu discourses tend to prohibit divorce, the actual restrictions on divorce vary greatly in practice among different subgroups and in different regions. At one end of the spectrum—as represented by the Lahu Shehleh (Hill 1985) and the Lahu Nyi (Walker 1970) in northern Thailand—divorce is fairly frequent and sometimes even occurs without stigma, especially for couples who have not established their own households. Among the Lahu in China, degrees of restriction on divorce also vary greatly (Lei and Liu 1999:87; Wang 2001:134; Wang and He 1999:110–113)

In the Lahu Na village clusters in Lancang, Qhawqhat is among the places where the traditional restrictions on divorce were very strict. According to the Qhawqhat elders I interviewed, it was very difficult to divorce prior to the 1950s. The households co-headed by those who were the core-kin members of the one who requested the divorce were obligated to help him or her pay heavy fines, including paddy field plots and cattle. Although not meeting the impossible requirements expressed in wedding speeches, these items were the villagers' most valuable items, and the amount tended to be extremely large for a normal household. Most of the fine was taken to compensate the other family, leaving a small proportion to cover the expenses of a ritual to purify the village. In addition, by suddenly tearing apart the close affinal networks of reciprocity built around a married couple, divorce brought about severe relational damages and caused shame and embarrassment to the relatives involved. Consequently, relatives tended to pressure a couple to remain in their marriage, no matter how dysfunctional it may have been. Some Qhawqhat elders I interviewed used the examples of some elderly couples in the village cluster to show how a marriage could be retained throughout a lifetime under difficult conditions, which brought public sympathy yet did not constitute valid reasons to request divorce. Among these marriages, while one spouse was normal, the other had serious problems, including being suspected of possessing the spirit (*tawr*), being severely addicted to opium or alcohol, being convicted of stealing, being incapable of working (because of disease), and being afflicted by leprosy.

Despite the extremely strong discursive and social prohibitions against divorce before the 1950s, divorces were occasionally granted in Qhawqhat. I recorded fifteen divorces occurring between the late 1930s and the early 1950s, and most of them involved forcibly arranged marriages. The parents who arranged their children's marriage could arrive at the decision to divorce after they had given up hope that the couple would ever get along and had balanced the economic and social costs of the decision. Since the wives were the ones who insisted on objecting to the arranged marriages, their parents had to appeal to the village co-heads for the divorce on behalf of their daughters. In addition to economic compensation, the parents had to implicitly confess that they had forced their child to marry, a behavior that would cause them to be considered "unwise parents." In addition to cases of arranged marriages, divorces were also granted when the marriage involved a member who was from another village cluster—a situation uncommon in Qhawqhat even in the mid-1990s. Two divorces among the fifteen cases I gathered belonged to this category. Such divorces were less costly to social relations because the geographic distances had prevented the affinal relatives from engaging in intensive reciprocity, especially that in labor cooperation. In addition, unlike those who live in the same village cluster, these relatives could avoid embarrassment in daily encounters with each other.

Since the beginning of the PRC regime, the divorce rates have undergone some changes. During the Mao era, even in situations in which Lahu tradition would have allowed divorce, the local cadres would not give permission. Many Lahu cadres considered divorce to be discouraged or even outlawed by the state, and they therefore typically vetoed the divorce requests to avoid the risk of making political mistakes that could jeopardize their careers. During the twenty-six years of the collectivist period (1956–1982), only three case of divorce occurred in Qhawqhat, all within the time frame of 1961–1965, when the village's commune-based administration was basically dissolved after the famine induced by the failure of the Great Leap Forward. Since the 1980s, however, the more relaxed state policies, compounding the reduced power of village cadres, have led to a rapid increase of divorce in Qhawqhat as well as elsewhere in Lancang. Since the 1990s, Lahu villagers have become more aware of the state legal system, and some Qhawqhat young people have gone to the district court to request divorces.

ELOPEMENT

For the individuals who have no hope of attaining a divorce yet are determined to escape from a dysfunctional marriage, eloping is an option. In the areas where Lahu traditional restrictions on divorce are strong, elopement is an extremely difficult choice because the action in principle declares the couple's social death in the community. Meanwhile, it is an enormous challenge for the couple to survive elsewhere. The unfeasibility of elopement is depicted by the love-pact suicide stories in Lahu songs and folklore in which two devoted young lovers weigh their options between elopement and love-pact suicide when their parents oppose their marrying each other. In these stories, the couple decides to abandon the first strategy after considering the lack of a viable destination as well as the lack of the financial and social means to escape.

Constituting an extreme violation of norms and social stability, elopement used to be considered one of the worst crimes, and failed attempts were severely punished by customary law in many Lancang Lahu Na villages prior to the 1950s. Several Qhawqhat elders recalled an incident in which a young married woman whose husband was an opium addict attempted to elope with an unmarried young man in the 1940s. They were discovered and caught soon after they left Qhawqhat and were severely beaten and humiliated. Some elders said that the convicted couple could have been beaten to death because they had not only committed adultery but had also abandoned their parents, families, and relatives. Despite the potential risk of life in failing, two more incidents of elopement took place in Qhawqhat in the late 1940s, and both succeeded. In the first case, the husband ran away because his wife was rumored to have the dangerous spirit. In the second case, a woman in an arranged marriage eloped with an unmarried young man.

According to Qhawqhat elders, running away from their village (including elopement) was rarely heard of before the late 1930s. Indeed, it was extremely difficult for most Lahu villagers in Lancang to survive if they suddenly decided to run away from their villages because they were then detached from their kinship networks, land, and cattle. Nevertheless, heavy taxes and military conscription in the 1940s forced the members of some households to run away from their home villages after selling all their land in a futile effort to pay back the local loan sharks. According to my retrospective surveys in a Qhawqhat village that had only thirty-two households in 1947, three households escaped between 1947 and 1949. Villagers were sympathetic to those escapees because they were experiencing similar economic and military pressures. Along with the large numbers of political and economic escapes, the incidence of elopement also increased.

The drastic increase in Lahu interactions with outsiders since the 1940s also lessened the isolation of the Lahu villagers, enhancing the possibility of reestablishing life in other Lahu areas. Many of the escapees from Qhawqhat were later said to have settled in an area of Lancang County that is adjacent to Myanmar (Burma). Since this area was very sparsely populated and the forest was abundant, it was not very difficult for newcomers to receive permission from a village to use their surrounding land for slash-and-burn cultivation. Some newly established villages in this area particularly welcomed the newcomers in order to increase the village population as a defense against the threats from organized robbers in the 1940s that resulted from social instability at the end of the ROC (Republic of China) regime. To add to the ease of the newcomers' resettlement, the heads of those villages even lent them seed without interest. The highly increased survival chances in a new Lahu area also encouraged and provided opportunities for some Lahu villagers who strongly intended to escape from their dysfunctional marriages.

During the Mao era (1949–1976), however, running away again became extremely difficult and risky for Lahu villagers, and I recorded not a single case of successful elopement in the Qhawqhat village cluster. During this period, the jewel in the crown of Chinese state control was the household registration system, which recorded each person by household and provided a means of monitoring political activities. Since no one could change the location of his or her household registration without authorization, physical mobility was severely limited. While the strict household registration system made internal migration within the China extremely difficult, attempting to cross into Burma without state permission could result in being imprisoned on a charge of treason.[4] During the Cultural Revolution, the roads into and out of most Lahu villages were guarded by the civil militia (made up of local villagers), and the major roads crossing the border were guarded by the People's Liberation Army (PLA). Those who were caught escaping, especially those who bore "bad class labels," were sent back to the village, where they were forced to work during the day and receive "criticism," often involving verbal and physical abuse, during the evening. Among the many Qhawqhat villagers who attempted to escape were two pairs of illicit couples from the First Production Team of Qhawqhat Brigade who attempted to elope to Burma in 1970 but were caught and punished. In general, the extreme state control over the population prevented some villagers from eloping during this period.

Since the state relaxed its policies in the 1980s, the incidents of elopement in Lancang have increased drastically. In the Qhawqhat village cluster, I recorded fifty-three women who secretly "ran away" from the village between 1986 and 1996. Of these fifty-three women, fifteen of them ran away to escape a difficult marriage. For instance, Siq Mei ran away in 1990 (when she was twenty-two) after failing to divorce her husband, who was addicted to gambling and ran their household into deep debt. In several cases, the wife ran away with some unmarried female peers after quarreling with her husband.

The radical increase in the number of individuals who have run away from Lahu villages since the 1980s resulted mainly from the development of a commodity economy, which undermined the household registration system and dramatically increased the opportunity for physical mobility. More and more Lahu men have begun to work as contract laborers and as traders outside the villages. Most of these activities are limited to the Lahu area: Lancang County, Menglian County, and the adjacent areas in Myanmar. The mobility of Lahu women, however, is oriented mainly towards the rural Han areas outside Yunnan province, mainly in northern and northeast China, such as Henan, Jiangsu, Guangdong, and Shandong. Since the 1980s, women have become desirable commodity in the "marriage market" in China (Anagnost 1997:135). Many Lahu women who "ran away" were actually abducted by underground traffickers (Fang 1998). Many of these women were sold, explicitly or implicitly, to be wives to the male Han peasants who were unable to afford the inflated bride-prices in these areas.

LOVE(-PACT) SUICIDES

When divorce and elopement are impossible, death seems to be the last option for those who are determined to break up undesirable marriages. Such individuals choose to end their marriage through suicide rather than by passively waiting for natural deaths or aggressively murdering their spouses, a phenomenon that is absent in both Lahu oral literature and the social memories of all the village clusters I visited. In most cases, together with their star-crossed lovers, many committed so-called "love-pact suicide."

Love-pact suicide constitutes a popular motif in Lahu oral literature. In the widespread Lahu folk stories and songs, love-pact suicide is typically depicted as a tragic solution for two unmarried lovers torn between their devoted affection and insurmountable parental objection to their marriage (Gen 1997:169; Wang and He 1999:310). Despite the popularity of love-pact suicide stories, it was extremely rare for Lahu villagers act out such drama in real life before the 1950s. The only Lahu elder I interviewed in all the Lahu village clusters I visited who could recall a single case of love-pact suicide prior to 1950 was Cal Chid, the oldest Qhawqhat resident (ninety-seven years old in 1996).

Since 1950, however, love-pact suicide has plagued many rural Lahu who reside on the west side of the Lancang River in southwest China. The number of victims of love-pact suicides was so large during the later half of the twentieth century that villagers tended to respond to my retrospective surveys by the phrase "[there were] too many to recall." After many failed attempts, I had to change my strategy from conducting surveys on a village cluster as a whole to focusing on one production team (village) at a time. The results of my surveys and interviews in Qhawqhat, one of the village clusters in Lancang where suicide rates were extremely high, showed seventy-two deaths resulting from love-pact suicides between 1950 and 1996. The number of incidents was astoundingly high considering that the average population of Qhawqhat during this period was only around 2,000. Of all the victims, only one couple were both single when they committed suicide. For the illicit couples, love-pact suicide was believed to be the best means, if not the only viable one, to end their marriages in order to legitimize their attachment in the afterlife.

My research suggests that the outbreak of love-pact suicides resulted mainly from a clash between Lahu values and institutions and radical social changes introduced by state policies since 1949. As discussed in the previous section, the practice of collectivism and the political upheavals during the Mao era greatly undermined the indigenous institutions that promote cohesion in husband-wife dyads, resulting in a drastic increase in the number of extramarital affairs. Meanwhile, restrictions on divorce and the punishment of those involved in illicit relationships were both increased, thereby trapping many Lahu youth in fatal dilemmas. Corresponding to its high rate of love-pact suicides, Qhawqhat is among the Lahu Na village clusters in which tradition clashed most strongly with state policies during the Mao era. In such places, the Lahu traditions were very strict in maintaining marital stability, and the implementation of state policies was in full force.

The story of the Qhawqhat villagers San Mei and Li Shif, who committed love-pact suicide in 1975 (both were in their mid-twenties), exemplifies the impact of state policies during the Mao era. According to some of San Mei's old friends, before San Mei's marriage, she was deeply in love with Cal Thawd, whose father was a "landlord," a negative label designating someone as a class enemy of the state. Some Qhawqhat cadres vetoed their marriage proposal because San Mei's family was classified as "poor peasants," a class label considered progressive in the political rhetoric of the Mao era. Eventually, San Mei gave in and unhappily married another Qhawqhat man with a "good" class background. Heartbroken after San Mei's marriage and unwilling to endure discrimination resulting from the class label of his family, Cal Thawd risked his life and succeeded in escaping to Myanmar. Several years later, San Mei began to develop a close relationship with Li Shif when they joined the intensive project to build roads for Qhawqhat. As with most other victims of love-pact suicides in Qhawqhat, they committed suicide when some people began to suspect their relationship. Upon their deaths, some villagers suspected that San Mei used Li Shif as a substitute for Cal Thawd, expressing her regret for having given up their commitment under social pressures.

During the period of the clash between Lahu traditions and the radical social changes imposed by state policies, the popularity of love-pact suicide in Lahu oral literature served as a powerful catalyst for the outbreaks of love-pact suicide. According to the confidences of some Lahu whose close friends or lovers had committed suicide, many star-crossed lovers sang love-pact suicide songs to each other outside the village at night, typically accompanied by their peers who sat in front of a bonfire that separated the group by sex. The singing provided the lovers with highly emotionally and aesthetically charged experiences in making such life-and-death decisions. When singing such songs, some singers not only strengthened their faith in the world of the dead as depicted in Lahu traditions, but also romanticized a religious reality far beyond that represented in normative beliefs. For instance, in stark contrast to the constant food shortage during the period of collectivism, the world of the dead was described as a place where each ear of grain was "as long as a horse tail" and the action of committing suicide became "going to Xeul Sha's world of plenty" (Du 1995:214). Some extremely powerful singing sessions created a Siren effect that lured some sympathetic friends to commit collective suicide with the star-crossed lovers (Du 1995:207).

The rich Lahu oral literature has convinced many youths that they can achieve their dream marriages and live a more abundant life in the world of the dead, forming a stark contrast to Romeo and Juliet, whose suicides resulted from misunderstanding and despair. Bearing such an optimistic anticipation of a romantic and abundant future, the Lahu "victims" of love-pact suicides typically interacted with their relatives in a positive manner prior to their deaths. Many villagers recalled that most of them conducted some good deeds—such as collecting extra firewood and giving small gifts—for their respective families before committing suicide (Du 1995:215). According to the confidences of some surviving close friends, many illicit lovers acted in such a way to express their affection to their close relatives and to apologize for abandoning worldly responsibilities in exchange for their own happiness in the afterlife.

Despite the overall amicable attitudes of those who committed love-pact suicides, dominant public opinion harshly condemns them because most of them used death to terminate their marriages in favor of illicit relationships. To express their anger and revenge for the enormous shame and hurt brought upon them, relatives tended to bury such victims separately, preventing them from fulfilling their dream marriage in the world of the dead. In some cases, the relatives even threw thorns into the crude grave before casting down the corpse. According to many Lahu villagers I interviewed, especially the elders, such treatment served to simultaneously punish the illicit couples in the afterlife and to warn the young witnesses who may have secretly intended to follow their example.

Paradoxically, the victims of love-pact suicides seem to reinforce the Lahu gender ideal as much as they challenge it. On the one hand, they abandon the ideal by failing to fulfill even the minimal social expectations for a marriage, i.e., sustaining its formal stability until the natural death of one spouse, regardless of its disharmony or even dysfunction. On the other hand, however, by giving up their lives in the faith that they can achieve perfect marriages in the world of the dead, they passionately dedicate themselves to the full realization of the dyadic ideal within the framework of Lahu cosmology.

CONCLUSION

The degree to which the dyadic gender ideal is realized in Lahu lives depends mainly on the endurance, stability, and harmony of individual marriages.

Recognizing the gap between ideal and practice, many Lahu indigenous traditions found in Lahu Na areas such as Qhawqhat aim to minimize this gap. While categorizing and marginalizing social deviants, institutional strategies to maintain marital stability also include promoting husband-wife cohesion, punishing extramarital relationships, and prohibiting divorce regardless of the quality of the marriages. Despite the enormous coherence of the Lahu institutions and norms in promoting the ideal of husband-wife dyads prior to 1949, some marriages still collapsed and many others sustained great tensions and conflicts. The discrepancy between gender ideals and marital practices increased drastically when radical social changes introduced by the CCP inadvertently undermined the coherence of Lahu gender ideals and family structures. Marital conflicts in many Lahu areas reached their peak during the Mao era—when constant political upheavals generated enormous social chaos and at the same time disrupted Lahu traditions most severely—resulting in the outbreak of an "epidemic" of love-pact suicides.

It is interesting that institutionalized gender equality prevails even in the midst of extreme discrepancy between the dyadic gender ideals and their realization in practice. First, gender-blind principles are applied to categorizing, as well as discriminating against, the individuals who deviate from gender norms (the "peculiar"). By the same token, in a given Lahu village cluster, both men and women are subjected to the same forms and degrees of social restrictions on extramarital relations along with punishment if they violate customary law. Regarding forced parental interventions in mate choice, both the authoritarian and the powerless (or even victims) tend to constitute male-female pairs, reflecting generational hierarchy, rather than gender inequality. By committing love-pact suicide, some Lahu men and women jointly sacrificed their lives in order to attain the ideal husband-wife union in the world of the dead, although many of them simultaneously dismantled their marriages in the world of the living.

CONCLUSION

RETHINKING GENDER EQUALITY

IN THE CONCLUDING chapter, I discuss how this study can enhance our understanding of gender equality. I first summarize how gender equality constitutes a basic social reality of the Lahu people in rural Lancang, a phenomenon that disproves the perpetual denials of the existence of gender-egalitarian societies. I then examine the cultural particularity of gender equality by exploring the historical, sociocultural, and environmental factors that foster the development of the Lahu gender system and facilitate its extraordinary congruence and resilience. Finally, I explore several underlying principles of gender equality in a cross-cultural setting.

GENDER EQUALITY AS SOCIAL REALITY

As discussed in the introductory chapter, both academia and popular opinion typically offer either a negative or an ambiguous answer to the basic question, "Is there any gender-egalitarian society on earth?" The denial of—or the difficulty in recognizing—gender-egalitarian societies is rooted in both utopian ideals and double standards for hierarchy and equality, which often turn the notion of the universality of female subordination into a self-fulfilling prophecy. In order to break through the idealistic biases, I define a gender-egalitarian society as one whose dominant ideology, institutions, and social practices value male and female members equally regardless of the roles they play. Only after the removal of various utopian blinders that distort cross-cultural studies can we recognize the existence of gender-egalitarian societies, despite their scarcity and imperfection. The case study of the Lancang Lahu presented in the preceding chapters provides insight into one of these rare societies.

Ideologically, the equal value placed on male and female is deeply rooted in the Lahu dyadic worldview that centers on the concept *awl cie* ('pairs'), which suggests a single entity that is made of two similar yet distinguishable components. Such a worldview cherishes gender equality by uniting male and female into dyads, in which the two sexes are evaluated according to their joint identity rather than being treated as separate social categories. Specifically, Lahu mythology declares that both sexes share an identical human nature and morality, even denying any epistemological predestination of sex difference in reproduction. Congruent with this cosmological order, traditional ideals tend to set identical standards for men and women, blending femininity with masculinity in spirituality, morality, personality, and body aesthetics. The ideological focus on the husband-wife dyad, as expressed by the maxim "Chopsticks only work in pairs," further crystallizes the worldview. After being simultaneously initiated into adulthood through their wedding, a couple is expected to share the same responsibility, authority, and prestige throughout their lives and in the afterlife.

Among many Lahu in rural Lancang, the unitary ideology is still widely realized in gender roles at the beginning of the twenty-first century. Most important, social norms expect a married couple to function as a single labor team that performs a variety of tasks, including domestic and outdoor activities as well as pregnancy, childbirth, and childrearing. While labor sharing leaves little room to develop gender asymmetry, the few gender-specific tasks are not associated with any value differentiation. Likewise, asserting that households and villages are manageable only when a pair of male-female masters rule together, the dyadic ideal also expects a married couple to jointly hold the responsibility and authority of leadership. Despite the drastic erosion of indigenous political structures, husband-wife co-headship is still common at the household level and observable at the levels of the village and the village cluster in a few places.

Significantly, the gender-unitary ideology and role allocations are solidly grounded in the kinship system and interhousehold organization. Beyond practicing bilateral principles that undermine gender discrimination, the Lahu kinship system goes a step further by tracing relatives through husband-wife pairs, thereby providing a married couple with circles of kinship relations that connect them structurally with other couples and individuals. Accordingly, the forms and intensity of interhousehold reciprocity in economic and ritual activities are oriented toward household head couples, empowering men and women as joint social entities.

Of course, the gender system of the Lancang Lahu is by no means perfect, despite the extreme coherence and resilience of the gender-unitary principle in their social life. While disharmony, conflicts, and the dissolution of some marriages challenge the ideal husband-wife dyad, certain traditions that are intended to ensure the stability of marriages, such as arranged marriage and the prohibition against divorce, often cause more problems than they solve. The internal tensions and conflicts of the Lahu gender system have been exacerbated by externally imposed social changes, especially since the 1950s. Nevertheless, institutionalized gender equality still prevails even in the midst of the discrepancy between ideal and practice, manifesting itself especially in the gender blindness of social restrictions and the punishment of deviant behaviors. Most dramatically, responding to the shared oppression caused by the lack of freedom to choose a mate and to divorce, some Lahu men and women have committed love-pact suicide in pairs in order to attain their imagined perfect marriages in the world of the dead.

Despite the gap between ideal and practice, the equality between the two sexes continues to be a basic social reality for most Lahu villagers in rural Lancang in 2002. Shaped by the dyadic worldview expressed by the proverb "Chopsticks only work in pairs," the foreign term "gender equality" is translated into Lahu as "men and women are the same" and is taken as a matter of course. As a real-life example of a gender-egalitarian society, the Lahu gender system enables us to transcend the long-enduring and fruitless debate over the universality of female subordination.

THE CULTURAL PARTICULARITY OF GENDER EQUALITY

From a cross-cultural perspective, it is rare to find that the principle of gender unity exists not just in ideology, but also in practice. Sanday's (1981:59) cross-cultural study of the creation myths of 112 societies found that the gender-origin symbolism of 32 percent of them focuses on couples, revealing the motif of male-female unity. However, in most of these societies, the unitary theme usually serves merely as a symbolic representation of gender relations rather than operating as a congruent motif that dominates ideology, sex roles, and social structures. For example, Sanday found no close correlation between joint gender roles in labor allocation and the motif of gender unity in mythology. Specifically, fathers have close proximity to infants in only 34 percent of the societies where gender-origin symbolism is centered on the couple. In contrast, fathers in 28 percent of such societies have either no close proximity or only rare instances of close proximity to their infants (Sanday 1981:61). More surprisingly, sexually integrated technological activities are found in only 9.1 percent of such societies (Sanday 1981:85).

The extraordinary coherence of Lahu gender unity, especially in rural Lancang, is derived from particular historical, sociocultural, and ecological contexts. Although historical records are too scarce to reveal the roots of such a system, the available information hints at a few contributing factors. According to both written documents (Gen 1997:54; Lei and Liu 1999:24–25) and Lahu oral literature (Cal Yawl 1989:79–81; Liu 1988:97), Lahu ancestors had a long history of practicing hunting and gathering. From a cross-cultural perspective, the hunter-gatherer subsistence pattern is frequently associated with egalitarianism in general and with gender equality in particular (e.g., Begler 1978; Harris 1993:59; Leacock 1983).

The Lahu dyadic worldview is shared, in various forms and to different degrees, by some other ethnic groups who are closely related to the Lahu linguistically and culturally, suggesting some common cultural heritage. Linguistic parallelism, or the tendency to make pairs in language structures, is a common feature of the Tibeto-Burman language family, of which the Lahu language is a subbranch (F. K. Lehman 1999, personal communication). Additionally, strong cultural emphases on pairs tend to be manifested in the worldviews of many ethnic groups closely related to the Lahu such as the Lisu (Durrenberger 1989:35; Klein-Hutheesing 1990:53; Wohnus and Hanks 1965) and the Yi (Liu 2001:273; Mueggler 2001b:154–157).[1] In particular, the Yi metaphor "It takes two legs to walk" (Stevan Harrell 1999, personal communication) greatly resembles the Lahu motto "Chopsticks only work in pairs." Interestingly, rituals that worship male-female ancestors are observed not only among the Lolopo (Yi) (Liu 2001:273; Mueggler 2001b: 158), whose language is particularly close to the Lahu language (Bradley 2001:202; Harrell 2001:7; Mueggler 2001a:14), but also among some other ethnic groups in Southwest China that are linguistically unrelated or remotely related to the Lahu, such as the Bulang (Mu 1999:78–80) and the Zhuang (Wilkerson 1999).

In addition to historical factors, Southeast Asia seems to provide a favorable cultural climate for the Lahu gender system. Although most Lahu people live within the territory of the People's Republic of China, their indigenous traditions bear cultural traits more typical of Southeast Asia than of East Asia. Dominant East Asian traditions are well-known for their gender hierarchy, which is based on Confucianism. In contrast, Southeast Asia is of-

ten considered remarkable for women's high status, although gender ideologies and practice in the region demonstrate great diversity, inconsistency,
ambiguity, and dynamics across cultures as well as in different historical and
politico-economic contexts.[2] Factors considered contributive to women's
high status in the region include swidden cultivation combined with hunting-and-gathering activities (Klein-Hutheesing 1995:76), bilateralism (Karim
1995; Winzeler 1996), wet-rice cultivation, low-density population, and weak
state control (Winzeler 1974, 1996). Until the 1950s, all of these factors applied
to the social lives of the Lahu villagers of Lancang.

Lahu gender equality in rural Lancang stands out even among the societies in southwest China and Southeast Asia that are considered remarkable
for the equal value they place on men and women, such as the Moso (or the
Na), the Kodi, the Javanese, the Balinese, and the Iban.[3] In my opinion, extreme cultural elaboration of gender unity, as well as environmental and sociocultural isolation, seems to explain the extraordinary salience, congruence, and resilience of the institutionalized equality between Lahu men and
women in rural Lancang.

Male-female dyads constitute the overarching theme of Lahu oral literature, which may be considered "Lahu high culture." Passed down from generation to generation, the rich oral tradition powerfully and coherently in-
terweaves origin myths and migration legends with contemporary rituals,
customs, and beliefs (Cal Yawl 1989; Lei and Liu 1995). Until the late 1980s,
singing traditional songs still dominated ritual events, courtship, and entertainment in most Lancang villages. Extreme examples of the aesthetic power generated by such "high culture" can be seen in the fact that some youths
were so enchanted by suicide songs sung by star-crossed lovers that they
committed suicide with them in order to continue enjoying their friendship
and songs in the afterlife (Du 1995:207).

The extreme environmental isolation of the mountainous areas west of
the Lancang River, including Lancang County, contributes greatly to the
ethnic and cultural homogeneity of the Lahu people in general and the congruence and resilience of their gender system in particular. Lahu villages in
the area are typically located in the middle of precipitous mountains and
have poor transportation infrastructures. Until the early 1950s, within the
present-day Lancang County there were only dirt trails, which were impassable even for horses and cattle during the rainy season (Li 1985:79). Meanwhile, difficult road conditions also hindered the connections between Lancang County and the interior of China. For example, it took nearly a month
to travel from Lancang to Kunming, the capital city of Yunnan province (Li

1985:80). Since the mid 1950s, the Chinese government has sponsored large-scale road construction, greatly enhancing connections between Lancang County and its neighboring counties as well as the interior of China. Nevertheless, in the 1990s, most roads in rural Lancang still consisted of "substandard" dirt tracks, which were often impassable for vehicles in the harsh climate (Zhang et al. 1996:302).

The strong determination of Lahu ancestors to maintain their political autonomy and cultural homogeneity greatly reinforced the isolating effect of their natural environment. Beginning in the late eighteenth century, Lahu ancestors raised arms against imperial control more than twenty times, and they usually migrated to more isolated regions after major defeats, resulting in de facto political autonomy at the level of the village cluster until the 1940s.[4] Contrary to the common association between warfare and female subordination in band and village societies (Divale and Harris 1976; Harris 1993:62), Lahu military confrontations with the imperial armies seemed to have indirectly contributed to the society's gender equality by strengthening husband-wife bonds.[5] According to Lahu migration legends, in addition to their major military confrontations with imperial armies, Lahu ancestors also retreated to deep forests from an agricultural region when another ethnic group began to dominate the area.[6] Conforming to the historical defenses for political autonomy and cultural homogeneity, Lahu traditions also discourage interethnic marriages, which remain very rare in most Lahu villages (Lei and Liu 1999:80).

Whereas the Lahu in rural Lancang still retain a high degree of ethnic and cultural homogeneity at the beginning of the twenty-first century, it is obvious that the gender-unitary principle has been greatly weakened since the 1950s and will become more incoherent and less influential in the future. As a result of the political and economic incorporation of Lancang into national and global systems, the isolation and cohesion of Lahu culture and society have been increasingly undermined. For example, with more and more village clusters of Lancang County gaining access to electricity (72 percent in 2000), television and other forms of mass-media entertainment have replaced the singing of Lahu folk songs in rural life. It is unrealistic to expect the Lahu youth who grow up watching Gongfu (Kung-Fu) movies and TV shows such as *Baywatch* to develop a coherent worldview of male-female dyads as illustrated in Lahu origin myths and other oral literature.

Despite the rapid social transformations among the Lahu people, there are still reasons to be optimistic about the endurance of the indigenous core

FIGURE 15 Lahu children enjoy modern entertainment. The group on the left watches television in a private shop. The group on the right pays money to watch a Kung-Fu movie in the video room. Photograph by Shanshan Du

value of gender unity, although in various forms and to different degrees. It is unimaginable that external influences will quickly be able to destroy the institutions and the practice of husband-wife teams and the underlying social structures of the kinship system in Lahu villages. Although fewer and fewer Lahu individuals are able to articulate their "high culture" by singing or reciting origin myths and migration legends, the principle of male-female unity will probably remain a powerful, though subtle, influence in shaping their worldview for a long time to come. After all, it is difficult to rapidly transform what the dominant ideology has portrayed as "natural" for many generations; the difficulty of such a transformation is best illustrated by the continuing influence of gender dichotomy in the dominant Euro-American societies in spite of profound challenges by women's movements. In addition, nurtured by the relaxed ethnic policies since the 1980s, Lahu culture has undergone revivals marked by the return of traditional practices in rural areas and by the increase of ethnic awareness and a passion to preserve their cultural heritage on the part of urban Lahu. Riding on the waves of cultural revivals, the indigenous worldview, especially the dyadic principle, has been both reemphasized and reinvented.

The coherence and resilience of the Lahu gender-unitary motif is rooted in particular sociocultural and ecological contexts; this motif and its by-product of gender equality operate as integral parts of the indigenous culture. In this sense, while many features of Lahu gender equality are very admirable, they are not directly applicable to the practices of other societies. However, Lahu indigenous ideology and institutions in rural Lancang can at least inspire us to explore the diversity of gender equality from a cross-cultural perspective.

THE DIVERSITY OF GENDER EQUALITY

In addition to offering an example of a gender-egalitarian society and speculating about its particular sociocultural and environmental contexts, this study also suggests that equality comes in different forms, which may go beyond feminist utopias. According to its outward manifestations—which include an extreme sociocultural blindness towards sex difference—Lahu gender equality is very close to the so-called "sameness" ideals promoted by some feminist schools (e.g., Beauvoir 1972 [1949]; Ferguson 1993; Fraser 1997). Nevertheless, fundamental differences exist between the core values of the Lahu gender system and those of the major feminist schools that advocate gender-blind values. For example, binding individuals into presumably inseparable husband-wife teams and defining adulthood and prestige according to team achievements, the ideology of gender dyads goes against the grain of individualism, which is the philosophical root of liberal feminism. Likewise, because it is grounded on monogamous marriages and households, the gender equality of Lahu society is at odds with orthodox Marxism, which traces the origin of female subordination to the emergence of private property and monogamous marriage (Engels 1972 [1884]). After all, it is primarily through the institution of marriage that Lahu women contribute and share equally with men in both economic life and the decision-making processes. In addition, the Lahu unitary principle may also be distasteful to some extreme radical feminists who believe that men as a group are the ultimate source of female subordination and who therefore set their hopes for gender equality on promoting separation of the sexes (e.g., Greer 1992; MacKinnon 1987; Radicalesbians 2000:236).

Beyond the contrasts between the Lahu gender system and the ideals of several feminist strands, differences also exist among gender-egalitarian societies, especially in their underlying principles of equality. This phenomenon is much more difficult to recognize than the mere existence of such societies. However, like the significance of comparative studies of gender hierarchy, the comprehension of cultural diversity is also crucial to the understanding of gender equality. After all, while sex differences are universal, societies vary in their local understanding of such differences, in their perceptions of the fundamental relationships between the sexes, and in the symbolic and social significance of such relations. In the remainder of this section, I classify three types of gender attributes—unity, complementarity, and triviality—showing how each may serve as an underlying principle for gender equality. I make such preliminary classifications in order to expand the analytical capacity to recognize the diversity of gender equality, not to attempt to pigeonhole gender-egalitarian societies into a few prototypes.

Let me start with a brief review of the motif of gender unity that I have examined through the example of the Lancang Lahu. Since this motif symbolically and socially emphasizes the joint entities of male and female, the two sexes are bound to each other in value, interest, obligation, authority, and social status. In other words, gender equality is fostered in the unity of the two sexes rather than achieved by a careful distribution of equal power and prestige between male and female. When the unitary motif dominates the ideology and institutions of a society, gender equality is enjoyed as a by-product of male-female unity. Derived from the unitary principle, gender equality is expressed in the form of "same-thus-equal." Specifically, this principle maximizes gender similarities and mutuality by highlighting the entities that are made complete by incorporating both males and females, such as male-female deities, conjugal couples, parents, and parental spirits. Accordingly, while distinguishing men from women and recognizing certain superficial differences between them, such a gender framework minimizes the symbolic and social significance of sex differences. From the unitary perspective, male and female are essentially similar and, therefore, equal. Fairly consistent sociocultural elaboration of gender unity has been recorded among the Andaman Islanders (Ortner 1996; Radcliffe-Brown 1922) and some indigenous Andean groups living in Ecuador (Hamilton 1998) and Bolivia (Harris 1978).

The complementary gender motif—which highlights the mutual dependence and complementarity of male and female—provides a contrasting underlying principle of gender equality. By emphasizing the interdependence between the sexes, this motif identifies men and women as reciprocal partners with shared interests—both benefiting from their harmonious cooperation—rather than as competitors with conflicting interests. Since such a viewpoint considers each sex fully reliant on reciprocity with the other, it attaches equal value to men and to women as well as to the different roles they play. Therefore, when the motif of gender complementarity dominates the ideology and social institutions of a society, gender equality is also manifested.

Rooted in the principle of complementarity, this kind of gender equality is typically expressed in the form of "different-but-equal." In particular, while stressing the reciprocal interdependence of the two sexes, this principle highlights the differences between men and women rather than emphasizing their similarities in a single inseparable unity. While "man" and "woman" constitute two separate social categories in the complementary motif, the different attributes and role assignments of the two sexes are equally valued. Meanwhile, gender relations are characterized by cooperation and reciprocity rather than by competition and opposition. For example, while the people of Onitsha, Nigeria, made clear gender distinctions in both symbolism and social institutions, such distinctions served to maintain and perpetuate the reciprocal system between men and women (Nzegwu 1994). Strong emphasis on gender complementarity is also recorded among peoples such as the Iroquois of North America (Wallace 1969) and the Ashanti of West Africa (Fortes 1950; Sanday 1981:28–33), as well as on the present-day kibbutz communes in Israel (Melford 1996).

Every known society distinguishes "male" from "female," at least biologically and linguistically. However, this fact by no means suggests that gender is universally and uniformly significant, as is commonly assumed in feminist discourse. Contrary to the unitary and complementary motifs—in which gender is salient symbolically and institutionally—the third underlying principle of gender equality is what I call "gender triviality." By "gender triviality" I mean the scarcity and social insignificance of the symbolic elaboration of "men," "women," and their relationships in a given culture. Since gender in this context is insignificant in ideological and social institutions, men and women are similarly considered as individuals and members of a community regardless of their sex difference. By minimizing gender differentiation in both ideological and practical arenas, gender triviality leaves little space for discrimination against the members of either sex. In this sense, gender equality is achieved in the most effortless way, i.e., simply by ignoring gender itself. Based on the principle of gender triviality, gender equality manifests itself in the form of "same-thus-equal"—i.e., men and women are equal because of the gender-blind attitudes of dominant ideologies and institutions.

Whereas gender triviality and the motif of gender unity similarly foster gender equality in the form of cultural indifference to sex differences, they weigh the significance of gender differently. Specifically, in contrast to the societies that have little symbolic and social elaboration of the relationships between men and women, gender constitutes the source of core symbolism in societies that are dominated by the unitary motif. Examples of a few egalitarian societies that trivialize gender and, correspondingly, glorify individual autonomy and collective cooperation, will serve to clarify this distinction. The first example is the Vanatinai islanders of New Guinea (Lepowsky 1993). The ideological insignificance of gender manifests itself in their ideal personalities, which promote characteristics of individual autonomy (such as strength, wisdom, and magical power) and those that enhance communal solidarity (such as sharing, generosity, and nurturing) (Lepowsky 1993:116, 119, 283). The ideological triviality of gender is reflected in the overlapping of sex roles. Most significantly, while individuals who possess desirable characteristics often attain prestige as "big men" or "big women" through their extraordinary hard work and generosity, there is a high degree of tolerance of idiosyncrasy and variation among all members of the society. Structurally, the Vanatinai matrilineal system is counterbalanced by other gender-blind institutions such as the bilocal pattern of postmarital residence, which obligates a married couple to live alternately with their two natal families for many years (Lepowsky 1993:47).

A similar unelaborated gender ideology (Barry Hewlett 2000, personal communication) and ethical orientation toward collectively grounded individualism (Hewlett 1991) mark the Aka of the Western Congo. The core values of the Aka include individual equality, independence, and autonomy as well as sharing and cooperation (Hewlett 1991:27–28). Both men and women regularly participate in net hunting and in intensive and intimate infant care. The depth of this society's patrilineage is remarkably shallow, corresponding to weak lineage identity (Hewlett 1991:22) and close relations between a married couple and their relatives from both sides. The overall gender triviality is also observed in the traditional lifestyles of some other hunting-and-gathering societies. As Leacock (1978:247–248) points out, in many band societies, male and female are "autonomous" but "equal" in decision-making and hold "separate" but "equal" tasks.

Therefore, not only do gender-egalitarian societies exist, they also differ in their underlying principles of gender equality. Such differences are rooted in the diversity of the dominant cultural perceptions of men and women.[7] The case of the Lahu people in rural Lancang and further comparative studies of gender-egalitarian societies can enhance our understanding of the diverse meanings of "gender equality" across cultures. Such understanding encourages us to reflect on the goals, challenges, and strategies for promoting gender equality in our own societies.

NOTES

INTRODUCTION

1. The principle of gender dichotomy also prevails in a number of other societies, such as many Islamic cultures (e.g., Delaney 1991; Inhorn 1996) and many groups in highland Papua New Guinea (Herdt 1987, 1993).
2. For reflections on the debate, see Felski (1997), Jaggar (1994), Hekman (1999), Squires (1999, ch. 4), and Weedon (1999).
3. For anthropological studies of women's studies in the 1970s and 1980s, see the review articles by Quinn (1977) and Mukhopadhyay and Higgins (1988). Presuming the universality of female subordination, many studies centered on the search for its universal determinants, which are represented by the presumed common associations between women and nature (Ortner 1996 [1972]) and the domestic sphere of social life (Rosaldo 1974).
4. Sherry Ortner (1996: 175) recognized recently that her earlier work had overemphasized menstruation taboos and wrote that "it was fair to view them [the Andaman Islanders] as egalitarian, despite the presence of certain items of special male privilege and authority."
5. For discussions on inconsistency between dominant ideologies and institutions of female subordination and social practices in imperial China, see Ebrey (1984), Ko (1994), McMahon (1994), and Watson (1986, 1991).
6. Although I use the term "sex" to focus on some universal features, I by no means deny particularities and transformation. Specifically, I recognize the existence of ambiguities between the sexes (e.g., Butler 1990; Fausto-Sterling 2000; Herdt 1993), the potential for great diversity among members of the same sex, and the dynamics of sex difference in both individual life spans and human evolutionary history (Tarli, Borgognini, and Repetto 1997; Zihlman 1997). My use of "gender" includes only dual genders because it reflects the Lahu indigenous concept and the theoretical focus of this book. I do ac-

knowledge that some societies indeed recognize ambiguity or multiplicity genders, such as the *hijira* of India (Nanda 1990), the *berdatche* and women-men among American Indians (Blackwood 1984; Roscoe 1993), as well as the third gender in Papua New Guinea (e.g., Herdt 1993; Morris 1994).

7. For criticisms of the dichotomous perceptions of "sex" and "gender," see reviews by Hawkesworth (1997), Morris (1995), Nicholson (1994), Worthman (1995). When in analytical need of a means of emphasizing the multiple layers of biosocial interactions (Worthman 1995), I combine the two terms into "sex/gender," echoing Rubin's (1975:159) "sex/gender system."

8. For examples of ethnic minority groups in China that are more populous and visible than the Lahu, see Grunfeld (1996) and Shakya (1999) for the Tibetans, Gladney (1998) for the Hui, Schein (2000) for the Miao, Rudelson (1997) for the Uyghur, Litzinger (2000) for the Yiao as well as Harrell (2001a) and Mueggler (2001a) for the Yi. For recent studies on the perceptions of ethnic minorities in muliethnic regions of China, see Blum (2001) and Harrell (2001b).

9. For more details on Lahu religions and external influences, see Du (1996); Lei and Liu (1999, ch. 3); Walker (1995); Wang and He (1999, ch. 7).

10. This statement is based on my own fieldwork experiences and on publications in Chinese and English as well as personal communications with some Lahu specialists.

11. In sharp contrast to the corruption and cruelty in Banlo, I observed and heard many touching stories in other villages I visited about the warm-heartedness and selflessness of both villagers and local officials in helping each other during the disaster.

1. "EVERYTHING COMES IN PAIRS": A DYADIC WORLDVIEW

1. For studies of the diverse cultural manifestations of dualism, see Errington (1987) for mythology; Cunningham (1964) and Bourdieu (1990 [1980]) for the "house," Almagor (1989) for moieties, and Fox (1989) and Lancy and Strathern (1981) for languages.

2. Situated at the two ends of the spectrum in perceiving pairing relationships, the dichotomous and the dyadic frameworks also occupy the two extremes on the continuum of academic visibility. Not only does the dichotomous principle provide foundations for formal logic, but it is also universalized by some scholars as the unconscious structure of human mentality, presumably being projected in various cultural forms across human societies

(Levi-Strauss 1963). In contrast, the dyadic principle has drawn little scholarly attention, much of which is discussed under the category of "complementarity." Among many anthropological studies of dualism, the dyadic principle has drawn little theoretical attention although it has been recorded as prevailing in societies such as the Laymis of Bolivia (Harris 1978:24), the Balinese (Belo 1949:14; Geertz 1973:417–418), the Wana (Atkinson 1990: 65), and the Meratus (Tsing 1990:101) of Indonesia.

3. My data on Lahu oral literature derive both from my own fieldwork collections and from publications. Unless I specify improvisations, the verses I quote are those that are widespread in Lancang County and are considered to be traditional styles.

4. Lahu language does not distinguish gender in its pronouns—*yawd* refers both to "she" and "he." In Chinese translations, Xeul Sha is most frequently translated as "he" when distinction is needed. Sometimes, the author may use both "she" and "he" when referring to the same person on the same page without any explanation. In my writing, as a substitute for the English gendered pronoun, I use the paired pronoun—"he-she"/"she-he"—depending on the more or less arbitrary sequence in which the paired entities are named. For the sake of simplicity, I use the plural forms occasionally.

5. The depiction of the male twin as physically stronger is consistent with the popular Lahu notion that men are typically stronger than women. Although the few verses are closely related to some core Lahu values on characters—diligence, physical strength, and humility—they bear few implications for essentializing gender differences. Some versions of Lahu origin myths link the lack of coordination to a pair of assistants of Xeul Sha, Cal Lawl (male) and Na Lawl (female), thus disassociating Xeul Sha from the only error in creation (Cal Yawl 1989: 8-9). In contrast, some Chinese translations of the Lahu creation myth refer to Xeul Sha as one single male god, not explaining the reason why the earth was created larger than the sky (e.g., Du 1999; Walker 1995:3).

6. I can vividly recall Cal Kheu's strong reactions while pointing out that Xeul Sha was a male-female pair and criticizing some other academic misrepresentations (Hu 1996; Du and Hu 1996) when I began to learn Lahu folklore from him during my first field trip in 1987. While outlining Lahu creation myths, Cal Kheu quoted the verses in some versions that distinguished the identities of Xeul Sha. Cal Kheu's opinions are highly credible owing to his extraordinary mastering of the both the depth and the diversity of Lahu oral literature.

7. While the elders I interviewed all asserted that Xeul Sha was a pair (some specifying their sex identities), most youths said that they did not know and that it did not matter; others suggested that I ask elders. Among the youths who did offer answers, some replied Xeul Sha was one and a few identified Xeul Sha as a male and a female.

8. Jacquetta Hill, personal communications, 1998.

9. Kang is a Lahu measuring unit for volume.

10. Following the same structural patterns, the origin myths detailed how the twins sought advice from Xeul Sha after each accomplishment and received hoes and seeds as well as step-by-step guidance on agricultural skills such as weeding, seasons, and harvesting methods.

11. See Gen (1997:183–185), Liu (1988:114–118), Lei and Liu (1995:156–161), and Walker (1995).

12. The story then goes to tell how Xeul Sha taught them to snare the beasts and trap the birds, followed by many similar plots that are filled with challenges to the human twins and examples of their being helped by Xeul Sha.

13. Trees and bamboo typically coexist in most Lahu areas.

14. The pervasiveness of parallelism is also found in many Tibetan-Burman languages (Lehman 1998, personal communications), such as that of the Yi (Harrell 1998, personal communications).

15. The doubled odd number "seven-seven," together with "three-three" and "nine-nine," is often used as an archaic poetic term to mean 'many', 'countless', and 'innumerable.' My interpretation is that odd numbers, as incomplete entities, possess the potential to expand into a complete pair and for this reason are used to express the concept of 'many.'

2. HUSBAND-WIFE DYADS IN THE LIFE CYCLE

1. For ethnographic examples, see Michael Allen (1998), Herdt (1981), Hogbin (1970), Adams (1992), and Sykes (1996).

2. Since the 1970s, convenient access to plastic containers and bags has dramatically reduced people's use of the traditional lunch box while working in the fields.

3. *Chaw mawd* (*chaw* means 'person', *mawd* means 'elder', 'old', or 'senior') is among the most significant and complicated Lahu concepts. Referring to a part of the life cycle, *chaw mawd* means members who are in the stage that begins at one's marriage and reaches beyond death. As I will discuss in

chapter 5, *chaw mawd* is also used as a kin term, the connotations of which overlap with the meaning that marks stages of life.

4. The celebration of the successful life of deceased elders is also found in many other cultures (Gottlieb 1992).

5. I was told that the deceased parent can also pass a spiritual curse during the ritual to punish a couple who may have mistreated their parents or parents-in-law. This is rare and is not reflected in the term for the ritual.

6. According to some elderly interviewees, some Lahu village clusters or families adopted cremation in order to prevent the heads of their deceased relatives from being taken by the neighboring Wa. The Wa people practiced headhunting before the 1950s and sometimes used the heads of the newly deceased for their sacrifice rituals when they failed to get them from the living.

7. It is worthwhile to note that, compared to the detailed stages of the life cycle in the world of the living, the life cycle in the world of the dead is vague. Even though many Lahu state that recently deceased elders are transformed into infants, the burial ritual symbolically recognizes them as adults in the world of the dead.

8. For example, in the early 1990s, a Qhawqhat couple decided to have two sequential gunshots to announce the death of their seventeen-year-old son, who had been poisoned when spraying pesticides, and many relatives showed up to offer emotional support.

9. Before my departure form Qhawqhat in the summer of 1996, a woman name Na Shi suddenly became acutely sick while working in the field and died a few hours after returning home. Although Na Shi was only a junior adult because none of her three children were married, her mortuary rituals were the same as those for an elder. According to some Qhawqhat villagers, both her family and neighbors respected Na Shi because of her hard work and gentleness and were especially sympathetic to her tragic death at work when her children were either above or close to marriage age. Additionally, her family was economically prosperous enough to arrange a large-scale funeral.

10. This forms sharp contrasts with the common tendency to associate the sexes with opposite attributes, as exemplified by the dominant Euro-American societies (Frye 1996; Jay 1981; Lippa 2002) and by the Han Chinese traditions (Black 1986; Jankowiak 1993:168–169; 2002:365–367).

11. The ethnic groups having beliefs similar to those of the Lahu include the Dai, the Jingpaw (Sang 1983), and the Miao (Wenfeng Gu 1995, personal com-

munication), predominantly in Yunnan and Guizhou. Norma Diamond (1988) examined the Han beliefs about Miao regarding poisoning. According to my discussion with Wenfeng Gu, a Miao ethnographer, similar beliefs are also held by the Miao themselves in both Yunnan and Guizhou.

12. It seems that standards for polite voice level in both Han Chinese and dominant American cultures are far above what is considered "gentle" among the Lahu.

13. In order to highlight the attractiveness of the partner, a man or woman may debase him- or herself using such phrases as "my body is as a short palm tree along the river, grows big but not tall, grows crooked rather than straight."

14. According to my own data and communications with Jacquetta Hill.

15. The Lahu denial of the existence of homosexuality seems comparable to that of the Han Chinese in the 1980s (Brownell 1995:230).

3. "HUSBAND AND WIFE DO IT TOGETHER": UNIFYING GENDER IN LABOR

1. See Du (2000) for a review of the conceptual development of the study of the sex/gender allocation of labor. In particular, see Engels (1972:120), Freud (1966), Dinnerstein (1977), Firestone (1970), and O'Brien (1981) for the biologically determined version of "the sexual division of labor," and Murdock and Provost (1973), Brown (1970), Burton and White (1984), Draper (1997), and Hurtado and Hill (1990) for cross-cultural studies of the concept.

2. I collected the texts in Qhawqhat, yet some singers told me that similar expressions were widespread in the Lancang area.

3. The Lahu seem to round the typical nine months of pregnancy up to a ten-month period due to the lunar calendar they traditionally use.

4. My data on postpartum recovery is limited to interviews. For cross-cultural studies on infant care, see DeLoache and Gottlieb (2000), Gottlieb (2000), and Hewlett (1991).

4. "MALE-FEMALE MASTERS": HUSBAND-WIFE DYADS IN LEADERSHIP

1. If the groom is an eldest son of the family and his younger siblings are still unable to work as full laborers, the couple may symbolically live with the bride's parents for three months (sometime even three days) before they move to the groom's parents. Similarly, if the bride's family has a labor

shortage, the couple may live with the bride's parents until some of her younger siblings grow up. In extreme cases, several couples I interviewed in Qhawqhat were obligated to live with the bride's parents for seven or eight years, and most of them moved directly to their new houses afterwards.

2. The altars for village guardian spirits were all destroyed during the Cultural Revolution, and some villages were unable to restore them even when state policies were relaxed in the 1980s.

3. See Barlow (1993, 1994) and Brownell (2002) for theoretical discussions on gender constructions in China. For more in-depth descriptions of the complexity of women's lives in urban and rural China during different periods of the CCP regime, see Bossen (2002), Honig and Hershatter (1988), Jacka (1997), Judd (1994, 2002), Rofel (1999), Stacey (1983), and Wolf (1985). Also see Gladney (1994), Harrell (1995), Litzinger (2000, 2002), and Schein (2000, 2002[1997]) for discussions on the relationships between gender, ethnicity, and the Chinese state.

4. During the period from 1949 to 1995, there was only one female cadre out of a total of 117 individuals who ever held core government posts in Lancang County (Zhang et al. 1996:472–476). Likewise, there was only one female cadre out of the eighty-four individuals holding critical offices of the Party Committee of Lancang County between 1950 and 1995 (Zhang et al. 1996: 425–428).

5. Some elders recalled that Cal Pul read Buddhist scriptures in Chinese during ritual performances. Interestingly, he also wrote Chinese couplets for villagers to post on their doors during the Lahu New Year despite the fact that very few villagers were literate.

6. The beliefs in the special ritual and mystical power of blacksmiths are also found among some other Loloish-speaking groups in China, such as the Jinuo (Du Yuting 1996) and some other ethnic groups in Southeast Asia (F. K. Lehman 1999, personal communication). Similar to the Lahu, the Jinuo also associate the position of blacksmith with male-female pairs. However, rather than holding the position jointly with his earthly wife, a Jinuo leading blacksmith was traditionally initiated into his position by ritually marrying the goddess of blacksmiths, who was believed to fall in love and empower him because of his dreams and extraordinary experiences (Du Yuting 1996:196–205).

7. *Ful* means 'Buddha' or 'Buddhist' and *yiel* means 'grandfather' and is typically used as a form of respectful address for a man of an older generation.

8. In order to achieve a more quantitative comprehension of my informants' emphasis on husband-wife teams in evaluating the merits of potential vil-

lage leaders, I presented some adults of both sexes with a hypothetical grading of each individual of two couples on an imagined numerical scale. The husband of the first couple was graded a full five points and the wife was graded only three points (for a total of eight points). In contrast, the husband of the second couple was graded four points, and the wife had a full five points (for a total of nine points). When asked which couple they would have chosen, all chose the second couple because their overall qualification was higher.

9. As this shows, the officials tend to focus on the celebrity or influence of indigenous leaders rather than on the complexity and meanings of indigenous offices.

10. Inspired by the paired leadership of Fulqhat, I began to ask about household headship, and learned of the system of household co-heads that existed widely in Lancang.

5. UNIFYING GENDER IN KINSHIP AND INTERHOUSEHOLD ORGANIZATION

1. Membership in a double descent group can be designated through either the male or the female. In this case, while both genders appear to be included in the system at large, membership in each group is ultimately designated exclusively through the line of only one gender (e.g., Forde 1950, Gottlieb 1992).

2. Although anthropologists have used many concepts to explore kinship systems in bilateral societies, such systems have remained so fugitive and elusive that many studies shift their analytic focus from kinship to some other institutions. The concepts used to grasp kinship in nonunilineal societies include "nonunilinear" (Davenport 1959), "kindred" (e.g., Freeman 1961; Keesing 1966; Murdock 1964), "cognatic" or "cognation" (Carsten and Hugh-Jones 1995; Kemp and Hüsken 1991; Murdock 1960), "bilaterality" (Lambert 1977), and "kin-set" or "kinship matrix" (Gulliver 1971). Nevertheless, there is a general agreement that the bilateral kinship system is "loosely structured" (Embree 1950; Moerman 1969; Punyodyana 1980), "problematic," or "notoriously elusive" (Carsten and Hugh-Jones 1995). Consequently, attentions shift from kinship to other institutions, including "house" (Bourdieu 1990; Carsten and Hugh-Jones 1995; Cunningham 1964; Lévi-Strauss 1982), the *lignage* (Goody 1983), the "household" (C. Geertz 1960; H. Geertz 1961; Freeman 1970), and/or the "family" (Freeman 1958; H. Geertz 1961;

Goody 1983; Harrell 1997). The Lahu case shows that alternative principles of kinship organization, such as gender unity, may also serve as a coherent principle for effective kinship structures in some bilateral societies.

3. In the case of the wife's MB, the linking parent is the wife's mother. In the case of the husband's MB, the linking parent is the husband's mother.

4. The Lahu emphasis on siblinghood runs along lines similar to those of cultures in Southeast Asia (Kipp 1986; Luong 1984; McKinley 1981), Oceania (Marshall 1981; Smith 1983), and lowland South America (Kensinger 1985). These studies have explored the interactions between sibling relatedness and the principles of descent, affiliation, and affinity (see Ong and Peletz 1995) with the effect of softening the rigid gender dichotomy typically produced in alliance studies.

5. Gulliver (1971:17) originally used the term "kin-set" to define the bilateral kin—both cognatic and affinal—with whom an individual ego bears operational links. I borrow the term "kin-set" because it avoids the confusion caused by the inadequacy of the term "kindred," for which the exclusiveness or inclusiveness of affinal relations has been controversial both semantically and ethnographically (e.g., Freeman 1961; Gulliver 1971; Keesing 1966; Murdock 1964). Differing slightly from Gulliver, I use the term to define the recognized bilateral members of kin—both consanguineous and affinal—of a couple, or dyadic ego.

6. For examples of kinship theorists' concern with the issue, see Needham (1971:18) and Schneider (1981:402).

7. Lahu "mutual help" resembles the reciprocal system (*panganrau*)practiced among the members of the *dangau* family of the Ma'anyan of Borneo (Hudson 1972) and the *togon rojong* reciprocal labor activities in some central Indonesian villages (Koentjaraningrat 1961).

8. Rather than forming an unstable alliance whose solidarity is merely illusorily objectified by the household as an institution (Lévi-Strauss 1987:155), the consanguinity and affinity among the Qhawqhat Lahu strongly consolidate with each other both in category and in interhousehold organization. Unlike some societies whose emphasis on marriage and affines ultimately perpetuates patriliny and thus the principle of gender dichotomy (Dumont 1983; Wilkerson 1995), the consolidation of consanguinity and affinity is fostered by and, in turn, reinforces, the orientation toward the husband-wife dyad in Lahu kinship structure. Most significantly, since Lahu prefer village endogamy, strong affinal bonds reflect an underlying premise that the spouse-taker and the spouse-giver share the labor of the spouse who

moves out of his/her natal household. In this sense, Lahu marriage is fundamentally a system of sharing instead of exchange, which provides a wider base for intense gender unity within a marriage.

9. The lender bears the loss in making the loan because food shortages tend to occur during the months before the harvest, and the grain borrowed at this time is usually dry and light compared to the fresh grain to be returned after the harvest.

10. Qhawqhat elders share memories of the high and accumulative interests in the 1940s, a period when the taxes of the Guomindang government were extremely heavy, and many villagers had to borrow from nonrelatives, even loan sharks.

11. No interhousehold ritual obligation is required for the other lower levels of soul-calling rituals, *ha qho* (offering made to some animist object) and *chaw mawd ned te* (propitiating the spirits of deceased parents and parents-in-law).

12. Household co-heads discuss their labor allocation informally on various occasions, and they often make decisions concerning the next day during the evening meal. Such discussions occur mainly between the head couple, but other adult members may also participate.

6. THE DYSFUNCTION AND COLLAPSE OF GENDER DYADS: DIVORCE, ELOPEMENT, AND LOVE-PACT SUICIDE

1. This incident occurred in the early 1950s, when the village was still surrounded by forest and there were still many wild animals around Lahu villages. According to some elders, tigers and leopards occasionally invaded the village to steal pigs and small cattle. Since 1958, both the forest and the wild animals have disappeared, especially after massive deforestation related to such political campaigns such as "the Great Leap Forward" and "Learn from Dazhai [in Agriculture]" (e.g., Oi 1989:98). Increasing population density has also contributed to rapid deforestation in the area.

2. Following the customary laws, not only had the man stayed in his marriage until my last fieldtrip, but none of the Qhawqhat villagers mentioned this case or any others to me when I solicited examples of their customary laws. I learned of the case unexpectedly, along with the prohibition by Qhawqhat customary laws against revealing convicted cases, when a close friend of mine who came from Qhawqhat and who had witnessed the punishment as a child was commenting on another issue. I was permitted to use the case

in my publications as long as I disguised the identities of the individuals involved.

3. The effects of CCP policies on women's status vary in different domains. The effects concerning Han marriage and the family—the very heart of the subordination of Han women (Jacka 1997; Johnson 1983; Stacey 1983)— seem to be the most unsatisfactory (e.g., Johnson 1983; Stacey 1983; Jankowiak 1993).

4. In contrast to Qhawqhat residents, inhabitants of border villages, who enjoyed both easier geographical exit and more lenient state policies, found escape much easier and less risky.

CONCLUSION

1. In contrast to the Lahu tradition, however, male-dominant ideology as well as patrilineage and patrilocality are observed among the Yi (Harrell 2001b:98–99; Mueggler 2001a:91–92; Hill 2001; Hill and Diehl 2001), the Lisu (Durrenberger 1989:36; Klein-Hutheesing 1990:109, 123), the Akha (or the Hani) (Kammerer 1988, 1998; Hanks 1988; Yang 1992), and some other ethnic groups who are closely related to the Lahu linguistically.

2. See Klein-Hutheesing (1995), Steedly (1999:437–438), Van Esterik (1982), and Winzeler (1996), for descriptions of the high status of women in Southeast Asia. In contrast, see Brenner (1998), Eberhardt (1988), Errington (1990:8), Ong and Peletz (1995), and Tsing (1990) for discussions of the inconsistency, ambiguity, and changes of gender status in the region and in specific cultures.

3. For ethnographic studies on gender among the Moso (or the Na), see Cai (2001) and Zhou (2001). See H. Geertz (1961), Jay (1969), Hatley (1990), Keeler (1990), and Tanner (1974) for studies on the Javanese. For details on the Balinese, see Belo (1949), Boon (1990), Errington (1987), and C. Geertz (1973:56). See Hoskins (1990) for the Kodi and Freeman (1958, 1970, and 1981) for the Iban in Sarawak.

4. Many Lahu elders I interviewed said that their ancestors came to Lancang from Mumie Mimie (the present-day Lincang) many generations ago after being defeated by the imperial armies.

5. Some cross-cultural studies suggest a correlation between a drastic decrease in population and bilocal residence, which allows a couple to live with or near either the husband's or the wife's parents and therefore offers them more relational resources for survival (Ember and Ember 1972; Service

1962:137). Taking the interpretations a step further, survival challenges in rapidly depopulated societies may strengthen the husband-wife bond and promote the centralization of bilateral social networks. In this sense, Lahu depopulation resulting from failed major revolts between the late 1700s and the early 1900s may have contributed to institutionalized gender equality by generating strong husband-wife ties and bilateral social organization. Such a speculation is supported by the association between warfare and gender equality found in some other Southeast Asian societies (Winzeler 1996:162–163).

6. According to some Lahu folklorists and scholars, this area was the present-day Dali, and the people who came into power were the ancestors of the present-day Bai.

7. It is worthwhile noting that, no matter how compelling and central a gender motif is in a given society, it often coexists with competing motifs. For example, as far back as Ancient Greece, Plato's representation of men and women as split halves who desire to reunite into original wholeness (Heilbrun 1973: xiii) provides a splendid portrayal of the model of gender unity that exists alongside the dominant motif of gender dichotomy in Western traditions.

BIBLIOGRAPHY

Adams, Monni. 1992. "Celebrating Women: Girls' Initiation in Canton Boo, Wè/Guéré region, Côte d'Ivoire," *Ethnographie* 110: 81–115.

Agassi, Judith B. 1989. "Theories of Gender Equality: Lessons from the Israeli Kibbutz," *Gender and Society* 1, no. 2: 160–186.

Ahern, Emily M. 1975. "The Power and Pollution of Chinese Women." In Margery Wolf and Roxanne Witke, eds., *Women in Chinese Society*, pp. 193–214. Stanford: Stanford University Press.

Allen, Michael. 1998. "Male Cults Revisited: The Politics of Blood Versus Semen," *Oceania* 68, no. 3: 189–199.

Almagor, Uri. 1989. "The Dialectic of Generation Moieties in an East African Society." In David Maybury-Lewis and Uri Almagor, eds., *The Attraction of Opposites: Thought and Society in the Dualistic Mode*, pp. 143–169. Ann Arbor: University of Michigan Press.

Anagnost, Ann. 1997. *National Past-Times: Narrative, Representation, and Power in Modern China*. Durham: Duke University Press.

Appell, Laura W. R. 1991. "Sex Role Symmetry Among the Rungus of Sabah." In Vinson H. Sutlive, Jr. ed., *Female and Male in Borneo: Contributions and Challenges to Gender Studies*, vol. 1, pp. 1–35. Williamsburg, Va.: Borneo Research Council.

Atkinson, Jane Monnig. 1990. "How Gender Makes a Difference in Wana Society." In Jane Monnig Atkinson and Shelly Errington, eds., *Power and Difference: Gender in Island Southeast Asia*, pp. 59–94. Stanford: Stanford University Press.

Bacdayan, Albert S. 1977. "Mechanistic Cooperation and Sexual Equality Among the Western Bontoc." In Alice Schlegel, ed., *Sexual Stratification: A Cross-Cultural View*. New York: Columbia University Press.

Barlow, Tani E. 1993. "Introduction." In Tani E. Barlow, ed., *Gender Politics in Modern China: Writing and Feminism*. Durham: Duke University Press.

——1994. "Politics and Protocols of *Funü*: (Un)making National Woman." In Christina K. Gilmartin, Gail Hershatter, Lisa Rofel, and Tyrene White, eds., *Engendering China: Women, Culture, and the State*, pp. 339-359. Cambridge: Harvard University Press.

Baxter, Janet. 1997. "Gender Equality and Participation in Housework: A Cross-National Perspective," *Journal of Comparative Family Studies* 28, no. 3: 220–247.

Beauvoir, Simone de. 1972 [1949]. *The Second Sex*. Translated by H. M. Parshley. Harmondsworth: Penguin.

Begler, Elsie B. 1978. "Sex, Status, and Authority in Egalitarian Society," *American Anthropologist* 80: 571–588.

Belo, Jane. 1949. *Bali: Rangda and Barong*. Monographs of the American Ethnographical Society, no. 16. Seattle: University of Washington Press.

Benston, Margaret. 1969. "The Political Economy of Women's Liberation," *Monthly Review* 21, no. 4 (September): 13–27.

Black, Alison H. 1986. "Gender and Cosmology in Chinese Correlative Thinking." In Caroline W. Bynum and Stevan Harrell, eds., *Gender and Religion: On the Complexity of Symbols*. Boston: Beacon Press.

Blackwood, Evelyn. 1984. "Sexuality and Gender in Certain Native American Tribes: The Case of Cross-Gender Females," *Signs* 10: 27–42.

Bleier, Ruth. 1984. *Science and Gender: A Critique of Biology and Its Theories on Women*. New York: Pergamon Press.

Bloch, Maurice and Jonathan Parry. 1982. "Introduction: Death and the Regeneration of Life." In Maurice Bloch and Jonathan Parry, eds., *Death and the Regeneration of Life*, pp. 1–44. Cambridge: Cambridge University Press.

Blum, Susan D. 2001. *Portraits of "Primitives": Ordering Human Kinds in the Chinese Nation*. Lanham: Rowman & Littlefield.

Bock, Philip K. 1987. " 'Neither Two Nor One': Dual Unity in 'The Phoenix and the Turtle,'" *Journal of Psychoanalytic Anthropology* 10, no. 3: 251–267.

Bohannan, Laura. 1952. "A Genealogical Charter," *Africa* 22, no. 4: 301–315.

Boon, James A. 1990. "Balinese Twins Times Two: Gender, Birth Order, and 'Household' in Indonesia/Indo-Europe." In Jane Monnig Atkinson and Shelly Errington, eds., *Power and Difference: Gender in Island Southeast Asia*, pp. 209–233. Stanford: Stanford University Press.

Bossen, Laurel. 2002. *Chinese Women and Rural Development: Sixty Years of Change in Lu Village, Yunnan*. Lanham: Rowman and Littlefield.

Bourdieu, Pierre. 1990 [1980]. The Kabyle House or the World Reversed? In *The Logic of Practice*. Translated by Richard Nice. Stanford: Stanford University Press.

Bradley, David. 2001. "Language Policy for the Yi." In Stevan Harrell, ed., *Perspectives on the Yi of Southwest China*, pp.195–213. Berkeley: University of California Press.

Brenner, Suzanne A. 1998. *Domesticating Desire: Women, Wealth, and Modernity in Java*. Princeton: Princeton University Press.

Brown, Judith K. 1970. "A Note on the Division of Labor by Sex," *American Anthropologist* 72: 1073–1078.

Brownell, Susan. 1995. *Training the Body for China: Sports in the Moral Order of the People's Republic*. Chicago: University of Chicago Press.

——. 2002. "Introduction." In Susan Brownell and Jeffrey N. Wasserstrom, eds. *Chinese Femininities/Chinese Masculinities: A Reader*, pp. 1–41. Berkeley: University of California Press.

Brownmiller, Susan. 1976. *Against Our Will: Men, Women, and Rape*. New York: Bantam.

Bryson, Valerie. 1999. *Feminist Debates: Issues of Theory and Political Practice*. New York: New York University Press.

Buckley, Thomas and Alma Gottlieb. 1988. A Critical Appraisal of Theories of Menstrual Symbolism. In *Blood Magic: The Anthropology of Menstruation*. Berkeley: University of California Press.

Burton, Michael L. and Douglas R. White. 1984. "Sexual Division of Labor in Agriculture," *American Anthropologist* 86, no. 3: 568–583.

Butler, Judith. 1990. *Gender Trouble: Feminism and the Subversion of Identity*. New York: Routledge Press.

Cai, Hua. 2001 [1997]. *A Society Without Fathers or Husbands: The Na of China*. Translated by Asti Hustvedt. New York: Zone Books.

Cal Yawl. 1989. *Ladhol Qameul Lirdaw* [A Collection of Lahu Folksongs]. Edited by Zhiqing Peng and Zheng-fang Liu. Kunming: Yunnan Nationalities Publishing House.

Carsten, Janet and Stephen Hugh-Jones. 1995. Introduction. In *About the House: Lévi-Strauss and Beyond*. Cambridge: Cambridge University Press.

Chafetz, Janet S. 1990. *Gender Equality: An Integrated Theory of Stability and Change*. Newbury Park: Sage Publications.

Chang Hong'en, ed. 1986. *Lahu Yu Jianzhi* [The Concise Annals of the Lahu Language]. Beijing: Nationalities Publishing House.

Chen Jongguang and Li Guanghua, eds. 1986. *Lahuzu Jianshi* [A Concise History of the Lahu]. Kunming: Yunnan People's Publishing House.

Cheng Zhifang, ed. 1983. *Wazu Shehui Lishi Diaocha* [An Investigation of Wa Society and History]. Kunming: People's Publishing House.

Clark, Gracia. 1999. "Mothering, Work, and Gender in Urban Asante Ideology and Practice," *American Anthropologist* 101, no. 4: 717–729.

Collier, J. 1988. *Marriage and Inequality in Classless Societies*. Stanford: Stanford University Press.

Colquhoun, Archibald R. 1970. *Amongst the Shans*. New York: Paragon.

Cunningham, Clark. 1964. "Order in the Antoni House," *Bijdragen tot de Taal-Land- en Volkenkunde* 120: 34–68.

Daly, Mary. 1979. *Gyn/Ecology*. London: The Women's Press.

Davenport, W. 1959. "Nonunilinear Descent and Descent Groups," *American Anthropologist* 61: 557–572.

de Botton, Alain, ed. 1999. *The Essential Plato*. Translated by Benjamin Jowett with M. J. Knight. New York: Quality Paperback Book Club.

Delaney, Carol. 1991. *The Seed and the Soil: Gender and Cosmology in Turkish Village Society*. Berkeley: University of California Press.

DeLoache, Judy S. and Alma Gottlieb. 2000. "If Dr. Spock Were Born in Bali: Raising a World of Babies." In Judy S. DeLoache and Alma Gottlieb, eds., *A World of Babies: Imagined Childcare Guides for Seven Societies*, pp. 1–27. Cambridge: Cambridge University Press.

de Munck, Victor D. and Andrey Korotayev. 1999. "Sexual Equality and Romantic Love: A Reanalysis of Rosenblatt's Study on the Function of Romantic Love," *Cross-Cultural Research* 33, no. 3: 265–277.

Diamond, Norma. 1988. "The Miao and Poison: Interactions on China's Southwest Frontier," *Ethnology* 27, no. 1: 1–25.

Dinnerstein, Dorothy. 1977. *The Mermaid and the Minotaur: Sexual Arrangements and Human Malaise*. New York: Harper Colophon Books.

Divale, William T. and Marvin Harris. 1976. "Population Warfare and the Male Supremacist Complex," *American Anthropologist* 78: 521–538.

Dong, Ai et al., eds. 1995. *Shuangjiang Lahuzu Wazhu Bulangzu Daizu Zizhixianzhi* [The Annals of the Shuangjiang Lahu, Wa, Bulang, and Dai Autonomous County]. Kunming: Yunnan People's Publishing House.

Doucet, Andrea. 1995. "Gender Equality and Gender Differences in Household Work and Parenting," *Women's Studies International Forum* 18, no. 3: 271–284.

Douglas, Marry. 1984 [1966]. *Purity and Danger: An Analysis of the Concepts of Pollution and Taboo*. London: Routledge.

Draper, Patricia. 1997. "Institutional, Evolutionary, and Demographic Contexts of Gender Roles: A Case Study of !Kung Bushmen." In Mary Ellen Morbeck, Alison Galloway, and Adrienne L. Zihlman, eds., *The Evolving Female: A Life-History Perspective.* pp. 220–232. Princeton: Princeton University Press.

Du, Shanshan. 1987. "*Lahuzu de Yinyang Bianzhengguan* [Lahu Yin/Yang Dialectics]." In Yuan Renyuan, ed., *Yunnansheng Shehui Kexueyuan Yanjiusheng Luwunxuan* [A Selection of Papers of the Graduate Students of the Yunnan Academy of Social Sciences], pp. 100–111. Kunming: Yunnan People's Publishing House.

——. 1994. "A Life and Death Ethical Dilemma," *Anthropology Newsletter* 35, no. 2 (February 1994): 2.

——. 1995. "The Aesthetic Axis in the Construction of Emotions and Decisions: Love-Pact Suicide Among the Lahu Na of Southwest China." In Michael Flaherty and Carolyn Ellis, eds., *Social Perspectives on Emotion*, vol. 3, pp. 199–221. Greenwich, Conn.: JAI Press,

——. 1996. "Cosmic and Social Exchanges: Blessings Among the Lahu of Southwest China and the Feast-of-Merit Complex in Highland Southeast Asia." In Cornelia Ann Kammerer and Nicola Tanenbaum, eds., *Merit and Blessing in Mainland Southeast Asia*, pp. 52–78. New Haven: Yale University Southeast Asia Monograph Series.

——. 1999. Review of *Mvuh Hpa Mi Hpa: Creating Heaven, Creating Earth: An Epic Myth of the Lahu People,* edited by Anthony R. Walker. *Crossroads: An Interdisciplinary Journal of Southeast Asia Studies* 12.

——. 1999a. "Gender, Ethnicity, Nature, and Culture in a Socialist State: The Case of the Lahu People of Southwest China." Paper presented at the Annual Meeting of the American Ethnological Society, Portland, March 1999.

——. 2000. " 'Husband and Wife Do It Together': Sex/Gender Allocation of Labor Among the Qhawqhat Lahu of Lancang, Southwest China." *American Anthropologist* 102, no. 3: 520–537.

——. 2001. "Negotiating Buddha's Gender and Marital Status: Syncretized Mahayana Buddhism Among the Lahu of Southwest China." Paper presented at the 100th Annual Meeting of the American Anthropological Association, Washington D. C., November 2001.

Du, Shanshan and Hu Calkheu. 1996. "*Xeulsha Yu Calnu Calpie de Guanxi: Lahu Zhishangshen de Zhangzi Zhangnü* [The Relation between Xeulsha and Calnu Calpei: The Senior Daughter and Son of the Lahu Supreme Parental God]," *Minzu Diaocha Yenjiu* [The Journal for Ethnographic Research] 12: 69–75.

Du Yuting. 1996. *Jinuozu Wenxue Jianshi* [A Brief History of Jinuo Literature]. Kunming: Yunnan Nationalities Publishing House.

Dumont, Louis. 1970. *Homo Hierarchicus*. Chicago: University of Chicago Press.

——. 1983. *Affinity as a Value: Marriage Alliance in South India, with Comparative Essays on Australia*. Chicago: University of Chicago Press.

Durrenberger, Paul E. 1989. *Lisu Religion*. Northern Illinois University Series on Southeast Asia, Occasional Paper, no. 13. Dekalb: Northern Illinois University.

Eberhardt, Nancy. 1988. "Introduction." In Nancy Eberhardt, ed., *Gender, Power, and the Construction of the Moral Order: Studies from the Thai Periphery*. Center for Southeast Asian Studies, Monograph 4, pp. 3–10. Madison: University of Wisconsin.

Ebrey, Patricia. 1984. "Women in the Kinship System of the Southern Sung Upper Class." InRichard W. Guisso and Stanley Johannesen, eds., *Women in China: Current Directions in Historical Scholarship*. Youngstown, N.Y.: Philo Press.

Ember, Carol R. and Melvin Ember. 1972. "The Conditions Favoring Multilocal Residence," *Southwest Journal of Anthropology* 28: 382–400.

Embree, J. F. 1950. "Thailand–A Loosely Structured Social System," *American Anthropologist* 52: 181–193.

Engels, Fredrich. 1972 [1884]. *The Origin of the Family, Private Property and the State*. Translated by Alec West. Edited by Eleanor B. Leacock. New York: International Publishers.

Errington, Shelly. 1987. "Incestuous Twins and the House Societies of Insular Southeast Asia," *Current Anthropology* 2, no. 4: 403–444.

——. 1990. "Recasting Sex, Gender, and Power: A Theoretical and Regional Overview." In Jane Monnig Atkinson and Shelly Errington, eds., *Power and Difference: Gender in Island Southeast Asia*, pp. 1–58. Stanford: Stanford University Press.

Fang, Bay. 1998. "China's Stolen Wives: Thousands Are Abducted and Sold by Traffickers," *U.S. News and World Report*, October 12: 35–38.

Fausto-Sterling, Anne. 2000. *Sexing the Body: Gender Politics and the Construction of Sexuality*. New York: Basic Books.

Felski, Rita. 1997. "The Doxa of Difference," *Signs* 23, no. 1: 1–22.

Ferguson, Kathy. 1993. *The Man Question: Visions of Subjectivity in Feminist Theory*. Berkeley: University of California Press.

Firestone, Shulamith. 1970. *The Dialectic of Sex: The Case for Feminist Revolution*. New York: William Morrow.

Firth, Rosemary. 1995. "A Woman Looks Back on the Anthropology of Women and Feminist Anthropology." In Wazir Jahan Karim, ed., *"Male" and "Female" in Developing Southeast Asia*, pp. 3–10. Oxford: Berg Publishers.

Forde, Daryll. 1950. "Double Descent Among the Yakö." In A. R. Radcliffe-Brown and Daryll Forde, eds., *African Systems of Kinship and Marriage*, pp. 285–332. London: Oxford University Press.

Fortes, Meyer. 1949. *The Web of Kinship Among the Tallensi*. London: Oxford University Press.

——. 1950. "Kinship and Marriage Among the Ashanti." In A. R. Radcliffe-Brown and D. Forde, eds., *African Systems of Kinship and Marriage*, pp. 252–284. London: Oxford University Press.

——. 1958. "Introduction." InJack Goody, ed., *The Developmental Cycle in Domestic Groups*, pp. 1–14. Cambridge: Cambridge University Press.

Fox, James J. 1974. " 'Our Ancestors Spoke in Pairs': Rotinese Views of Language, Dialect, and Code." InRichard Bauman and Joel Sherzer, eds., *Explorations in the Ethnography of Speaking*, pp. 65–85. Cambridge: Cambridge University Press.

——. 1989. "Category and Complement: Binary Ideologies and the Organization of Dualism in East Indonesia." In David Maybury-Lewis and Uri Almagor, eds., *The Attraction of Opposites: Thought and Society in the Dualistic Mode*, pp. 33–56. Ann Arbor: University of Michigan Press.

Fraser, Nancy. 1997. *Justice Interruptus: Critical Reflections on the "Postsocialist" Condition*. New York: Routledge.

Freeman, J. D. 1958. "The Family System of the Iban of Borneo." In Jack Goody, ed., *The Developmental Cycle in Domestic Groups*, pp. 15–52. Cambridge: Cambridge University Press.

——. 1961. "On the Concept of Kindred," *Journal of the Royal Anthropological Institute of Great Britain and Ireland* 91, no. 2: 192–220.

——. 1970. *Report on the Iban*. London: Athlone Press.

——. 1981. "Some Reflections on the Nature of Iban Society." Occasional Paper, Research School of Pacific and Asian Studies. Canberra: Australian National University.

Freud, Sigmund. 1966 [1933]. *The Complete Introductory Lectures on Psychoanalysis*. Translated and edited by James Strachey. New York: W. W. Norton.

Frye, Marilyn. 1996. "The Necessity of Difference: Constructing a Positive Category of Women," *Signs* 21, no. 4: 991–1010.

Fulop, Naomi. 1986. "Sociobiology, Social Policy, and Sexual Equality: The Kibbutz as a Test Case," *Critical Social Policy* 6, no. 1: 91–103.

Gan Sizhen, et al., ed. 1991. *Honghe Xianzhi*. [The Annals of the Honghe County]. Kunming: Yunnan People's Publishing House.

Geertz, Clifford. 1960. *The Religion of Java*. Chicago: University of Chicago Press.

———. 1973. Deep Play: Notes on the Balinese Cockfight. In *The Interpretation of Cultures: Selected Essays*. New York: Basic Books.

Geertz, Hildred. 1961. *The Javanese Family: A Study of Kinship and Socialization*. New York: The Free Press.

Gen Xiao. 1997. *Lahu Wenhua Lun* [On Lahu Culture]. Kunming: Yunnan University Press.

Gillogly, Kate. 2000. "Dancing the Night Away: Lisu New Year Celebrations and Ethnic Display." Paper presented at the Annual Meeting of the Association for Asian Studies, San Diego.

Gladney, Dru. 1994. "Representing Nationality in China: Refiguring Majority/Minority Identities." *Journal of Asian Studies* 53, no. 1: 92–123.

———. 1998. *Ethnic Identity in China: The Making of a Muslim Minority Nationality*. Fort Worth, Tex.: Harcourt Brace College Publishers.

Goody, Jack. 1983. *The Development of the Family and Marriage in Europe*. Cambridge: Cambridge University Press.

Gottlieb, Alma. 1986. "Cousin Marriage, Birth Order and Gender: Alliance Models Among the Beng of Ivory Coast," *Man* 21: 697–722.

———. 1990. "Rethinking Female Pollution: The Beng Case (Cote d'Ivoire)." In Peggy R. Sanday and Ruth G. Goodenough, eds., *Beyond the Second Sex: New Directions in the Anthropology of Gender*, pp. 113–138. Philadelphia: University of Pennylvania Press.

———. 1992. "Passion and Putrification: Beng Funerals in Disarray." Paper presented at the 8th Annual Meeting of the Satterthwaite Colloquium on African Ritual and Religion, Satterthwaite, England, April 1992.

———. 2000. "Luring Your Child Into This Life: A Beng Path for Infant Care." In Judy S. DeLoache and Alma Gottlieb, eds., *A World of Babies: Imagined Childcare Guides for Seven Societies*, pp. 55–89. Cambridge: Cambridge University Press.

Greenhalgh, Susan and Jiali Li. 1995. "Engendering Reproductive Policy and Practice in Peasant China: For a Feminist Demography of Reproduction," *Journal of Women in Culture and Society* 20, no. 31: 601–641.

Greer, Germaine. 1971. *The Female Eunuch*. London: Paladin.

———. 1992. "The Backlash Myth," *The New Republic* 207: 20–22.

Griffin, Susan. 1984 [1978]. *Women and Nature: The Roaring Inside Her*. London: Women's Press.

Grunfeld, A. T. 1996. *The Making of Modern Tibet*. Armonk, N.Y.: M. E. Sharpe.

Gullett, Gayle. 2000. *Becoming Citizens: The Emergence and Development of the California Women's Movement, 1880–1911*. Urbana: University of Illinois Press.

Gulliver, P. H. 1971. *Neighbors and Networks: The Idiom of Kinship and Social Action Among the Ndendeuli of Tanzania.* Berkeley: University of California Press.

Haas, Linda. 1990. "Gender Equality and Social Policy: Implications of a Study of Parental Leave in Sweden," *Journal of Family Issues* 11, no. 4: 401–423.

Hamilton, Sarah. 1998. *The Two-Headed Household: Gender and Rural Development in the Ecuadorean Andes.* Pittsburgh: University of Pittsburgh Press.

Hanks, Jane R. 1988. "The Power of Akha Women." In Nancy Eberhardt, ed., *Gender, Power, and the Construction of Moral Order: Studies from the Thai Periphery,* pp. 13–31. Monograph 4. Madison: University of Wisconsin Center for Southeast Asian Studies.

Harrell, Stevan. 1995. "Introduction: Civilizing Projects and the Reaction to Them." In Stevan Harrell, ed., *Cultural Encounters on China's Ethnic Frontiers,* pp. 3–36. Seattle: University of Washington Press.

——. 1997. *Human Families.* Boulder, Colo.: Westview Press.

——. 2001a. "Introduction." In Stevan Harrell, ed., *Perspectives on the Yi of Southwest China,* pp. 1–17. Berkeley: University of California Press.

——. 2001b. *Ways of Being Ethnic in Southwest China.* Seattle: University of Washington Press.

Harris, Marvin. 1993. "The Evolution of Human Gender Hierarchies: A Trial Formulation." In Barbara D. Miller, ed., *Sex and Gender Hierarchies,* pp. 57–79. Cambridge: Cambridge University Press.

Harris, Olivia. 1978. "Complementarity and Conflict: An Andean View of Women and Men." In J. S. La Fontaine, ed., *Sex and Age as Principles of Social Differentiation,* pp. 21–40. London: Academic Press.

Harvey, Edward B., John H. Blakely, and Lorne Tepperman. 1990. "Toward an Index of Gender Equality," *Social Indicators Research* 22: 299–317.

Hatley, Barbara. 1990. "Theatrical Imagery and Gender Ideology in Java." In Jane Monnig Atkinson and Shelly Errington, eds., *Power and Difference: Gender in Island Southeast Asia,* pp.177–207. Stanford: Stanford University Press.

Hawkesworth, Mary. 1997. "Confounding Gender," *Signs* 22, no. 31: 650–685.

Hayden, B., M. Deal, A. Cannon and J. Casey. 1986. "Ecological Determinants of Women's Status Among Hunter/Gatherers," *Human Evolution* 1, no. 5: 449–474.

Heberer, Thomas. 1989. *China and its National Minorities: Autonomy or Assimilation?* Armonk, N.Y.: M. E. Sharp.

Heilbrun, Carolyn G. 1973. *Toward a Recognition of Androgyny.* New York: Alfred A. Knopf.

Hekman, Susan J. 1999. *The Future of Differences: Truth and Method in Feminist Theory*. Cambridge: Polity Press.

Herdt, Gilbert H. 1987. *Guardians of the Flutes: Idioms of Masculinity*. New York: McGraw-Hill.

———. 1993. "Introduction: Third Sexes and Third Genders." In Gilbert H. Herdt, ed., *Third Sex Third Gender: Beyond Sexual Dimorphism in Culture and History*, pp. 21–81. New York: Zone Books.

Hewlett, Barry S. 1991. *Intimate Fathers: The Nature and Context of Aka Pygmy Paternal Infant Care*. Ann Arbor: University of Michigan Press.

Hill, Ann M. 1998. *Merchants and Migrants: Ethnicity and Trade Among the Yunnanese Chinese in Southeast Asia*. Yale Southeast Asian Studies Monograph, no. 47. New Haven: Yale University.

———. 2001. "Captives, Kin, and Slaves in Xiao Liangshan." *The Journal of Asian Studies* 60, no. 4: 1033–1049.

Hill, Ann M. and Eric Diehl. 2001. "A Comparative Approach to Lineages Among the Xiao Liangshan Nuosu and Han." In Stevan Harrell, ed., *Perspectives on the Yi of Southwest China*, pp.51–67. Berkeley: University of California Press.

Hill, Jacquetta. 1985. "The Household as the Center of Life Among the Lahu Shehleh of Northern Thailand." In K. Aoi, K. Morioka, and J. Suginohara, eds., *Family and Community Changes in East Asia*, pp. 504–525. Tokyo: Japan Sociological Society.

Ho, David Y. F. 1987. "Fatherhood in Chinese Culture." In Michael E. Lamb, ed., *The Father's Role: Cross-Cultural Perspectives*, pp. 227–245. Hillsdale, N.J.: Erlbaum.

Hogbin, Ian. 1970. *The Island of Menstruating Men: Religion in Wogeo, New Guinea*. Prospect Heights, Ill.: Waveland Press.

Honig, Emily and Gail Hershatter. 1988. *Personal Voices: Chinese Women in the 1980s*. Stanford: Stanford University Press.

Hoskins, Janet. 1990. "Doubling Deities, Descent, and Personhood: An Exploration of Kodi Gender Categories." In Jane Monnig Atkinson and Shelly Errington, eds., *Power and Difference: Gender in Island Southeast Asia*, pp. 273–306. Stanford: Stanford University Press.

Hu Calkheu. 1991. *Lahuzu Zucheng he Lahuzu Liangda Zhixi de Laili Kaozheng Lunshu* [A Discussion on the Lahu Ethnonym and the Origins of the Two Major Lahu Branches]. Presented in the Seminar on Lahu History, Lancang.

———. 1996. *Xeu Sha de Zhangzi Zhangnü* [The Senior Daughter and Son of Xeul Sha]. *Minzu Diaocha Yenjiu* [The Journal of Ethnographic Researches] 12: 64–68.

Hudson, Alfred B. 1972. *Padju Epat: The Ma'anyan of Indonesian Borneo*. New York: Holt, Rinehart and Winston.

Hurtado, Magdalena A. and Kim R. Hill. 1990. "Seasonality in a Foraging Society: Variation in Diet, Work Effort, Fertility, and Sexual Division of Labor Among the Hiwi of Venezuela," *Journal of Anthropological Research* 46, no. 3: 293–346.

Imray, Linda and Audrey Middleton. 1983. "Public and Private: Making Boundaries," In Eva Gamarnikow, David Morgan, June Purvis, and Daphne Taylorson, eds., *The Public and the Private*, pp.12–28. London: Heinemann.

Inhorn, Marcia C. 1996. *Infertility and Patriarchy: The Culture and Politics of Gender and Family Life in Egypt*. Philadelphia: University of Pennsylvania Press.

Jacka, Tamara. 1997. *Women's Work in Rural China: Change and Continuity in an Era of Reform*. Cambridge: Cambridge University Press.

Jaggar, Alison M. 1983. *Feminist Politics and Human Nature*. Lanham, Md.: Rowman and Littlefield.

——. 1994. "Sexual Difference and Sexual Equality." In *Living with Contradictions: Controversies in Feminist Social Ethics*, pp. 18–27. Boulder, Colo.: Westview Press.

Jankowiak, William. 1992. "Father-Child Relations in Urban China." In Barry S. Hewlett, ed., *Father-Child Relations: Cultural and Biosocial Contexts*, pp. 345–363. New York: Aldine De Gruyter.

——. 1993. *Sex, Death, and Hierarchy in a Chinese City: An Anthropological Account*. New York: Columbia University Press.

——. 2002. "Proper Men and Proper Women: Parental Affection in the Chinese Family." In Susan Brownell and Jeffrey N. Wasserstrom, eds., *Chinese Femininities/Chinese Masculinities: A Reader*, pp. 361–383. Berkeley: University of California Press.

Jay, Nancy. 1981. "Gender and Dichotomy," *Feminist Studies* 7, no. 1: 39–56.

——. 1992. *Throughout Your Generations Forever: Sacrifice, Religion, and Paternity*. Chicago: University of Chicago Press.

Jay, Robert R. 1969. *Javanese Villagers*. Cambridge: MIT Press.

Johnson, Kay Ann. 1983. *Women, the Family, and the Peasant Revolution in China*. Chicago: University of Chicago Press.

Jordan, Brigitte. 1993. *Birth in Four Cultures*, 4th. ed. Prospect Heights, Ill.: Waveland Press.

Judd, Ellen. 1994. *Gender and Power in Rural North China*. Stanford: Stanford University Press.

——. 2002. *The Chinese Women's Movement Between State and Market*. Stanford: Stanford University Press.

Kammerer, Cornelia A. 1988. "Shifting Gender Asymmetry Among the Akha of Northern Thailand." In Nancy Eberhardt, ed., *Gender, Power, and the Construction of Moral Order: Studies from the Thai Periphery*. Center for Southeast Asian Studies Monograph 4, pp. 53–71. Madison: University of Wisconsin.

——. 1998. "Descent, Alliance, and Political Order Among the Akha," *American Ethnologist* 25, no.4: 659–674.

Karim, Wazir J. 1995. "Bilateralism and Gender in Southeast Asia." In Wazir J. Karim, ed., *"Male" and "Female" in Developing Southeast Asia*, pp. 35–74. Oxford: Berg Publishers.

Keeler, Ward. 1990. "Speaking of Gender in Java." In Jane Monnig Atkinson and Shelly Errington, eds., *Power and Difference: Gender in Island Southeast Asia*, pp. 127–152. Stanford: Stanford University Press.

Keesing, R. 1966. "Kwaio Kindreds," *Southwestern Journal of Anthropology* 22: 346–353.

Kemp, Jeremy and Frans Hüsken. 1991. "Cognatic Kinship in Southeast Asia." In Jeremy Kemp and Frans Hüsken, eds., *Cognation and Social Organization in Southeast Asia*, pp. 1–14. Leiden: KITLV Press.

Kensinger, K., ed. 1985. "The Sibling Relationship in Lowland South America." Working Papers on South American Indians, no. 7. Bennington, Vt.: Bennington College.

Kipp, R. 1986. "Terms of Endearment: Karo Batak Lovers as Siblings," *American Ethnologist* 13, no. 4: 632–645.

Klein-Hutheesing, Otome. 1990. *Emerging Sexual Inequality Among the Lisu of Northern Thailand: The Waning of Dog and Elephant Repute*. Leiden: E. J. Brill.

——. 1995. "Gender at the Margins of Southeast Asia." In Wazir Jahan Karim, ed., *"Male" and "Female" in Developing Southeast Asia*, pp.75–97. Oxford: Berg Publishers.

Ko, Dorothy. 1994. *Teachers of the Inner Chambers: Women and Culture in Seventeenth-Century China*. Stanford: Stanford University Press.

Koentjaraningrat. 1961. *Some Social-Anthropological Observations on Gotong Rojong Practices in Two Villages of Central Java*. Translated by Claire Holt. Ithaca: Cornell Modern Indonesia Project.

Kopytoff, Igor. 1971. "Ancestors as Elders in Africa," *Africa* 41, no. 2: 128–142.

Krosenbrink-Gelissen, Lilianne. 1993. " 'Traditional Motherhood' in Defense of Sexual Equality Rights for Canada's Aboriginal Women," *Native American Studies* 7, no. 2: 13–16.

——. 1996. "Sexual Equality as an Aboriginal Right: Canada's Aboriginal Women in the Constitutional Process on Aboriginal Matters, 1982–1987," *Law and Philosophy* 8:147–160.

Laderman, Carol . 1983. *Wives and Midwives: Childbirth and Nutrition in Rural Malaysia*. Berkeley: University of California Press.

———. 1991. *Taming the Wind of Desire: Psychology, Medicine, and Aesthetics in Malay Shamanistic Performance*. Berkeley: University of California Press.

Lambert, Berndt. 1977. "Bilaterality in the Andes." In Ralph Bolton and Enrique Mayer, eds., *Andean Kinship and Marriage*. A Special Publication of the American Anthropological Association, no. 7. Washington, D. C.: American Anthropological Association.

Lancy, David F. and Andrew W. Strathern. 1981. " 'Making Twos': Pairing as an Alternative to the Taxonomic Mode of Representation," *American Anthropologist* 83, no. 4: 773–793.

Leacock, Eleanor. 1978. "Women's Status in Egalitarian Society: Implications for Social Evolution," *Cultural Anthropology* 19, no. 2: 247–275.

———. 1983. "Interpreting the Origins of Gender Inequality: Conceptual and Historical Problems," *Dialectical Anthropology* 7:263–284.

Lehman, F. K. 1963. *The Structure of Chinese Society*. Urbana: University of Illinois Press.

———. n.d. "The Relevance of the Founders' Cult for Understanding the Political Systems of the Peoples of Northern Southeast Asia and its Chinese Borderlands." In Cornelia Ann Kammerer and Nicola Tanenbaum, eds., *Founders' Cults*. Southeast Asia Monograph Series. New Haven: Yale University

Lei Bo and Liu Huihao, eds. 1995. *Lahuzu Wenxue Jianshi* [A Concise History of Lahu Literature]. Kunming: Yunnan Nationalities Publishing House.

Lei Bo and Liu Jinrong, eds. 1999. *Lahu Wenhua Daguan* [Perspectives on Lahu Culture]. Kunming: Yunnan Nationalities Publishing House.

Lepowsky, Maria. 1993. *Fruit of the Motherland: Gender in an Egalitarian Society*. New York: Columbia University Press.

Lerner, Gerda. 1993. *The Creation of Feminist Consciousness: From the Middle Ages to 1870*. New York: Oxford University Press.

Lévi-Strauss, Claude. 1963. *Structural Anthropology*. Translated by Claire Jacobson and Brooke Grundfest Schoepf. New York: Basic Books.

———. 1969 [1949]. *The Elementary Structures of Kinship*. Translated by James H. Bell, John R. von Sturmer, and Rodney Needham. Boston: Beacon Press.

———. 1982 [1975]. *The Way of the Masks*. Translated by Sylvia Modelski Seattle: University of Washington Press.

———. 1987. *Anthropology and Myth: Lectures 1951–1982*. Translated by Roy Willis. Oxford: Blackwell.

Lewis, Paul and Elaine Lewis. 1984. *Peoples of the Golden Triangle: Six Tribes in Thailand*. New York: Thames and Hudson.

Li Huiquan and Yang Chen, eds. 1989. *Jiangcheng Hanizuyizu Zizhixianzhi* [The Annals of the Jiangcheng Autonomous County of the Hani and the Yi]. Kunming: Yunnan People's Publishing House.

Lippa, Richard A. 2002. *Gender, Nature, and Nurture.* Mahwah, N. J.: Erlbaum.

Littleton, Christine A. 1994. "Reconstructing Sexual Equality." In Alison M. Jaggar, ed., *Living with Contradictions: Controversies in Feminist Social Ethics,* pp. 28–34. Boulder, Colo.: Westview Press.

Litzinger, Ralph. 2000. *Other Chinas: The Yao and the Politics of National Belonging.* Durham: Duke University Press.

———. 2002. "Tradition and the Gender of Civility." In Susan Brownell and Jeffrey N. Wasserstrom, eds., *Chinese Femininities/Chinese Masculinities: A Reader,* pp. 412-434. Berkeley: University of California Press.

Liu Huihao, ed., 1988. *Lahuzu Minjian Wenxue Jicheng* [A Collection of Lahu Folk Literature]. Beijing: Publishing House for Chinese Folk Art.

Liu, Xiaoxing. 2001. "The Yi Health Care System in Liangshan and Chuxiong." In Stevan Harrell, ed., *Perspectives on the Yi of Southwest China,* pp.1–17. Berkeley: University of California Press.

Luong, H. V. 1984. "'Brother' and 'Uncle': An Analysis of Rules, Structural Contradictions, and Meaning in Vietnamese Kinship," *American Anthropologist* 86, no. 2: 290–315.

Mackerras, Colin. 1994. *China's Minorities: Integration and Modernization in the Twentieth Century.* Hong Kong: Oxford University Press.

MacKinnon, Catharine A. 1987. "A Feminist/Political Approach: Pleasure under Patriarchy." In James H. Geer and William T. O'Donohue, eds., *Theories of Human Sexuality,* pp. 65–90.New York: Plenum Press.

Man, E. H. 1883. "On the Aboriginal Inhabitants of the Andaman Islands." *Journal of the Anthropological Institution* 12, no. 1: 117–175; 12, no. 3: 327–434.

Marshall, Mac, ed. 1981. *Siblingship in Oceania: Studies in the Meaning of Kin Relations.* Ann Arbor: University of Michigan Press.

Matisoff, James A. 1988. *The Dictionary of Lahu.* Berkeley: University of California Press.

Maybury-Lewis, David. 1989. "The Quest for Harmony." In David Maybury-Lewis and Uri Almagor, eds., *The Attraction of Opposites: Thought and Society in the Dualistic Mode,* pp.1–17. Ann Arbor: University of Michigan Press.

McMahon, Keith. 1994. "The Classic 'Beauty-Scholar' Romance and the Superiority of the Talented Woman." In Angel Zito and Tani E. Barlow, eds., *Body, Subject and Power in China,* pp. 227–252. Chicago: University of Chicago Press.

McKinley, Robert L. 1981. "Cain and Abel on the Malay Peninsula." In M. Marshall, ed., *Siblingship in Oceania: Studies in the Meaning of Kin Relations*, pp. 335–387. Ann Arbor: University of Michigan Press.

Mead, Margaret. 1963 [1935]. *Sex and Temperament in Three Primitive Societies*. New York: Morrow.

Meillassoux, C. 1984 [1975]. *Maidens, Meal, and Money: Capitalism and the Domestic Community*. Translated by Felicity Edholm. Cambridge: Cambridge University Press.

Mill, Harriet Taylor. 1970 [1851]. "Enfranchisement of Women." In Alice S. Rossi, ed., *Essays on Sex Equality*, pp. 89–122. Chicago: University of Chicago Press.

Milne, Leslie. 1970. *Shans at Home*. New York: Paragon.

Moerman, Michael. 1969. "The Study of Thai Society: Summary Comments." In Hans-Dieter Evers, ed., *Loosely Structured Social Systems: Thailand in Comparative Perspective*. Cultural Report Series no. 17, pp. 128–132. New Haven: Yale University Southeast Asia Studies.

Morris, Rosalind C. 1994. "Three Sexes and Four Sexualities: Redressing the Discourses on Gender and Sexuality in Contemporary Thailand." *Positions* 2: 15-43.

———. 1995. "All Made Up: Performance Theory and the New Anthropology of Sex and Gender," *Annual Review of Anthropology* 24: 567–592.

Mu Wenchun. 1999. *Bulangzu Wenhua Daguan [A Holistic Perspective on the Bulang]*. Kunming: Yunnan Nationalities Publishing House.

Mueggler, Erik. 2001a. *The Age of Wild Ghosts: Memory, Violence, and Place in Southwest China*. Berkeley: University of California Press.

———. 2001b. "A Valley-House: Remembering a Yi Headmanship." In Stevan Harrell, ed., *Perspectives on the Yi of Southwest China*, pp.144–169. Berkeley: University of California Press.

Mukhopadhyay, Carol C. and Patricia Higgins. 1988. "Anthropological Studies of Women's Status Revisited: 1977–87," *Annual Review of Anthropology* 17: 461–495.

Murdock, George P. 1960. "Cognatic Forms of Social Organization." In George P. Murdock, ed., *Social Structure in Southeast Asia*, pp.1–14. Chicago: Quadrangle Books.

———. 1964. "The Kindred," *American Anthropologist* 66, no. 1: 129–132.

Murdock, George P. and Caterina Provost. 1973. "Factors in the Division of Labor by Sex: A Cross-Cultural Analysis," *Ethnology* 12: 203–225.

Nanda, Serena. 1990. *Neither Man Nor Woman: The Hijras of India*. Belmont, Calif.: Wadsworth Publishing Co.

Needham, Rodney. 1971. "Remarks on the Analysis of Kinship and Marriage." In Rodney Needham, ed., *Rethinking Kinship and Marriage*, pp. 1–19. London: Tavistock Publications.

——. 1973. "Introduction." In Rodney Needham, ed., *Right and Left: Essays on Dual Symbolic Classification*, pp. xi–xxxix. Chicago: University of Chicago Press.

Nicholson, Linda. 1994. "Interpreting Gender," *Signs* 20, no. 11: 79–105.

Nyman, Charlott. 1999. "Gender Equality in 'the Most Equal Country in the World?' Money and Marriage in Sweden," *The Sociological Review* 47, no. 4: 766–793.

Nzegwu, Nkiru. 1994. "Gender Equality in a Dual-Sex System: The Case of Onitsha," *Canadian Journal of Law and Jurisprudence* 7, no. 1: 73–95.

O'Brien, Mary. 1981. *The Politics of Reproduction*. New York: Routledge and Kegan Paul.

Oi, Jean C. 1989. *State and Peasant in Contemporary China: The Political Economy of Village Government*. Berkeley: University of California Press.

Ong, Aihwa and Michael G. Peletz. 1995. "Introduction." In Aihwa Ong and Michael G. Peletz, eds., *Bewitching Women, Pious Men: Gender and Body Politics in Southeast Asia*, pp. 1–18. Berkeley: University of California Press.

Ortner, Sherry. 1996 [1972]. Is Female to Male as Nature Is to Culture? In *Making Gender: The Politics and Erotics of Culture*. Boston: Beacon.

——. 1996 [1990]. Gender Hegemonies. In *Making Gender: The Politics and Erotics of Culture*. Boston: Beacon.

——. 1996. So, Is Female to Male as Nature Is to Culture? In *Making Gender: The Politics and Erotics of Culture*. Boston: Beacon.

Oyewumi, Oyeronke. 1997. *The Invention of Women: Making an African Sense of Western Gender Discourses*. Minneapolis: University of Minnesota Press.

Plath, David and Jacquetta Hill. 1992. *Candles for New Years: The Lahu of Northern Thailand*. Videotape.

Punyodyana, Boonsanong. 1980. "Loosely Structured Social System: A Thai View." In Hans-Dieter Evers, ed., *Sociology of South-east Asia: Readings on Social Change*, pp. 181–98. Kuala Lumpur: Oxford University Press.

Quinn, Naomi. 1977. "Anthropological Studies on Women's Status," *Annual Review of Anthropology* 6: 181–225.

Radcliffe-Brown, A. R. 1922. *The Andaman Islanders*. Cambridge: Cambridge University Press.

——. 1950. "Introduction." In A. R. Radcliffe-Brown and Daryl Forde, eds., *African Systems of Kinship and Marriage*, pp. 1–85. Oxford: Oxford University Press.

Radicalesbians. 2000. "The Women-Identified-Women." In Barbara A. Crow, ed., *Radical Feminism: A Documentary Reader*, pp. 233–237. New York: New York University Press.

Richard, Audrey. 1950. "Some Types of Family Structure Amongst the Central Bantu." In A.R. Radcliffe-Brown and Daryl Forde, eds., *African Systems of Kinship and Marriage*, pp. 207–251. Oxford: Oxford University Press.

Rofel, Lisa. 1999. *Other Modernities: Gendered Yearnings in China After Socialism.* Berkeley: University of California Press.

Roscoe, Will. 1993. "How to Become a Berdache: Toward a Unified Analysis of Gender Diversity." In Gilbert Herdt, ed., *Third Sex Third Gender: Beyond Sexual Dimorphism in Culture and History*, pp. 329–372. New York: Zone Books.

Rosaldo, Michelle Z. 1974. "Woman, Culture, and Society: A Theoretical Overview." In Michelle Z. Rosaldo and Louise Lamphere, eds., *Woman, Culture and Society*, pp. 17–42. Stanford: Stanford University Press.

Rosaldo, Renato. 1989. *Culture and Truth: The Remaking of Cultural History.* Boston: Beacon Press.

Rubin, Gale. 1975. "The Traffic in Women: Notes on the 'Political Economy' of Sex." In Rayna Reiter, ed., *Toward an Anthropology of Women*, pp. 157–210. New York: Monthly Review Press.

Ruddick, Sara. 1989. *Maternal Thinking: Towards a Politics of Peace.* Boston: Beacon Press.

Rudelson, Justin J. 1997. *Oasis Identities: Uyghur Nationalism along China's Silk Road.* New York: Columbia University Press.

Ruf, Gregory A. 1998. *Cadres and Kin: Making a Socialist Village in West China 1921–1991.* Stanford: Stanford University Press.

Sacks, Karen. 1979. *Sisters and Wives: The Past and Future of Sexual Equality.* Westport, Conn.: Greenwood Press.

Sanday, Peggy R. 1981. *Female Power and Male Dominance: On the Origins of Sexual Inequality.* Cambridge: Cambridge University Press.

Sang Yaohua. 1983. *Dehong Mouxie Diqu de "Pipagui" Hai Zai Hai RenPipa* [Spirit Still Harms People in Some Areas of Dehong]. Yanju Jikan [The Collections of Research Essays] 2: 289–296. Kunming: Yunnan Sheng Lishi Yanjusuo.

Sanit Wongsprasert. 1974. "Lahu Agriculture and Society." Ph.D. diss., University of Sydney.

——. 1989. "Opiate of the People? A Case Study of Lahu Opium Addicts." In John McKinnon and Bernard Vienne, eds., *Hill Tribes Today: Problems in Change*, pp. 173–90. Bangkok: White Lotus.

Schein, Louisa. 2000. *Minority Rules: The Miao and the Feminine in China's Cultural Politics.* Durham: Duke University Press.

——. 2002 [1997]. "Gender and Internal Orientalism." In Susan Brownell and Jeffrey N. Wasserstrom, eds., *Chinese Femininities/Chinese Masculinities: A Reader*, pp. 385–411. Berkeley: University of California Press.

Schlegel, Alice. 1972. *Male Dominance and Female Autonomy: Domestic Authority in Matrilineal Societies*. New Haven: HRAF Press.

Schneider, David M. 1961. "The Distinctive Features of Matrilineal Descent Groups." In David M. Schneider and Kathleen Gough, eds., *Matrilineal Kinship*, pp.1–29. Berkeley: University of California Press.

——. 1981. "Conclusions." In Mac Marshall, ed., *Siblingship in Oceania: Studies in the Meaning of Kin Relations*, pp. 389–404. Ann Arbor: University of Michigan Press.

Sered, Susan. 1999. *Women of the Sacred Groves: Divine Priestesses of Okinawa*. New York: Oxford University Press.

Service, Elman R. 1962. *Primitive Social Organization: An Evolutionary Perspective*. New York: Random House.

Shakya, Tsering. 1999. *The Dragon in the Land of Snows: A History of Modern Tibet since 1947*. New York: Columbia University Press.

Shostak, Marjorie. 1981. *Nisa: The Life and Words of a !Kung Woman*. Cambridge: Harvard University Press.

Shwey Yoe. 1901. *The Burman: His Life and Notions*. London: Macmillan.

Siim, Birte. 1987. "The Scandinavian Welfare States–Towards Sexual Equality or a New Kind of Male Dominance?," *Acta Sociologica* 30 , no. 3/4: 255–270.

Smith, D. R. 1983. *Palauan Social Structure*. New Brunswick: Rutgers University Press.

Solanas, Valarie. 2000. "SCUM (Society for Cutting Up Men) Manifesto." In Barbara A. Crow, ed., *Radical Feminism: A Documentary Reader*, pp. 201–222. New York: New York University Press.

Spiro, Melford E. 1996 [1979]. *Gender and Culture: Kibbutz Women Revisited*. New Brunswick: Transaction Publishers.

Squires, Judith. 1999. *Gender in Political Theory*. Cambridge: Polity Press.

Stacey, Judith. 1983. *Patriarchy and Socialist Revolution in China*. Berkeley: University of California Press.

Steedly, Mary M. 1999. "The State of Culture Theory in the Anthropology of Southeast Asia," *Annual Review of Anthropology* 28: 431–454.

Stone, Linda. 1997. *Kinship and Gender: An Introduction*. Boulder, Colo.: Westview Press.

Sykes, Karen. 1996. "Making the Papua New Guinean Women: The Extension of Women's Initiation Process to Secondary Education in Central New Ireland," *Pacific Studies* 19, no. 4: 99–127.

Tanner, Nancy. 1974. "Matrifocality in Indonesia and Africa and Among Black Americans." In Michelle Z. Rosaldo and Louise Lamphere, eds., *Woman, Culture and Society*, pp. 129–156. Stanford: Stanford University Press.

Tarli, Silvana, M. Borgognini, and Elena Repetto. 1997. "Sex Difference in Human Populations: Changes Through Time." In Mary E. Morebeck, Alison Gallaway, and Adrenne L. Zihlman, eds., *The Evolving Female: A Life History Perspective*, pp. 198–208. Princeton: Princeton University Press.

Tsing, Anna Lowenhaupt. 1990. "Gender and Performance in Meratus Dispute Settlement." In Jane Monnig Atkinson and Shelly Errington, eds., *Power and Difference: Gender in Island Southeast Asia*, pp. 95–126. Stanford: Stanford University Press.

Van Esterik, Penny. 1982. "Introduction." In Penny Van Esterik, ed., *Women of Southeast Asia*. Northern Illinois University Series on Southeast Asia, Occasional Paper, no. 9, pp. 1–15. Dekalb: Northern Illinois University.

Walker, Anthony. 1970. *Lahu Nyi (Red Lahu): Village Society and Economy in North Thailand*. Chiang Mai: Tribal Research Center.

———. 1974. "The Division of the Lahu People," *Journal of the Siam Society* 62, no. 1: 1–26.

———. 1992 [1982]. "Lahu Nyi (Red Lahu) Village Officials and Their Ordination Ceremonies." In Anthony R. Walker, ed., *The Highland Heritage: Collected Essays on Upland Northern Thailand*, pp. 265–292. Singapore: Suvarnabhumi Books.

———. 1986. "Transformations of Buddhism in the Religious Ideas and Practices of a Non-Buddhist Hill People: The Lahu Nyi of the Northern Thai Uplands," *Contributions to Southeast Asian Ethnography* 5: 65–91.

———. 1992. "Opium: Its Production and Use in a Lahu Nyi (Red Lahu) Village Community." In Anthony R. Walker, ed., *The Highland Heritage: Collected Essays on Upland North Thailand*, pp. 111–144. Singapore: Suvarnabhumi Books.

———. 1995. *Mvuh Hpa Mi Hpa: Creating Heaven, Creating Earth*. Chiang Mai: Silkworm Books.

Wallace, Anthony F. C. 1969. *The Death and Rebirth of the Seneca*. New York: Random House.

Wang Jun. 1983. *Lahuzu* [The Lahu People]. In Du Yuting, ed., *Yunnan Shaoshuminzu* [Minority Nationalities in Yunnan]. pp. 239–263. Kunming: Yunnan People's Publishing House.

Wang Xiaozhu, ed. 2001. *Lahuzu: Lancang Nuofu Xiang Nanduan Laozhai* [The Lahu People: The Nanduan Village of Nuofu Xiang, Lancang]. Kunming: Yunnan University Press.

Wang Yingcai. 1990. *Nüren Huaiyun Shenghaizi de Youlai* [The Origin of Pregnancy and Childbirth of Women]. In Shiguan Yang, ed., *Lahuzu Minjiangushi* [Lahu Folk Stories], pp.40–41. Kunming: Yunnan People's Publishing House.

Wang Zhenghua. 1996. *Jinnian Guonei Lahuzu Yanjiu Zhong de Fanyi Shiyi Cuowu Huixi* [An Analysis of the Errors in the Translations and Interpretations in Recent Lahu Studies]. *Yunnan Minzuxueyuan Xuebao* [The Journal of the College of Yunnan Nationalities] 2: 84–89.

Wang Zhenghua and He Shaoying. 1999. *Lahuzu Wenhuashi* [The History of Lahu Culture]. Kunming: Yunnan Nationalities Publishing House.

Watson, James L. 1982. "Of Flesh and Bones: The Management of Death Pollution in Cantonese Society." In Maurice Bloch and Jonathan Parry, eds., *Death and the Regeneration of Life*, pp. 155–186. Cambridge: Cambridge University Press.

Watson, Rubie S. 1986. "The Named and the Nameless: Gender and Person in Chinese Society," *American Ethnologist* 13, no. 4: 619–631.

——. 1991. "Afterwards: Marriage and Gender Inequality." In Rubie S. Watson and Patricia B. Ebrey, eds., *Marriage and Gender Inequality in Chinese Society*, pp. 347–368. Berkeley: University of California Press.

Watson-Franke, Maria-Barbara. 1992. "Masculinity and the 'Matrilineal Puzzle'," *Anthropos* 87: 475–488.

Weedon, Chris. 1999. *Feminism, Theory and the Politics of Difference*. Oxford: Blackwell.

Weisner, Thomas and Ronald Gallimore. 1977. "My Brother's Keeper: Child and Sibling Caretaking," *Current Anthropology* 18: 169–190.

Whiting, John W. M. and Beatrice B. Whiting. 1975. "Aloofness and Intimacy of Husband and Wives: A Cross-Cultural Study," *Ethos* 3, no. 2: 183–208.

Whyte, Martin K. 1978. *The Status of Women in Preindustrial Societies*. Princeton: Princeton University Press.

Wilkerson, James R. 1995. "Rural Village Temples in the P'enghu Islands and Their Late Imperial Corporate Organization." In *Ssu-miao yu min-chien wen-hua yen-t'au hui lun-wen-chi* [Collection of Papers from the Seminar on Temple and Folk Cultures], pp. 68–95. Taipei: Wen-Chien Hui.

——. 1999. "Anticipating Memory: 'Celebrating Longevity' in Jingxi County, Guangxi Zhuang Self-Governing Region." Paper presented at the Annual Meeting of the American Anthropological Association, Chicago.

Winzeler, Robert L. 1996. "Sexual Status in Southeast Asia: Comparative Perspectives on Women, Agriculture and Political Organization." In Penny Van Esterik, ed., *Women of Southeast Asia*, 2nd ed. Northern Illinois University

Series on Southeast Asia, Occasional Paper, no. 17, pp. 139–169. DeKalb: Northern Illinois University.

Wohnus, William H. and L. M. Hanks. 1965. "The Brother and Sister Who Saved the World: A Lisu Tale." In Lucien M. Hanks, Jane R. Hanks, and Lauriston Sharp, eds., *Ethnographic Notes on Northern Thailand*, pp. 67–71. Ithaca: Cornell University Southeast Asia Program.

Wolf, Margery. 1972. *Women and the Family in Rural Taiwan*. Stanford: Stanford University Press.

——. 1975. "Women and Suicide in China." In Margery Wolf and Roxanne Witke, eds. *Women in Chinese Society*, pp. 111–142. Stanford: Stanford University Press.

——. 1985. *Revolution Postponed: Women in Contemporary China*. Stanford: Stanford University Press.

Worthman, Carol M. 1995. "Hormones, Sex, and Gender," *Annual Review of Anthropology* 24: 593–616.

Xing, Huang. 1992. "On Writing Systems for China's Minorities Created by Foreign Missionaries," *International Journal of the Sociology of Language* 97: 7–85.

Xu, Yong'an. 1993. "*Nanzha Fosi Diaocha* [An Investigation of Nan Zha Buddhist Temple]." In Yong-an Xu, ed., *Simao Lahu Chuantong Wenhua Diaocha* [An Investigation of Traditional Culture of the Lahu in Simao]," pp. 264–274. Kunming: Yunnan People's Publishing House.

——. 1993. "*Lancangxian Nanduancun Longzhupengzhai Lahuzu Chuantongwunhua Diaocha* [An Investigation of Lahu Traditional Culture in Longzhupeng Village of Nanduan, Lancang]." In Yong-An Xu, ed., *Simao Lahuzu Chuantongwunhua Diaocha* [An Investigation of Traditional Culture of the Lahu in Simao], pp. 1–58. Kunming: Yunnan People's Publishing House.

Yanagisako, Sylvia Junko. 1979. "Family and Household: The Analysis of Domestic Groups," *Annual Review of Anthropology* 8: 161–205.

Yanagisako, Sylvia J. and Jane F. Collier. 1987. "Toward a Unified Analysis of Gender and Kinship." In Jane Fishburne Collier and Sylvia Junko Yanagisako, eds., *Gender and Kinship: Essays Towards a Unified Analysis*, pp. 14–52. Stanford: Stanford University Press.

Yang Cheng, ed. 1992. *Luchun Xianzhi* [The Annals of the Luchun Autonomous County]. Kunming: Yunnan People's Publishing House.

Zhang Dongfeng and Peng Yuancan. 1982. "*Lancangxian Mugaqu Dabanlizhai Lahuzu Shehui Lishi Diaocha* [An Investigation of Lahu Society and History in Dabanli Village, Muga, Lancang]." In *Lahuzu Shehui Lishi Diaocha* [An Investigation of Lahu Society and History], vol. 1., pp. 39–54. Kunming: Yunnan People's Publishing House.

Zhang Qilong, Yue Faxing, and Zhang Xiaoga, eds. 1996. *Lancang Lahuzhu Zizhixian Zhi* [The Annals of the Lancang Lahu Autonomous County]. Kunming: Yunnan People's Publishing House.

Zhou Huashan. 2001. *Wufu Wumu de Guodu?* [A Land Without Father and Husband?]. Beijing: *Guangming Ribao* Publishing House.

Zihlman, Adrenne L. 1997. "Women's Bodies, Women's Lives: An Evolutionary Perspective." In Mary E. Morebeck, Alison Gallaway, and Adrenne L. Zihlman, eds., *The Evolving Female: A Life History Perspective*, pp. 185–197. Princeton: Princeton University Press.

INDEX

administrative office (*cungongsuo*), 20

adults (*chaw mawd*), 53, 57, 67, 143–44, 200–201n3

affinal elders, 146–47

agricultural conditions, 14

Aka people, 195

alcoholism, 164

aloneness (*awl tif*), 46–47

American Indian cultures, 5, 7

Andaman islanders, 193, 197n4

archives, 22–23

assistants (*zi yad*), 119

awl lid (principle), 85, 91–92, 107, 141, 151, 154, 160

awl viq awl ni, 144–45

awl yad, 146

baby-holding game, 94–96

band societies, 195–96

baozhang position, 118, 119–20

beeswax candle rituals, 30–31, 35, 54, 66

blacksmiths, 127–28, 131, 203n6

bone and marrow-blood and flesh metaphor, 80

Buddhism, 36, 120, 203n5

Buddhist monk-couple, 128–30, 134

Burma. *see* Myanmar

cadre system, 110, 116–17; female cadres, 134–35, 203n4

Cal Nud–Cal Pie, 40

Cal Tif–Na Tif (Only Man–Only Woman), 41–44

canonical parallelism, 49

chasing bees song, 102, 104

chaw mawd. See adults

chicken-bone divinations, 67

childrearing, 79, 91–97, 106

children, 53

China, borders, 10, 12

Chinese Communist Party (CCP): archives, 22–23; control of villages, 116–17; divorce and, 175–76

Chinese government, 11, 107; effect on Lahu leadership, 110, 115–17, 131–32; gender discrimination, 116–17, 120–25; households and, 110; local control system (*lülin*), 116; love-pact suicides and, 181–82

chopsticks metaphor, 1, 30, 51, 66, 186, 196

classification, 47–51, 198–99n2

class labels, 182

liberal feminism, 3–4, 6

life cycle, 24, 201n7; adults, 53, 57; children, 53, 68–69; elders, 53, 57, 58–59; husband-wife dyads in, 52–53; joint journey of married couples, 57–60; lone souls, 46–47, 52, 67–71; married youth/junior adults, 53, 57, 58, 70–71; parental spirits, 53, 57, 60–67, 89, 201n5; red-and-naked children, 53, 68–69; ritual reciprocity, 155–57, 186; senior elders, 53, 57, 59–60; wedding ceremony, 53–57; young children, 53, 68–69

linguistic parallelism, 48–51

Lisu people, 45

Lolopo people, 188

lone souls, 46–47, 52, 67–71

Mahayana Buddhism, 120

male-dominant societies, 5

male-female dyads. *see* husband-wife dyads

male-female masters of the household, 107–14; *see also* head couple; husband-wife dyad; leadership

male hostility, 2–3

Mao era, 18, 117; marriage and, 173–76, 179, 184, 207n3

market economy, 15, 158–59, 180

marriage, 42, 70; arranged, 166, 169–71, 177; collectivization period and, 172–73; courtship, 167, 170; cross-cousin/parallel cousin, 169; divorce *(bal dar)*, 55, 171, 174, 175–77; elopement, 178–80; finding one's own spouse, 166–68; intermarriage with Han, 96–97; labor obligations, 108, 150–51; in Mao era, 173–76, 179, 184, 207n3; monogamy, 11, 192; parental guidance, 166, 167; sexual relations, 170–71

Marriage Law (CCP), 175

marriage market, 180

Marxist-socialist feminism, 3, 6, 192

masculinity, 71–75; *see also* gender unity

menstruation taboos, 5, 197n4

methodology, 17–23

Miao people, 201–2n11

militia, 179

minority religious leader, 132

monogamy, 11, 192

moral values: *hie* (harshness), 73–74, 163; human, 41–44; *nud* (gentleness), 72–74, 163; in Senior Daughter–Son story, 38–41; speeches, 54–56

Motorola Corporation, 15

Myanmar (Burma), 179

Na Hie–Cal Hie, 39

New Rice Tasting Festival, 35, 59, 156

New Year Festival, 33, 35, 36, 45, 120, 128, 129, 156

Nie Xeul–Yad Xeul, 32–41

nud (gentleness), 72–74, 163

officials, 19, 20

Only Man–Only Woman, 41–44

opium, 164–65

oral literature, 19, 73, 188; dyads and, 48–49; love-pact suicides in, 180–83; *see also* folk-song tradition

CPSIA information can be obtained at www.ICGtesting.com
Printed in the USA
LVOW08s2104301215

468424LV00013B/30/P

9 780231 119573